LINGUISTICS AND YOUR LANGUAGE

Robert A. Hall, Jr., is Professor of Linguistics at Cornell University. Born in Raleigh, North Carolina, in 1911, he graduated from Princeton University in 1931, later receiving his M.A. from the University of Chicago and, in 1934, the degree of Doctor of Letters from the University of Rome. He taught at Puerto Rico, Princeton, and Brown before joining the Cornell faculty in 1946. His main fields of linguistic research, in addition to general linguistics, have been Italian and Romance philology, Hungarian, and pidgin and creole languages. During World War II, Professor Hall was in charge of the army Italian courses at Yale and the navy courses in pidgin English at Columbia. Fulbright Lecturer in Linguistics at the University of Rome in 1950–51, he also spent a year in Australia and New Guinea in 1954, studying pidgin English on a Guggenheim Fellowship. He is author of many publications on linguistics, including *An Analytical Grammar of the Hungarian Language, Spoken and Written French, A Short History of Italian Literature* and *Italian for Modern Living.*

LINGUISTICS AND YOUR LANGUAGE

Robert A. Hall, Jr.

Second, revised edition of
Leave Your Language Alone!

ANCHOR BOOKS
DOUBLEDAY & COMPANY, INC.
GARDEN CITY, NEW YORK

COVER DESIGN BY SIDNEY BUTCHKES
TYPOGRAPHY BY EDWARD GOREY

The Anchor Books edition of *Linguistics and Your Language* is published by arrangement with the Linguistica Press.

Anchor Books edition: 1960

To Joseph Dana Allen

Preface

This book is intended as a brief, popular discussion of a number of problems connected with language, and of the science of language—*linguistics*—and what it can contribute to the solution of these problems. There have been a number of recent expositions of linguistics, particularly Hockett's *A Course in Modern Linguistics;* their purpose, however, and their scope are somewhat different from those of this book. The aim of this book is not to give so thorough a discussion of linguistic science, as does Hockett, for instance; on the other hand, it stresses somewhat more than previous works the conclusions of linguistics and their implications for our society. It is, to a certain extent, a tract addressed to the general public, in favor of a scientific attitude towards language and of linguistic relativism and tolerance, but including only as much detailed scientific analysis as is necessary to justify or exemplify its statements and conclusions.

In accordance with our basic aim as stated above, we have reduced the discussion of technical methods and procedures to the minimum consonant with our purpose of presenting the results and implications of linguistics. Yet the technical aspect cannot be omitted entirely; otherwise the reader would have nothing but the author's unsupported word for many of the conclusions presented, and no way of seeing or judging for himself the procedures underlying the results. The main body of the text has been worded so as to avoid all use of special symbols such as those of phonetic transcriptions, always a point of difficulty for the non-specialist. Sections involving technical definitions, analytical reasoning, special symbolism, or detailed exemplifications have been put in smaller type; the reader who is interested in points of detail can find at least some of his curiosity satisfied in these sections, whereas the more general reader can pass them by.

Thanks are due to the following colleagues and friends who have read all or part of the book at various stages of its development, and from whose suggestions I have profited greatly, not hesitating even to "lift" at times whole phrases or sentences from their comments: Fred Agard, Bernard Bloch, William E. Bull, Joe and Allah Congress, J Milton Cowan, María Escudero, Gordon H. Fairbanks, Albert G. Hart, Archibald A. Hill, Charles F. Hockett, Henry M. Hoenigswald, Harry Hoijer, Kemp Malone, Raven McDavid, William G. Moulton, Kenneth L. Pike, Ernst Pulgram, Victor Reynolds, James Rosier, Henry Lee Smith, Jr., Jess Stein, C. K. Thomas, W. Freeman Twaddell, and Maria Weber. My wife, Frances A. Hall, has been of especial assistance in suggesting improvements in style and content. The Division of Modern Languages, of Cornell University, by publishing a preliminary multi-lithed edition in 1948 enabled me to obtain a greater initial diffusion of the work and beneficial suggestions from many of those mentioned above, than would otherwise have been possible.

Acknowledgments are due to the following, for permission to reprint material as specified: Irving Berlin Music Corporation, a verse from the song "Doin' What Comes Natur'lly," from "Annie Get Your Gun"; the Columbia University Press, a passage from Ralph Linton's *The Science of Man in the World Crisis;* Doubleday and Co., Inc., passages from Rudyard Kipling's

Just So Stories; E. P. Dutton and Co., a passage from the 1932 edition of J. G. Anderson's *Le Mot Juste;* D. C. Heath and Co., a diagram of the organs of speech from R. A. Hall, Jr.'s, introduction to Maria de Lourdes Sá Pereira's *Brazilian Portuguese Grammar;* Henry Holt and Co., Inc., several passages from Leonard Bloomfield's *Language;* Prof. John S. Kenyon, material from his article "Functional Varieties and Levels of Usage"; the Linguistic Atlas of the United States and Canada, several maps and charts from the *Linguistic Atlas of New England* and the prospectus therefor; the Linguistic Society of America, passages from Martin Joos' *Acoustic Phonetics* and from the journal *Language;* Charles Scribner's Sons, a passage from Edith Wharton's *The Custom of the Country.* An effort was made to obtain specific permission to quote a brief passage from P. G. Wodehouse's *Psmith, Journalist,* but no answer was received to the request.

Contents

LINGUISTICS AND YOUR LANGUAGE

PART I: THINGS WE WORRY ABOUT

1. Which Should I Say?

"Is it bad English to say *it's me* instead of *it is I?*"

"Isn't it incorrect to say *everybody should take off their hat,* instead of *everybody should take off his hat?*"

"Aren't *hisn, hern, ourn, yourn, theirn* illiterate?"

"Is it wrong to spell *nite, lite, fite* instead of *night, light, fight?* Isn't that debasing the English language?"

These questions are just a few samples of the kind of thing we are always worrying and asking about in connection with our language. There are some things that we constantly hear said (like *it ain't, those kind of people*) or see written (like *go slo*) all around us, that give us trouble. We have no trouble about most matters in our language; nobody is likely to criticize us for saying *I'm going home, he helped me,* or for using the spellings *smoke, delight,* or *debt.* On other points, however, like those just mentioned, some people are likely to raise objections to what they hear or see, but disapprove of: for instance, *I ain't, he done it, I gotta stay 'n work but I don' wanna,* or *forehead* pronounced to rhyme with *horrid.* Then they tell us we must not say it one way, we must say it another—*their* way—because what we've just said is "bad," "wrong," "incorrect," "ungrammatical," "uneducated," "ignorant," or something else equally uncomplimentary. The result is, we are confused and insecure; we develop conflicts within ourselves on such points, and, in the end, no longer know what we should say.

Then how can we find out what to say, in such a situation of conflict or doubt? The way of least resistance, in some respects, is to take the word of those who try to correct our speech, and to base our usage on that of "authorities" like dictionaries, grammars, or individuals whose word we are willing to take. If we simply accept their decrees without arguing, it saves us that much further unpleasantness, but then we may have considerable trouble changing our own ways to agree with what they want. The problem gets more difficult when the "authorities" disagree: one will condemn us for pronouncing *forehead* as "forrid", the other will object equally strongly to "forehead". As a matter of fact, if we are worried about any such point, we need accurate and reliable information on it to enable us to decide one way or the other. Is there any source for accurate and reliable information about language, which will be more dependable and less likely to throw us into an intellectual and emotional tailspin than the "authorities" that try to correct us?

There is. For the last hundred and fifty years, a number of scholars have been working on the study of language from a scientific point of view. They are often called simply *linguists;* but, as many people use the word *linguist* to mean a polyglot—somebody who knows a lot of languages—the person who has made a scientific study of language often prefers the term *scientific linguist* or *linguistic analyst.* The work they engage in is called *linguistics.* By now, linguistics has amassed a store of knowledge which is accurate and reliable enough to decide on such points as these we worry about. If we ask a linguistic analyst such questions as those we quoted at the beginning of this chapter, we are likely to get answers like these:

"It's not at all wrong to say *it's me;* on the contrary, *it's me* is normal and absolutely correct English, and the great majority of people use it."

"*Everybody should take off their hat* is perfectly all right."

"*Hisn, hern* and so forth are often heard from illiterate people, perhaps more often than from people who know how to read and write; but there is no necessary connection."

"It's no worse to spell *nite* for *night* than it is to spell *smoke* for earlier *smoak*, or *delight* for earlier *deleite*; and in no case is the change either for better or for worse—nor, in fact, does it have any relation to language at all, but merely to spelling."

Not only questions about "right" and "wrong" usage, but problems concerning other aspects of language, often arise to bother us, such as careful speech, the exact meaning of words, or the relative age and worth of different languages. Here again, linguistics offers reasonably reliable solutions for our problems, as in these typical questions and answers:

QUESTION	ANSWER
Isn't the ordinary pronunciation of *forehead*, rhyming with *horrid*, just due to corruption, to careless and sloppy habits of speech, leaving out most of the letters?	Pronouncing *forehead* to rhyme with *horrid* is not careless or sloppy at all, but the result of normal development; it would be that way whether the word had ever been written with letters or not, and there is no such thing as "corruption" in language.
Doesn't *nice* really mean "silly", so that we shouldn't use it to mean *nice*?	*Nice* means exactly what we mean by it at the present time. Some hundreds of years ago it meant "silly", but what it meant earlier is no guide to what it should mean now. The only

guide to what a word *should* mean is what it actually *does* mean in the mouths of the people who use it.

Which is older, English or Chinese?

Neither is older than the other; written representation of Chinese is found dating from an earlier time than that of English, but both languages have been spoken and handed down from generation to generation, since time immemorial.

Aren't English, French, and other civilized languages better than savage tongues like Eskimo or Hottentot, that don't even have any written language or literature?

English and French are *languages,* that is to say they are systems of habits of speech, exactly like Eskimo or Hottentot or any other language, without any necessary connection between their structure and the civilization of the people that speak them; and, as languages, Eskimo and Hottentot are just as good as English and French, though of course in different ways, and quite without regard to whether there is a way of writing them or not.

Scientific linguists are often asked questions of this sort, and give answers like those we have just seen. These are answers which should set our doubts at rest, which should show us that the worries and conflicts we have about our language are largely unnecessary and either do not exist or have a different basis from what we usually think. The linguist's answers should make us feel more secure in our normal, everyday behavior. Often, however, we do not get the full benefit of the analyst's reassurance; sometimes we are incredulous, or we feel angry and hurt. Many of us even *want* to be humiliated and abased by someone telling us our language is "bad" or "ungrammatical"; or else we have been told so often that speech can be "incorrect", that language can be "corrupted", that we can't believe the news that it isn't so.

The situation is paradoxical. Such answers as the linguistic scientist gives to our questions are not the products of a disordered imagination, or his own fanciful inventions. Each of them is backed up by the results of a hundred-and-fifty-year old science, linguistics. Each of them can be demonstrated in detail by logical argument and proof. Taken as a whole, they have certain implications which could, if properly understood and applied, produce a major improvement in our everyday relations with each other and in the way we train our children in schools and colleges.

But the science of linguistics and its revolutionary implications are still unknown to all but a very few people, even though it has been in existence for a century and a half, and has made a very enviable record of success and has piled up a sizeable body of knowledge. Why is this? People who work in linguistics have been trying to make their science and its results better known, for nearly a hundred years. But every effort comes up against a wall of opposition, of entrenched opposition in folk beliefs and in schools.

Result: so far, the benefits that might come from linguistic science have not been allowed to become known or available to the general public. That situation clearly needs to be remedied: linguistics and its results need to be made far more widely known, both for their own sake and for the good they can do. Hence this book. In this book we have a double aim, both destructive and constructive: to expose the fallacies of the folkloristic notions and of the school dogmas that stand in our way and block our understanding of language; and to build up in their stead a better-founded and more accurate grasp of the facts of language and how we go about finding those facts.

In the course of the discussion, moreover, there are certain basic principles that we shall try to get across, and towards which our arguments will be oriented, such as the following:

There is no such thing as good and bad (or correct and incorrect, grammatical and ungrammatical, right and wrong) in language.

There is no such thing as "written language". There is speech and there is writing; and of these two, speech is basic in human life and writing is a reflection of speech. Changing the writing is not changing the language.

A dictionary or grammar is not as good an authority for your own speech as the way you yourself speak.

Words do not have any "real" meaning as opposed to other, "false" meanings. Any meaning people give to a word is automatically its *real* meaning under those circumstances.

All languages and dialects are of equal merit, each in its own way.

When languages change, they do not "decay" or

become "corrupted"; a later stage of a language is worth neither more nor less than an earlier stage.

These are not the only points we shall be making, of course; there are a number of others that will be introduced in their proper place, but these are among the most important.

We can best investigate and discuss the matter in four stages:

First, the remaining three chapters of this part will take up more in detail some of the things we worry about: the problems of correctness, of writing and its relation to speech, and of a language's history in relation to its present importance and worth.

In Part II, we will try to get at least a summary idea of the facts about linguistic structure, about the way a language is built and what "makes it tick", as linguistic science has analyzed it.

Part III will take up language in its relation to human society: its specifically social function, its extension in space (linguistic geography) and its development in time (linguistic history).

Finally, in Part IV, it will be time to take up some of the ways in which linguistic science and its conclusions can give us a better basis than we now have for proceeding with regard to those problems of correctness, writing, and etymology that trouble us; language teaching; the question of an international language; and general problems of language as it relates to human behavior and as it functions in our society. We have two main points to make: 1) that a science of language exists; and 2) that we can learn something from it which will ease our troubles and help towards solving some of our problems connected with language.

Our basic technique will be much like that of the "shock treatment" that psychiatrists often use. When a person has built up a way of life based on harmful attitudes or beliefs, the psychiatrist has to sweep this false basis away before he can replace it by new, more realistic and therefore sounder ideas. Often enough, a temporary confusion or disorientation may result, because of bewilderment and loss of cherished illusions. But this is really a favorable sign, since it represents the beginning of a healthy attitude and true understanding of the problems involved. In the same way, our discussion will intentionally aim first at showing how little real foundation there is for many of the ideas we have about language, in order to replace them with a better understanding of its nature and function. Of necessity, therefore, our first part will be primarily negative in its approach, clearing the ground, as it were, for the more realistic and more helpful positive conclusions to be presented in the rest of the book.

One further point: this is not intended to be a complete treatment of every branch of linguistic science. Such a treatment would require a much longer book than this, a much more detailed and more technical book. Our aim here is, rather, to present all the essential facts and their implications, to help the reader understand the linguistic problems that face him, and to help him reach his own conclusions and act on them. We shall, therefore, keep away from the technical level as much as possible, though some technical discussion will of necessity creep in. As a result of this aim, we shall have to be, on some occasions, briefer in our statements and perhaps seem more dogmatic than we would in a more extended or more purely technical discussion. You can be sure of finding here the essentials of fact and argument; but, if you want more detailed information on any point that is treated summarily, you can find a fuller treatment in the books listed in the Appendix ("Some Useful Books", pp. 260–63).

2. Right vs. Wrong

"How many of these frequent errors in English do YOU make?"

"Do YOU say KEW-pon for KOO-pon, ad-ver-TISE-ment for ad-VER-tise-ment, or AD-ult for ad-ULT?"

"Almost everybody makes these blunders in English: *between you and I, it's me, those kind of books.*"

"Even the greatest writers sin against the laws of grammar."

We have all seen advertisements in newspapers or magazines, with messages like those just quoted, implying to the reader "Shame on you if you are one of those who sin!"—and, of course, offering to teach him better. It is easy, on the one hand, to see that those who talk or advertise in this way and offer to cure our errors in pronunciation or grammar are simply appealing to our sense of insecurity with regard to our own speech. On the other hand, we must also admit that this sense of insecurity does exist, in almost all except those who are hardened against criticism and disapproval, and renders us easily susceptible to appeals of this kind. Our problem now is, to look at some of the ways in which we are supposed to be speaking wrongly, and to see whether there really exists a choice between "right" and "wrong", and, if so, what "right" and "wrong" consist of.

Our first approach may be made through very ordinary, everyday instances of "mistakes" like *I ain't, he don't, we seen him, you done it* or *hisn.* Most of us know that these are pretty widely condemned as "errors", when used instead of the corresponding *I am not* or *I'm not, he doesn't, we saw him, you did it, his.* But what is it that makes them "mistakes" or "errors"? If we drive through a traffic light, steal somebody's property, or kill someone, we know exactly what provides sanctions against these actions: the law of the land; and we know what will punish us if we disobey the law: the government. Is there any law of the land to set up rules about our speech, or any branch of the government that will enforce them? Obviously not. There are books that contain rules for speaking and writing, and there are people who will raise objections and criticize us if we fail to follow these rules; but those books and those people have no legal authority over us (outside of the rather special and limited situation in the schoolroom, where of course the teacher can give us a bad mark for not obeying the rules). Not only have they no legal authority, they have no authority whatsoever conferred on them by any power. Some countries, it is true, have had regulators of language with a kind of authority, such as the national Academies of France and Spain, which were set up by the king with the specific duty of "regulating and preserving the purity of the language". Even in those countries, very few people ever took the Academies' authority over language too seriously; but, technically speaking, their authority did exist in a way. But no such authority has ever existed in any English-speaking country, nor does it seem likely that speakers of English would ever be willing to accept the decrees of an Academy or similar institution, or of a Ministry of Education.

And yet, if we say *I ain't, you done it,* or *hisn,* we *are* likely to run into trouble. Trouble with whom?— with everybody? No. A foreigner using some completely abnormal turn of phrase, such as *this must we first do,* will confuse the ordinary speaker of English considerably, and will run no chance of finding anybody who would accept that as normal English. He would have trouble with everybody. But with *I ain't* and the like, some people would not be in the slightest upset; in fact, more than a few would find those "incorrect" forms more normal than the supposedly "correct" usage that they "ought" to be following themselves and insisting on in others. With some other people, however, our use of *he don't* and similar expressions may get us into more or less serious trouble. Our hearers may correct us on the spot, and tell us "Don't say *I ain't,* say *I'm not;* not *hisn,* but *his";* or, even though they may not correct our usage then and there, they are nevertheless likely to hold it against us, and to allow it to determine their attitude toward us in one way or another. They may, perhaps, not consider us their social equals; they may not invite us to their home again; they may object to our marrying into their family; they may pick someone else, who says *I'm not* and *his,* to give a job or a promotion to; or some other form of unfavorable reaction may result from our using a form or word which is the wrong one for the given situation.

Usually, we are told and we believe that "correctness" is a characteristic of educated, intelligent people, whereas "incorrectness" is the special quality of uneducated, ignorant, or stupid people. But notice that exactly the type of situation we described above, where someone arouses an unfavorable reaction because of his language, can arise from the use of "correct" speech where the hearer does not use that kind of speech, or has a prejudice or other objection against it. It can be just as much of a *faux pas* to say *I saw him,* where your hearer expects and wants *I seen him,* as the other way around. One friend of mine found that, when he went to work in a Houston shipyard during the second World War, he was regarded as a snob for saying *those things* instead of *them things,* and he did not get full cooperation from his fellow-workers until he started to say *them things.* There are even some ways of speaking, some turns of expression, such as *am I not?,* which, no matter how "correct" they may be in theory, are just too artificial for almost any situation.

Notice also that the forms themselves are of equal worth as expressions of the ideas you are trying to communicate. *You done it* is just as good an expression of "doing" something, in past time, as *you did it,* and no present-day speaker of English will ever be confused as to what you mean. The same is true for *he don't* instead of *he doesn't;* for *we seen him* instead of *we saw him;* and for a host of others. In some cases, one might even argue that the "incorrect" form is actually somewhat preferable from the point of view of clarity or simplicity. The form *his,* in "correct" speech, is both an adjective (*his book*) and a pronoun (*that's his*); whereas the "incorrect" form *hisn* and the others parallel to it ending in *-n* (*hern, ourn, yourn, theirn*) are clearly marked, by their ending, as being possessive pronouns and nothing else. The argument runs similarly for *ain't.* To make the present-tense forms of the verb *be* negative, we must use, in "correct" speech, three different forms: *I'm not, he isn't, we (you, they) aren't;* whereas the "incorrect" *ain't* offers us one single form, exactly parallel to *can't, won't* or *don't,* and equally convenient. *He doesn't* instead of *he don't* is also an extra complication, seen to be needless when compared with *can't* or *won't.* We might make similar arguments in favor of other "incorrect" forms as well.

What is it, then, that makes some forms "incorrect" and others not? This is not a matter of legal or quasi-legal authority, as we have seen. It is not a matter of universal condemnation, nor yet of incomprehensibility; in fact, some "incorrect" forms, as we have just pointed out, would be clearer or simpler than the corresponding "correct" forms. It all boils down, really, to a question of acceptability in certain classes of our society, in those classes which are socially dominant and which set the tone for others. Whether a form is accepted or rejected does not depend on its inherent merit nor yet on any official approval given it, but purely on whether its hearers like it or not—on whether they will react favorably or unfavorably towards a person they hear using it. "Correct" can only mean "socially acceptable", and apart from this has no meaning as applied to language.

The social acceptability, and hence "correctness", of any form or word is determined, not by reason or logic or merit, but solely by the hearer's emotional attitude towards it—and emotional attitudes naturally differ from person to person, from group to group, from social class to social class. Forms and words also change in social acceptability in the course of time: in the early seventeenth century, conservative speakers and purists objected violently to *ye* and *you,* used in speaking to one person, instead of the earlier *thou* and *thee;* and there must have been a time when *cows,* instead of the older plural *kine,* seemed an objectionable innovation.

Nevertheless, the difference in social acceptability between *I ain't* and *I am not,* between *hern* and *hers,* and so forth, is a real fact. If my child is likely to run into trouble later on for saying *I done it* or *hisn,* I will try to keep him from getting into the habit of using those forms which are actually not acceptable socially and which may cause others to react unfavorably towards him. But, if I am sensible about it, I will realize that the reason I want him to avoid these "incorrect" forms is not any inherent badness or evil character that they may have, but a purely practical consideration, that of their social acceptability. His choice of language will be used by others as a purely arbitrary means of classifying him socially among the sheep or the goats. All we need to do in the case of *I ain't*, etc., is to re-word the traditional instructions, and say that we avoid using such turns of speech, not because they are "bad" or "wrong" or "ungrammatical", but because they are socially unacceptable. Of course, as soon as people in any given group stop treating, say, *he don't* as socially unacceptable, it automatically becomes "correct".

There is a close parallel between acceptable usage in language and "correct" behavior in other social customs, such as personal garb or table manners. What is it that makes it perfectly good manners to eat some things, such as bread-and-jam, with the fingers, and not others, like meat or vegetables? Certainly not the decree of any official or self-appointed authority; and certainly not any inherent feature or characteristic of what we eat or do not eat with the fingers. Some things that we eat with our fingers are much more messy than others that we would always take up with knife and fork. Here again, it is social acceptability that determines whether we may or may not eat a given item of food with our fingers, or wear a four-in-hand tie with a tuxedo. This acceptability varies from place to place, and from one period of time to another. Thus, in England it is perfectly good manners to pile your peas up on the back of your fork, using your knife as a pusher, and to eat the peas from the back of the fork; but it is very much frowned upon to keep changing the fork from the left hand to the right and back again, as Americans normally do. And the permissibility of, say, table behavior is constantly changing; for instance, I was brought up always to eat bacon with knife and fork or in a sandwich, whereas by now it has become much more widely "correct" to eat it with the fingers.

For cases like those we have been discussing up to now, the situation is clear: we will avoid forms like *I seen him, he don't* because they are used as shibboleths, disregard of which may lead to unfortunate results for us in our living and relations with others. There are many instances, however, where reality and what we are taught do not correspond as to the actual "correctness", the actual acceptability, of what we are told to avoid. Take the case of *it's me*. Grammarians tell us that a rule exists that "the verb *to be* never takes a direct object", and that hence we must always say *it is I* and never *it's me*. The rule itself is found in plenty of grammar books, but that is no guarantee of its accuracy or relevance; in reality, this rule is meaningless as a statement of the facts of English usage. It was taken over by English grammarians from Latin grammar, where it is an accurate statement of the facts of Latin usage: in Latin, you said *sum egō* "[it] am I", never *sum mē* "[it] am me". The facts of actual acceptable usage in English are quite different: we normally say, and have said for hundreds of years, *it's me, it's us*, and so forth.

This is not merely an unsupported assertion on my part; statistical studies have been made which show *it's me* to be by far the most frequent and normal usage in current English, as compared with *it is I*. Professor Charles C. Fries made a detailed study of many such points that are often the objects of dispute and condemnation, in his *American English Grammar*, by analyzing thousands of letters which had been written to the War Department by people of all levels of education and social standing. He found very clear documentary proof that many forms and many constructions that are often condemned are actually in perfectly good standing in the usage of educated persons, and hence by definition acceptable or "correct". He found, for instance, that it is normal to say *it's me, these kind of things, none of the children are here, everybody should take off their hat,* in standard English, and that there is no real difference in such respects between standard and vulgar speech. The story is told of a certain very puristic lady—let's call her Miss Fidditch—who was teaching her class very strictly to avoid *it's me:*

MISS FIDDITCH: You must always say *it is I.* The inflexible rule of grammar is that the verb *to be* never takes a direct object.

(A few minutes later:)

PRINCIPAL (outside the door, knocking): Who's there?

MISS FIDDITCH: It's me—Miss Fidditch.

Miss Fidditch was right when she said *it's me,* naturally and normally, in a give-and-take conversational situation and without reflecting; she was wrong when she tried to force on her class an artificial, unrealistic rule that applied to no one's, not even her own, usage in actual fact. And we all know the old story about the grammarian who said "Never use a preposition to end a sentence with."

We are often told that such-and-such a form or combination of forms is "in accordance with the rules of logic", which make other competing forms or combinations "illogical" and hence inadmissible. Such a rule as "*everyone* or *everybody* is singular and hence a word referring to it must be in the singular" is an instance of this, or the rule that "a double negative makes a positive" and that hence we mustn't say *I didn't see nobody* except when we really did see somebody. It is perfectly true that, in strictly ordered systems like mathematics or symbolic logic, a violation of the rules of discourse will introduce confusion and make a statement into its opposite or into something else from what was intended. The purists' error here lies in identifying language and logic, and expecting normal linguistic usage to be strictly logical. As a matter of fact, no language ever was strictly logical, nor can we make it so by preaching at its speakers. To begin with, we should have to define what "logical" meant—and we would find that each different language would, from the outset, give its speakers different ideas as to what "logic" is. To us, for instance, it seems logical, and, in fact, inescapable to say *one book*, but *two books, three books, five books*, using the form *books* when we refer to more than one of them, and thus distinguishing between "one" and "more than one" or (to use the traditional grammatical terms) singular and plural. To someone brought up speaking Hungarian, that difference seems useful in general—a Hungarian will say *könyv* for "book" and *könyvek* for "books", with *-ek* indicating the plural for him just as *-s* does for us—but when he has a numeral to tell him how many books there are, he uses, not the plural, but the singular form of the word for "book". The Hungarian says *egy könyv* "one book", *két könyv* "two book", and likewise *három könyv* "three book", *öt könyv* "five book" and so forth. To him it seems silly, needless and illogical to say "five books" where the indication of plurality is already given by the number, so that "five book" will do just as well. Which is more logical, English or Hungarian, in this respect? One could argue both ways, and perhaps the Hungarian way of saying "two book, three book" might prove to be more strictly logical. It all depends on what you are brought up to say.

The same thing holds for such points as the "double negative", which many persons condemn violently— *I didn't see nobody* instead of *I didn't see anybody.* They tell us that "logically" a double negative makes a positive, and that therefore *I didn't see nobody* "really" means *I did see somebody.* Here again, our traditional grammar rule is based on Latin, as it is in so many other instances—as if the rules of Latin could be applied to English. In Latin, those who spoke it about the time of Caesar, Cicero and Augustus normally took a double negative to mean a positive. So for them, *nōn nihil* "not nothing" meant "something", and *nōn vīdī nēminem* "I didn't see nobody" could only have meant "I saw somebody". That was right, logical and natural *for them,* because that was the way they used Latin. But later, in the course of the centuries, those who spoke Latin and the Romance languages which developed out of Latin, got in the habit of using a double negative with *negative* meaning. In Spanish, for instance, it is downright incorrect (because nobody will accept it) to say such a thing as *vi a nadie* in the meaning of "I saw nobody". You *must* say *no vi a nadie,* literally "I didn't see nobody", with the two negatives *no* "not" and *nadie* "nobody", whenever *nadie* "nobody" follows the verb; otherwise what you say is meaningless. It may be "illogical", and it may be "incorrect" from the point of view of Latin grammar; but in Spanish, French, and Italian, for instance, the requirement of a double negative is so absolute that no one would be able to get away with condemning it on the grounds of logic. The reason that the point can be raised at all in modern English is that we have a divided usage: in actual current speech, when there is no emphasis, a double negative and a single negative both have a negative meaning, and everybody will understand what we mean whether we say *I didn't see nobody* or *I saw nobody* or *I didn't see anybody*. But when we are putting emphasis on the verb or the pronoun, then *I DIDN'T see NObody* does have positive meaning, and would be normal as an answer, say, in contradiction to *You saw nobody*. The drift of our language is inevitably toward the use of the double negative; this is as normal and natural as anything else in English, and as logical in English as it is in Spanish and French.

Now with regard to this second group of "wrong" usages, the situation is essentially different from that of *ain't* and *hisn*. Such forms as *ain't* are both socially unacceptable and condemned by purists; whereas *it's me* and *those kind of things*, although grammarians may condemn them, are nevertheless in normal, everyday use by socially accepted people and hence are socially acceptable and by definition "correct". And when it comes to such pronunciations as KEW-pon, ad-ver-TISE-ment, AD-ult, the purists' condemnations are absolutely fanciful, without any rhyme or reason whatsoever. Both KEW-pon and KOO-pon, both ad-ver-TISE-ment and ad-VER-tise-ment, both AD-ult and ad-ULT are normal, regular, and acceptable variants; to call either member of these pairs "correct" and the other "incorrect" is quite arbitrary. Language is not an either-or proposition, in which no variation, no deviation from a strictly maintained party line is permissible; in many instances, such as those of *coupon* and *advertisement*, more than one alternative exists and both are equally acceptable or "correct".

Aside from these two types of "incorrectness" we have just discussed, there are other kinds of usage that are condemned, and (although this is not always realized) on somewhat different grounds. The largest group of forms of this sort are those which are under a social taboo of one kind or another. In our society, we tend to shy away from casual public discussion of certain topics, particularly two: sexual reproduction and elimination of bodily waste; and we carry over our repugnance to terms which imply casual discussion of these subjects. This is of course a real repugnance with the classes of people who set the dominant tone of what is and what isn't acceptable in our society, and it establishes a taboo which absolutely *must* be observed on pain of very severe social sanctions: if you use the so-called "four-letter" or taboo words in mixed company in any except the lowest classes of society, you will immediately be subjected to extreme disapproval, condemnation and ostracism. But there are two things to be noticed about these taboos of decency, real as they are: 1) they are partial, and 2) they are relative, in that they are peculiar to our West European society.

On the first point, that these taboos are partial, note that I can use the terms *sexual reproduction* and *elimination of bodily waste,* as I did in the preceding paragraph, without fear of reproach or condemnation, although I would never wish or dare to use, in conversing, lecturing, or writing this book, the equivalent taboo words—words which most readers probably know as well as I do. It offends our sense of "decency" to discuss those subjects casually or to imply casual discussion of them; but it is acceptable to use more formal, learned terms that imply serious discussion on a scientific level. In the meanwhile, of course, the "four-letter" words go on in the normal, everyday usage of folk who are untroubled by social taboos, and are the only terms they know for the activities and body parts connected with sex and elimination. Many of us have doubtless heard the anecdote of the doctor who kept asking a constipated patient if he had *defecated,* and, always receiving the answer "No", kept prescribing more and more laxatives until he finally (and with considerable reluctance) used the taboo word, when he found out that his patient's intestines had nearly been ruined by the excessive purgation. The patient simply didn't know the fancy word *defecate,* and kept giving the answer "No", whereas he would have known and understood the "four-letter" word from the beginning. Which was more sensible—for the doctor to observe the taboo and ruin the patient's intestines, or to use the "four-letter" word at the start and get the result he was aiming at?

Such taboos, also, although certainly very real, are relative. Not all societies have the same taboos. Most societies do not have our feeling that sex and elimination are indecent; on the other hand, another society may taboo the mention of one's relatives, or of dead people's names, or of certain game animals. With the Cree Indians, it is taboo to speak one's sister's name; the Cree will say that he "respects her too much", and he would feel as much repugnance towards mentioning her name as we would towards using a "four-letter" word. In some societies, especially in the islands of the Pacific, such taboos on one class of words or another have become very elaborate. We can imagine, for instance, a person from a society which tabooed the mention of one's relatives' names, as being highly shocked at such a comedy as *Charley's Aunt,* with its irreverent treatment of family relationships, whereas at the same time he might, without violating any of his society's taboos, sing his baby daughter a lullaby in which her sexual parts and their function were prominently mentioned. It would be extremely naive on our part to condemn such a person for not knowing the difference between decency and indecency: standards of decency, like other standards, are relative, not absolute, and no society can claim that its ideas of decency are right and all others wrong. So it is with our taboo words; they are condemned, it is true, and we would do extremely well to avoid using them in "decent" society; but the reason for avoiding them is, not that such words are inherently evil, but simply that they run counter to particular taboos of the dominant classes of our society.

Closely similar to the taboo on words that refer to sex and elimination is that on words that have a serious religious meaning, when they are used in any other connection: *Jesus, God, Christ, damn, hell* used as "swear-words". Here again, I can use any of these words in serious discussion: *Jesus Christ died to save us from damnation,* etc. But used frivolously, as in *Christ, am I tired!* or *Ouch! Damn it to hell!,* these words shock a great many of us. They used to shock still more people; in the 1880's, when Clarence Day, Sr., was in the habit of saying *damn!* in the middle of the pastor's sermon and elsewhere, it was a serious breach of etiquette—and part of our amusement over his behavior in that respect comes from the difference in attitude between that day and this. Objectively speaking, *damn it!* is simply a succession of sounds that we use when we are angry, and even *damn you!* implies no desire on our part that the person or persons spoken to should literally roast in hell-fire for eternity, but simply that we're more or less irritated at them. The "badness" of swear-words of this kind comes from the fact that some people—people who are dominant in our society—are displeased by them and will act unfavorably towards people who use them.

Another objection that we often hear made against

such a usage as *it's me* (instead of *it is I*) or *none of the boys are here* (instead of *none of the boys is here*) is that it is "ungrammatical" or that it does not "conform to the rules of grammar". The assumption involved here, whether we state it openly or not, is that there is such a thing as a body of rules, which are as fixed and unchangeable as the laws of the Medes and the Persians, which are called "grammar" and to which all language must conform or else be condemned as "ungrammatical". As a matter of fact, no such body of rules exists, or ever could exist. What passes for "grammar" in the usual textbook is really a conglomeration of rules, most of them taken from Latin grammars, some of them not, but often misstating the facts about English. We have already seen that the rule "the verb *to be* never takes a direct object" is a very good statement of the actual facts of Latin, but has no relation to the actual facts of English; and likewise for the double negative. Nor is there any reason why Latin should be taken as a model for all other languages, whether related or not. People used to think, and some still do, that Latin should be a universal model for language; the reason for this is that all during the Middle Ages in Western Europe, the language of learning and religion happened, through a historical accident, to be Latin. Educated people, just because they happened to get their education through Latin rather than through their native language, came to the conclusion that high intellectual activity and use or imitation of Latin were inseparable. We can easily see that such an idea was rather naive, and based on a false identification of two unrelated factors in the situation. Actually, Latin is just a language like any other, with its faults and shortcomings as well as its virtues, and its rules are far from being universally applicable. How would a speaker of Hungarian react to being told that

he must say *három könyvek* "three books" just because that is the way they say it in Latin or English or
some other language?

Many other "grammar rules", although not derived
from Latin grammar, are still quite inaccurate and unfounded: the best example of this is the "shall" and
"will" rules that we are taught with regard to the future
of English verbs. Most of us can never remember
those rules, and are always uneasy about whether we
are or are not making a mistake in their application: is
it *I shall go* or *I will go, he should go* or *he would go*?
We have been told that there is some difference in the
meaning of each member of these pairs, that one of
them indicates "determination" and the other "simple
futurity"—but which? As a matter of fact, there is no
wonder that we can't remember—because such a distinction does not really exist: in normal speech we
would usually say *I'll go, he'd go, we'll go.* Even with
the full forms, there is no distinction in meaning, except
the artificial distinction that we may have been taught
to make. Where did the grammar books get this rule?
A seventeenth-century English grammarian, one John
Wallis, sitting in his study, dreamed the rule up, manu-
factured it out of whole cloth, and put it in his book;
and later grammarians have copied and re-copied it,
each from his predecessor. Its relation to the facts of
the English language is completely null, and its origin
classifies it among works of fiction rather than of
science.

And even with rules that do state normal, current
usage accurately—have they any authority beyond that
of simple statements of fact? We have already seen
that there is no legal sanction, not even any semi-legal
academic backing, for any claim to "authority" in language and its use. Suppose that usage should change,
and that what we now say universally (such as *he goes,*

she sings) should go out of fashion and be replaced by some other usage which we now wouldn't accept (like *he go, she sing*). Would the old be "right" and the new be "wrong"? By no means; if people's habits and usage change, then there is no "authority", no law that can keep them from doing so, and the new is just as good as the old. Not necessarily better, of course: neither better nor worse, but just different. Some of us are inclined to think that because a habit, a custom, or a thing is old, it must necessarily be better than something new. This was the prevailing attitude all through ancient times and the Middle Ages, and has lasted even up to now in some matters like those of language; it is the only reason some grammarians have for preferring one usage to another.

Another norm that is often set up for deciding disputed points is the usage of great writers: do we find *it ain't, he don't* or split infinitives in great writers, men who must have had great knowledge of their own language in order to write their great books? First of all, though, we must ask *which* great writers—those of the present, or those of the past? Our choice is difficult here; if we go too far back, the literary language is obviously archaic, and nobody nowadays, not even the most conservative grammarian, would recommend every feature of Milton's or Dr. Johnson's prose for our modern usage. If we come too close to the present, it is hard to tell just who is a really great writer and who is not; and, even if we have our great writers picked out, we find that very often they use freely the very forms we want to condemn, especially the more "realistic" writers like Steinbeck and Farrell. Then let's restrict our choice of great writers to, say, the late nineteenth and early twentieth century, so that they will fit what we want to prescribe. Even so, we find that their actual usage was considerably freer than we want to think. Hence the defensive accusations we often hear dogmatic purists make, that "even the greatest writers" make this, that or the other "mistake".

Furthermore, just how much bearing does great literature and its language have on normal everyday usage? That great literature gives us examples of the *artistic* use of language, we can easily grant; and that studying the way a Thomas Hardy or a Henry James has manipulated his language will be of use to us if we want to write literature—likewise granted. But such men as Hardy or James (to say nothing of authors like Carlyle or Meredith) are not typical, they are exceptional, in their language as in their content; and the very fact that they are exceptional disqualifies them as examples for everyday, normal, non-literary usage. Wouldn't it be nice if we all tried to talk like great literature in our daily contacts? It would be almost like trying to handle everyday affairs in the style of grand opera.

The entire attempt to set up absolute standards, rigid norms, for regulating people's language is destined to failure from the outset, because, as we have seen in this chapter: 1) there is no authority that has either the right or the ability to govern people's usage; and 2) such an authority, even when it has been set officially (as were the French and Spanish Academies), can never find valid standards by which to govern usage. Logic, Latin grammar, the usage of literature, appeals to authority as such—none have any applicability. In our country, especially, attempts to prescribe rules, to set up a normative grammar, have been very widespread, and have battened on our insecurities, on our fears for our social standing in the face of linguistic shibboleths. But all such attempts have been, and will continue to be, failures.

Is there any definition at all that we can give for

"good" language? Only, I think, something like this: "good" language is language which gets the desired effect with the least friction and difficulty for its user. That means, of course, that "good" language is going to vary with the situation it is used in. In elegant or puristically inclined society, "good" usage will include *it isn't he, he doesn't,* and also *this kind of people, it is I,* since those forms will get the best results in favor and compliance with what we desire. In normal everyday situations with normal everyday people, *it isn't him, he don't, these kind of people, it's me* will be good usage, since ordinary people speak that way normally; and we won't be too worried about saying *damn!* unless our hearers have specific objections. With people who customarily say *it ain't him, he don't, we seen them, hisn,* those forms will be good usage, provided they serve to get results most effectively.

One type of confusion which often crops up at this point, and which we should be on our guard against, is that between language and style. We are often inclined to think that "correctness" is the same thing as good style, particularly in writing. Actually, the two are not the same, though the situation is parallel for both. "Good" style is simply that style of speaking or writing which is most effective under any given set of circumstances. When we speak of "good style", what we usually mean is clarity, absence of ambiguity, orderly structure, and the like—and these are, indeed, important in most situations. But they are not the same thing as type of language, and "good style" is possible in any dialect. Aesthetic considerations—whether a given way of expressing ourselves is pleasing or not to our listeners or readers—of course enter into the picture, too, with regard to "good" style. But all matters of aesthetics depend so much on individual preference, and differ so much not only from one language to another but from one speaker to another, that no one can presume to set up objective standards for them, nor legislate or make authoritative pronouncements on what is or is not pleasing to the ear or to the eye.

"Right" and "wrong", then, have no meaning, as applied to language, apart from the situations in which language is used. That is, by definition, we can never be wrong in our own language, when we use it as we have grown up speaking it, among our own family and friends. The ditch-digger who says *him and me ain't got none* and who uses swear-words and "four-letter" words freely is absolutely right—in his own language. His type of speech is not necessarily right for the language of other groups, just through the very fact that they speak differently. But when we condemn the ditch-digger's speech, we do so, not because of any inherent demerit of the way he talks, but because we take his speech as being characteristic of his social class. This factor in our speech attitudes is a relic from earlier, antidemocratic times, which accords very poorly with other aspects of our modern aspirations to true democracy.

When a person who has grown up using *him and me ain't got none* speaks in his normal, natural way and is told he is "wrong", therefore, all that this really means is that he is using these forms in a situation where his usage would make things harder rather than easier for him. But most often—in fact, we can say usually— neither the person making the "error" nor the one criticizing him understands this. As a result, speakers who have not been brought up speaking "correctly" are made to feel inferior, and either have to make a strong (and often poorly guided) effort to change their habits of speech, or else take shelter behind defensive feelings of hostility, mockery, etc., towards the approved type of speech. Current prescriptions of "right" and "wrong" thus serve only to divide our society, and to increase further the split between upper and lower, favored and unfavored classes—just at the time when greater unity, not greater division, is our crying need.

In short: the entire structure of our notions about "correctness" and "right" vs. "wrong" in language is not only inaccurate, erroneous and useless; it is definitely harmful, and we would do well to outgrow it. When purists tell us that we are using "bad" or "incorrect" or "ungrammatical" language, they are simply telling us that what we say would not be acceptable in the upper social levels; sometimes they are right as to the facts of the case, and sometimes they are just talking through their hats. What our purists give us in the way of rules and laws to observe has no authority, no validity aside from their own preference, and is often based on specious pseudo-logic or on the structure of a distantly related language, Latin, which has no relevance to English. If an "error" or "mistake" is frequent, if almost everybody makes it, if it is found in even the greatest writers, then it is no error: as the great Byzantine emperor and law-codifier Justinian put it, *communis error facit iūs*—a mistake that everybody makes is no longer a mistake. We need to look at our language realistically, not feeling "inferior" about it and taking nobody's word as to its being "right" or "wrong". Often enough, we may find we need to change our usage, simply because social and financial success depends on some norm, and our speech is one of the things that will be used as a norm. In a situation like this, it is advisable to make the adjustment; but let's do so on the basis of the actual social acceptability of our speech, not because of the fanciful prescriptions of some normative grammarian or other pseudo-authority.

3. Marks You Make with Your Fist

An episode in a current comic book shows the main characters of the story coming to a strange planet. They find a people who talk, but who have no writing. The heroes of the comic book produce the English alphabet and teach it to the inhabitants of the planet; at which point, one of the heroes remarks, "Now the people of this planet have a language."

A book for beginners in French used a way of spelling French which was not the ordinary way of spelling, but which was designed specifically and systematically to help the learner hear the sounds of the language and distinguish them clearly: for instance, *chaude* "hot" was written *SHÔD*, *mauvaise* "bad" was written *mô-VEZ*, *froide* "cold" was written *FRWAD*, and so on down the line. Most people who worked with the book liked this way of starting; but some wanted to know "When are we going to get to the *real* language?" And one professor who didn't like the book condemned it because (he said) writing *SHÔD* for the "real" French *chaude* or *mô-VEZ* for *mauvaise* was reducing the French language to the level of *I wanna* or *watcher gonna do* of the comic strips. Similar objections were raised to the phonetic transcription *KIE-ro* for Spanish *quiero* "I want" and to *KWAN-do* for Italian *quando* "when".

It's easy to see what is wrong in the two situations just described: the author of the comic book in the first paragraph, and the students who wanted the "real" language and the protesting professors in the second paragraph, were confusing writing and speech. But instances of this confusion are anything but rare; in fact, they are very typical of what we meet almost every day in public or private discussions of language. Defenders of the "purity" of the language write to the newspapers and protest against such spellings as *nite* for *night, thru* for *through, altho* for *although,* or against using an apostrophe in *it's* meaning "of it". We all know how little headway simplified spelling has made; opposition to any change in spelling has been so strong that, some years ago, when a widely read Mid-West newspaper had started to use a type of "simplified" spelling such as *aile* for *aisle,* it was forced to give up the attempt because of objections from outraged readers. Whenever we discuss language, we find it hard (if not impossible) to do so except in terms of letters and spelling: if I say *writin'* instead of *writing,* someone may tell me not to "drop my *g's*", and if I pronounce *thyme* with the initial sound of *think,* I may be told that I am "pronouncing the *h*" in *thyme.* Somewhat more sophisticated people, who are aware that sounds exist separately from letters and that the two don't always correspond, will usually talk of the "written language" and the "spoken language". We are often inclined to think that "written language" is more important than "spoken language", so that the spelling should serve as a guide to our pronunciation: as a result, we frequently pronounce a *t* in *often,* or make *again* rhyme with *rain.* In short, almost all of us tend to think of language in terms of writing and spelling and only secondarily, if at all, in terms of sounds; and we usually consider sounds subordinate to and determined by letters.

"Well," the reader may ask, "Why not? What's wrong with that idea? After all, doesn't writing have the value of being permanent, while the spoken word is fleeting and impossible to make permanent except by writing? Didn't Horace, two thousand years ago, point out that the written word remains as it is—*littera scripta manet* —and is consequently more reliable than the spoken word? Aren't there many languages which have sounds that can't be described or written accurately? Isn't even English an unphonetic language, with its vowels pronounced now one way and now another, and its consonants often not pronounced at all, as in the series *rough, bough, though, through, trough, hiccough?* Don't sounds vary from one dialect to the next, even from one person to the next, as in the different American pronunciations of *dog* (as "dahg" or "dawg")? Wouldn't we, therefore, do better to stick to writing, which is something we can see and understand clearly, rather than let the sound confuse us and lead us astray?"

Even at the risk of shattering cherished illusions, the answer to all these questions definitely has to be in the negative. When we think of writing as more important than speech, as having a priority over speech, as determining speech, we are putting the cart before the horse in every respect: historical origin, present-day function, and present-day importance of writing with respect to speaking. As a matter of fact, writing is essentially a way of representing speech, almost always an imperfect and inaccurate way. It came later in human development than speaking. In the sum total of human relations, even in the most civilized societies, writing is vastly less used than speaking. It is perfectly true that writing is very important in our modern civilization, and that there are even some things we can do with writing that we cannot do with speech; but it still is less important than speech. (Think of how much our daily lives would be slowed up, in fact brought practically to a standstill, if we were suddenly all stricken mute and forced to rely on writing alone for all our communication with each other!)

Each of these points needs more discussion in detail. We may not realize it, in fact our whole training in schools and colleges teaches us to think the opposite; but writing is an activity which grew up relatively late in the history of mankind, and which is still not known to a great part of the human race. Man has been a speaking being for a very long time—at least between five hundred thousand and a million years—but, on the other hand, he has known how to write for only a few thousand years, since the time hieroglyphic writing came into use in ancient Egypt and cuneiform writing was developed in Sumeria. If we assume that the beginnings of human speech may go back as far as five hundred thousand years, and writing for five or six thousand years, that means man has been writing for one hundredth the length of time he has been speaking. Even if we prefer, without evidence, to date the beginning of writing farther back, say as far as 8000 B.C., and to think of man as having known writing for ten thousand years, that still leaves the proportion of time as only one to fifty. Obviously, the invention of writing came extremely late in man's history; and human speech was already fully developed as a set of habits, and had existed for hundreds of thousands of years, when writing came into use. And its use was restricted to a very few people, mostly to the members of special groups such as priests or government officials, or at the most to members of the upper classes, until quite recently, until the past hundred or hundred-and-fifty years in Western Europe. Even now, the proportion of people who use writing in China, India, the East Indies, Africa, South and Central America, is relatively small. Yet certainly the great human masses of Asia and Africa are none the less human, and make no less use of language just because they do not know how to read and write. They talk to each other all the time, and live their lives quite successfully so far as linguistic communication goes, without any use of writing.

"Well, that's all right as far as it goes," someone may say, "but aren't you omitting half the story? There is spoken language, and nobody in his senses would deny its existence or even its priority in point of time, but there's written language too, and you're wanting to leave that out of the picture." Perhaps a clarification of terms might help here. If you want to use the term *language* to cover both what people say and what they write, well and good. So far in this discussion, we have tried to use the word *language* in such a way that its reference might be to either. The other alternative is to specifically delimit the meaning of the term *language* for the purposes of our discussion, and to agree that we will use that term to refer to speech activity, and some other term for writing activity—the word *writing* will do as well as any other. It does not matter which we do, provided we agree beforehand and stick to the meanings we agree on; after all, any word means simply whatever its users make it mean. But, no matter what words we use for the activities of speaking and writing, there still remains a basic fact: that those two activities are fundamentally distinct in their nature, and stand in a definite relation to each other. Speaking is an activity that we learn in our earliest childhood, from our second year onward; for every normal human being, speech is a set of habits which he uses in all his daily relations with his fellow men, and whose structure and system is pretty well set by the time he is six years old. (A six-year old child has the basic sounds and grammatical patterns of his lan-

guage down as well as he ever will have them, except
for a few minor fluctuations that iron out soon after-
wards.) Writing, on the other hand, is an activity that
we always learn *after* we learn to speak, if we learn it
at all. Writing is done with the hands, and is perceived
with the eyes; whereas we talk with our organs of
speech, and hear with our ears. Moreover, writing is a
derivative of speech; that is to say, the symbols we use
(whether they are hieroglyphs, cuneiform signs or
letters) are always based on speech, directly or indirectly, and are a more or less complete and accurate
representation of speech. There is no need of insisting
on the fact that systems of writing are often quite incomplete and inaccurate in their correspondence to
speech; English spelling is a notorious example. There
are other ways of communication, such as Morse tele-
graphic code or various cyphers, which in their turn
are based on writing—and therefore, through writing,
ultimately on speech. Even the so-called "gesture language" of the Plains Indians, to say nothing of the "fin-
ger language" of deaf-mutes, is ultimately based on
speech. Writing is based on speech, not the other way
around, as a moment's reflection will show; and codes
and cyphers and "gesture languages" are simply more
remote derivatives of speech.

In this situation, the use of the term *language* to refer to both speaking and writing is rather likely to lead
to difficulty, since such a use will bring confusion between two radically different activities, and will lead
to the implication that they are both on an equal level,
whereas the one (writing) is definitely subordinate in
historical origin and in present-day function to the
other (speaking). In short, as we have just seen, writing is a set of marks you make with your fist, whereas
speech is a set of noises you make with your face. Both
have the same object, communication with your fellow

men; but they are not equal, speaking being prior to writing. From now on, we shall use the term *language* exclusively to refer to activities involving speaking; and we would do well, from this point of view, to avoid the term "written language" as being, in a certain sense, a contradiction in terms: *language* can be, by our present definition, only spoken, and only *writing* is written.

Of course, writing is very useful, and no intelligent person would deny its great value and its extension in our modern civilization. Writing serves to represent speech, and thus to carry our words to places and to times that we cannot reach with our own voices—to the other side of the world, or to our descendants. Before mechanical means of voice-transmission and recording were invented (telephone, radio, tape, sound-film), writing was the only way we had of representing speech; but these means of sending or recording speech itself have tended to supplement, rather than replace writing, because of their mechanical complexity. Without speech itself, all human society as we know it would be impossible; without writing, our highly complex civilization would be impossible. For advanced technical work, writing is indispensable, and for some types of analysis, as in mathematics, writing makes possible some work that would not be possible with speech alone. But all these facts do not change the basic relation of writing to language, which is that of a derivative.

"But," I hear someone saying, "writing is fixed and clear, with a limited number of symbols, whereas speech (or language, if you choose to arbitrarily limit your term that way) is always vague, kaleidoscopic, without clear limits to its sounds, and cannot be adequately grasped without being reduced to writing."

Nothing could be farther from the facts. Every language, whether it has a system of writing to represent it or not, moves within a clearly definable range of significant speech-sounds, or *phonemes*.

This word *phoneme* is an important technical term, and just as essential in linguistics as *molecule* or *atom* are in chemistry, or *neutron* and *proton* in nuclear physics. It will be explained more in detail in Chapter 6 (pp. 89 ff.); for the purposes of this discussion, we can define a phoneme briefly as a unit of sound which makes a difference in the meaning of words. For instance, the English words *bit* and *pit* each consist of three significant units of sound, or phonemes, and differ from each other only in the first phoneme. Similarly, *bit* and *beat* each consist of three phonemes, and differ only in the second phoneme (the vowel sounds which we represent by the letter *i* for the vowel of *bit,* and by the two letters *ea* for the vowel of *beat*). And *bit* and *bid* differ from each other only in the last phoneme. By this method of contrasting pairs of words, we can establish a series of meaningful differences among sounds, and each difference serves to set up a pair of contrasting phonemes. Thus, from the words *bit, pit, beat* and *bid,* we establish the existence in English of the phonemes which are represented in spelling by the letters *b, p, i, ea, t* and *d.*

Now the differences between the phonemes of every language are 1) clearly noticeable to every native speaker of the language in question, and 2) easily analyzable and statable by one trained in linguistic analysis. Of course, the phonemes of one language are not the same as those of another language; but every language has meaningfully distinct sounds, or phonemes, and there is no such thing as an "inarticulate" or "unphonetic" language. What makes us think, often, that some language (say, French or German or Swahili or Potawatomi) is confused as to its sounds, and is simply "very nasal" or "very guttural" or "unpronounceable", is that its phonemes are not the same as ours, and often their range is not the same. We may have difficulty grasping the difference in sound between the French words *un* "one" (with nasalized vowel sound) and *eux* "they" (with non-nasalized vowel); but, on the other hand, the Frenchman will at first miss the very important difference between the vowels of English *beat* and *bit*. There is no more sense to our getting angry and calling French "unphonetic", than to the Frenchman's feeling that way towards English. We, as native speakers of English, have learned to make such a distinction as that between *beat* and *bit* ever since our childhood, and so it seems natural to us; but we did not learn to distinguish between nasal and non-nasal vowels, and so that seems unnatural. But the Frenchman's conditioning since childhood makes him feel the other way around. It is just a question of what you're brought up to think natural. All languages are articulate, pronounceable, and "phonetic" by definition—if they did not have clear distinctions between their phonemes they would not be languages.

Writing, as we know it in our Western European tradition, is essentially a symbolization of the significant sounds, the phonemes, of a language. (Chinese characters and similar "ideographic" systems of writing represent, not sounds, but units of linguistic form, or *morphemes* [to be taken up later, pp. 105 ff.]; but "ideographic" writing isn't relevant to our discussion here.) Writing is something completely arbitrary, and no letter has any innate or necessary connection with any particular sound; nor is any particular set of letters (such as our alphabet) especially holy or inviolable. People often object to letters or alphabets that they are not familiar with, and sometimes even regard a phonetic alphabet as a hindrance rather than a help in learning a foreign language. Such people apparently go on the assumption that the Lord created the universe, the world, the Garden of Eden, the animals and fishes and flowers, Adam and Eve, and the twenty-six letters of our alphabet—and that hence the alphabet we know and use for English must never be changed or used in any way other than what they already know. I used to think that this assumption was not usually stated outright, nor given clear-cut form in schools or elsewhere; but this very attitude towards the Roman alphabet is found, in so many words, at the end of Kipling's fanciful story "How The Alphabet Was Made", in *Just So Stories:*

> "And after thousands and thousands and thousands of years, and after Hieroglyphics and Demotics, and Nilotics, and Cryptics, and Cufics, and Runics, and Dorics, and Ionics, and all sorts of other ricks and tricks (because the Woons, and the Neguses, and the Akhoonds, and the Repositories of Tradition would never leave a good thing alone when they saw it), the fine old easy, understandable Alphabet—A, B, C, D, E and the rest of 'em—got back into its proper shape again for all Best Beloveds to learn when they are old enough."*

Kipling was being humorous, of course; but none the less, that is an excellent statement of the attitude that many people have in all seriousness.

In reality, it does not matter what letters are used to represent one sound or the other; provided the letters are used consistently, they give a good representation, and if they are used inconsistently (as in English spelling) they give a poor representation. In most civilizations, the spelling of the language has come to be fixed through custom, and becomes something to which people have an unreasoning emotional attachment, despite any shortcomings it may have. Such a fixed customary spelling as we have for English, French, German, etc., is usually called *conventional spelling* or

---

* From *Just So Stories*, by Rudyard Kipling, copyright 1902 by Rudyard Kipling, reprinted by permission of Doubleday & Company, Inc.

traditional orthography. Other systems of writing are often devised to give more accurate ways of representing the phonemes of language, often with peculiar or unfamiliar letters where the Roman alphabet does not suffice; such systems are called *transcriptions*, and are an indispensable tool for the linguistic analyst and for the language learner, as we shall see later (Chapter 6).

When we look at matters in this light, we see immediately that a great deal of what people currently think and say about language is, to put it mildly, set up on the wrong basis. To return to the characters in the comic book who said they were giving the hitherto illiterate people of their newly discovered planet a "language" by teaching them the ABC's, it should now be obvious why such a statement would be absurd. The people of the planet had a language already, by the very fact that they were able to talk; giving them a writing system was adding something to their civilization, by giving them a means of representing, of symbolizing, their language, but it was not giving them a language or even changing their language at all. The underlying assumption that the English alphabet would be quite satisfactory to give them is equally absurd, as the English alphabet is not automatically suitable for all other languages just by the fact of its existence and use in our civilization. And the professors who objected to spelling the French word for "hot" as *SHŌD*, or the Spanish for "I want" as *KIE-ro*, because that was reducing French or Spanish "to the level of *I wanna* of the comic strips", were making a hopeless confusion between language, i.e. speech, and writing. The French word for "hot" consists of three phonemes, one like our *sh*-sound, one like our *o*-sound, and one like our *d*-sound. It could be spelled any number of different ways: in conventional French spelling as *chaude,* in the alphabet of the International Phonetic

Association as ʃod, in other phonetic transcriptions as šod, chôd, shôd, or what have you. We could even, if there were any reason for so doing, transcribe it axq, by setting a = the sh-sound, x = the o-sound, and q = the d-sound. But the French word would still remain exactly the same word pronounced in exactly the same way, and meaning exactly the same thing in French. Similarly, you can take a person's picture in black and white or in color, with one type of lighting or another, with a box camera or a Leica, on film or on a glass plate —but no matter how you take the person's picture and no matter how good or bad a representation the picture gives of him, the person himself remains the same.

How could this confusion, which is so widespread, come about? The real nature of writing in its relation to language is so obvious, that it might seem strange that so much misunderstanding could arise about it. Probably the confusion is due to two things: the nature of our English spelling system, and the age at which we start to learn it. People whose languages have a simple, relatively accurate conventional spelling, like Italian, Hungarian, or Finnish, are not confused as to the relation of writing and speech, and are often surprised at the misunderstanding that spellers of English show. But our traditional orthography for English is quite far removed from the reality of speech, and our letters certainly do not stand in a wholly one-to-one relationship with the phonemes of our speech. It takes considerable effort and many years (as we all well know!) to completely master our English conventional spelling; and once we have learned it, it represents a considerable investment. Nobody likes to give up the fruits of any investment, and the more costly it is, the less we want to discard it; and so it is with the spelling of English. Once we have learned it, we have a strong emotional attachment to it, just because we have had considerable difficulty with it and have been forced to put in so much time and effort on learning it.

Furthermore, we learn to speak long before we are able to do any kind of reflective or analytical intellectual work; we learn to speak when we are small children, by a purely unreflecting process of repeated trial and error. But when we go to school and learn to write, we do so consciously and reflectingly. If, in our first school contacts with writing, we were taught a scientifically accurate phonemic spelling, which reflected all the facts of our speech itself, we would have very little trouble and would learn to use such a spelling in a year or two, as do Italian or Hungarian children. But we do not learn an accurate phonemic spelling; we learn our inaccurate, confused traditional English orthography, and we talk about it as we do so. When we were little children learning how to speak, we learned only to speak, not how to analyze our speech. When we are older and learn to spell, we also learn how to talk about spelling and how to analyze it: we are taught to name the letters, to tell how we replace letters by apostrophes or how we drop letters, and so forth. But we still learn nothing whatsoever about how to discuss speech and analyze it in its own terms; the only approach, the only vocabulary we end up with for discussing language is the approach and the vocabulary of spelling. Edith Wharton, in *The Custom of the Country*, says of one of her characters:

> Mrs. Spragg, when she found herself embarked on a wrong sentence, always ballasted it by italicizing the last word.

What Mrs. Wharton meant, of course, was "emphasizing" or "stressing" the last word; but the only term at her disposal was the word *italicizing*, the term that referred to spelling rather than to speech.

This entire situation has given results that are little short of disastrous for the understanding of the true nature of language, throughout the English-speaking world. Very few people have any clear idea of what they actually do when they speak—what organs of their body they use and in what way they use them. Many people find it difficult or downright impossible to conceive of sounds as such, or to hear differences in sound that are not directly related to differences in English spelling. Some even develop emotional blockings on the subject of phonetic analysis, because the strange appearance and use of special symbols in a transcription makes them "feel all funny inside", as one such person put it to me. When it comes to discussing sounds, the only way to identify many sounds in writing for the general reader who knows no phonetics, is to avoid all letters entirely, and to give cumbersome definitions like "the vowel sound of *bit*" or "the initial sound of *thing*"; for, if we were to speak of the *i* of *hit* or the *th* of *thing*, almost everyone would immediately read off those definitions as "the 'eye' (*i*) of *hit*" or "the 'tee aitch' (*th*) of *thing*." Likewise for a discussion of grammar or of syntax, we can recognize grammatical facts which we see reflected in the conventional spelling, like the vowel change in *sing sang sung;* but we find it hard to recognize or discuss those grammatical facts which are not indicated in writing, like the difference between the final consonant sounds of *house* (noun, as in *he has a big house*) and *house* (verb, as in *where can we house them?*), or the change in vowel sound between *you* (stressed, as in *is that you?*) and *you* (unstressed, as in *how do you do?*).

All kinds of misunderstandings and misrepresentations arise as a result of this spelling-induced confusion and ignorance. People often think that spelling a word out is the best way to tell someone how to pronounce it, and think that the names of the letters alone will give a key to the sounds that are involved. I once witnessed a prize example of this confusion when a high-school girl named Carlys (normally pronounced as if spelled *Carleece*, stress on last syllable) was trying to tell my four-year old boy Philip how to pronounce her name, which he had some difficulty with:

PHILIP: Hey, Craleeth!
CARLYS: No, no. Not Craleeth; Carlys. Say that.
PHILIP: Craleeth.
CARLYS: No, no, no. Carlys. CAR-LYS.
PHILIP: Craleeth.
CARLYS: No! Look; shall I spell it out for you?
PHILIP (not knowing what "spelling it out" meant): Yes.
CARLYS: See, ay, ahr, ell, wye, ess. Now say it.
PHILIP: Craleeth.
CARLYS: !!!

Many times we think that, because a word is spelled with a certain letter, we ought to pronounce some sound to correspond to that letter: we pronounce a *t*-sound in *fasten*, we pronounce three syllables in *Wednesday*, we sometimes even try to pronounce the initial *p* in words like *psychology* or *ptarmigan*. This kind of behavior is known as *spelling-pronunciation;* it almost never occurs where a language has a reasonably accurate system of spelling, but always crops up whenever the spelling ceases to represent the language adequately. Our pronunciation of *author* is a case in point. Older English had a word *autor*, meaning "creator, author", which had been borrowed from the French word *autor* of the same meaning, ultimately taken from Latin *auctor*. In the sixteenth century, people came to realize that many words previously spelled with *t* came from Latin or Greek sources in which they were spelled with *th,* such as *theater, thesis.* It came to be a mark of elegance and learning to write *th* instead of *t;* but some people carried their learning too far and wrote *th* even where it didn't belong, as in *author* for *autor.* Then more and more people, seeing the letters *th* in the elegant spelling of *author,* pronounced the *th* with the sound those letters stand for in *thing;* by now, that spelling-pronunciation has become general and we all pronounce *author* with that sound, not with the *t*-sound it originally had. Needless to say, spelling-pronunciation serves no good purpose, and only introduces confusion and misunderstanding into otherwise clear situations, like those of *autor* or *fasten.* That is, once upon a time *autor* was pronounced with a *t*-sound, and everybody was quite happy about it; now, everybody says it with a *th*-sound and is equally happy about it; but nothing has been gained by the change, and there was no need of the uncertainty that prevailed during the period of transition.

"Correct" spelling, that is, obedience to the rules of English spelling as grammarians and dictionary-makers set them up, has come to be a major shibboleth in our society. If I write *seet* instead of *seat, roat* instead of *wrote,* or *hite* instead of *height,* it makes no difference whatsoever in the English language, i.e. in my speech and that of others around me; yet we are all trained to give highly unfavorable reactions to such spellings, and to be either amused or displeased with people who know no better than to "misspell" in such a way. This shibboleth serves, as does that of "correct" speech, as a means of social discrimination: we can class people among the sheep or the goats according as they measure up to the standards we set in spelling. Spelling which is more nearly in accord with speech, and which we might logically expect to be considered better than the conventional spelling, thus comes to be, not praised, but blamed. Spelling "phonetically" becomes equivalent to spelling incorrectly. I once came across a reference to "phonetic" pronunciation, which at first puzzled me, since pronunciation can by definition never be anything but phonetic; it later turned out that the writer was referring to inaccurate pronunciation of a foreign language, such as French *est-ce que vous avez* "have you?" pronounced in a way which he transcribed *ess-ker-vooz-avay*. He had come to use the term "phonetic" as equivalent to "incorrect", through the folk use of the term *phonetic spelling* in the meaning of "incorrect spelling".

When we write down the exact words of people whose speech we consider "incorrect", we often purposely misspell their words to indicate their pronunciation and give the reader an idea of what social level they belong to; the realistic novels of Erskine Caldwell, John Steinbeck and others are full of these spelling devices: for instance, *Elviry done tole me she ain' a-gwineta do no sich thing fer nobuddy.* This shocks purists who are attached to "correct" spelling at all costs; but it is spreading more and more as an element of realism, which of course derives its force from the contrast between normal "correct" spelling and pronunciation, and the "incorrect" speech implied by the "incorrect" spelling. A further development of this device is so-called *eye-dialect*, in which misspellings are used to represent normal pronunciations, merely to burlesque words or their speaker. We all pronounce *women* in the same way; but if we spell it *wimmin*, we imply "The person quoted is one who would use a vulgar pronunciation if there were one." Likewise the spellings *licker* instead of *liquor, vittles* instead of *victuals, sez* instead of *says,* and the host of reduced forms such as *I wanna* for *I want to, ya oughta* for *you ought to, watcher gonna do* for *what are you going to do,* or *I hafta* for *I have to.*

This last group of examples may not, at first, seem accurate, because we are often not aware how much we reduce and telescope such combinations in normal speech; but just try observing yourself and see how many times a day you actually use the full, separate forms of the words in such an expression as *what are you going to do,* or *I have to do it.* In fact, *I have to* with a *v*-sound in *have* would be not only unusual, it would be abnormal. But, because of our conventions of spelling, the more realistic and accurate spellings like *I wanna* or *I hafta* are relegated to the comic strips and are made the objects of prejudice, which can be appealed to in whipping up opposition to phonetic transcription or to the writing of, say, the Italian word for "when" as *KWAN-do* instead of the conventional *quando.*

The situation with respect to spelling is much the same as it is with regard to "correct" speech in our society. In each case, an irrational, meaningless standard is set up as a shibboleth for people to conform to, which in many instances puts a premium on lack of realism and on unnaturalness in speech or its representation. In particular, our society's emphasis on the irregularities of English spelling has brought many of us to a point where we cannot distinguish between speech and writing, and where we cannot even conceive of sounds as existing distinct from and prior to letters. Consequently, anyone who goes through our schooling system has to waste years of his life in acquiring a wasteful and, in the long run, damaging set of spelling habits, thus ultimately unfitting himself to understand the nature of language and its function unless he puts in extra effort to rid himself of all the misconceptions and prejudices that our system has foisted on him.

4. What Price History?

Just somebody's say-so is hardly a valid standard to hold language to; neither is spelling, as we have seen in the last two chapters. Well, what are we going to do about it? If the present time is not a good norm for us to follow, how about the past? Things were usually better in the past than they are now, many people think; isn't that so in the case of language? As a matter of fact, such a notion is pretty widespread. People are often telling us that we find "pure" English in Shakespeare and the King James Bible, and that our modern language is corrupted from what it was in earlier, better times. Consequently, they tell us that we should use words only in the meanings they had in Shakespeare's or Milton's time: for instance, that if we use the word *nice* to mean "pleasant, agreeable", we are using the word wrongly, since it earlier meant— and hence "really" means—"fine, delicate, subtle" (as in *a nice distinction*).

Is there any validity to such a claim? No scientific linguist will admit there is. In the first place, our speech, like all other speech, goes back to that of our indefinitely distant ancestors in the remote past, hundreds of thousands of years ago. If we set value simply on the age of a form or of a meaning as such, then we ought to make our usage accord with the earliest usage that ever existed. But where are we going to stop? Take the instance of *nice*: true, at an earlier time *nice* meant "fine"—and at a still earlier time it meant "silly". *Nice* was borrowed by English in the Middle Ages from Old French, in which it meant "foolish".

"Very well," someone may say, "let's restrict the use of *nice* to the meaning 'foolish', and condemn all later corruptions such as the meanings 'fine' and 'pleasant, agreeable'." No, we can't stop there; for Old French *nice* went back to a Latin word *nēscius,* which meant "ignorant".

"Then we'll have to purify the word *nice* still further, restricting it to the meaning 'ignorant'; if we say *Joe's a nice boy,* that ought to mean really 'Joe's an ignorant boy'." We can't stop there either. Latin *nēscius* is derived from the Latin root *scī-* "to know", so that *nēscius* meant "not knowing". Now Latin was descended from a language which is usually called Indo-European; and the root which in Latin had the form *scī-* "to know", in Indo-European had a form which we represent by *sqēi-* and which meant "to cut, to separate" (developing in Latin through the meaning "to distinguish" into that of "to know"). So *nice,* going back to a negative derivative of Indo-European *sqēi-* "to cut", ought to mean "not cutting".

"Well, that must have been its original meaning, wasn't it; for wasn't Indo-European the language out of which all others developed?" Sorry; wrong in both parts of the question. Indo-European was simply the language out of which Latin, Germanic, Slavic, Celtic, Indic and various other groups of languages developed; it was, however, just a language like all others, and it had hundreds of thousands of years of history behind it, like all other languages. That the Indo-European root *sqēi-* had not always meant "to cut" is pretty certain, for language is always changing; what it may have meant before Indo-European times, we have no way of knowing, because our evidence does not go that far back. But we have no right to assume that *any* stage of language in the last few hundred thousand years gives us the "original" or "true" form or meaning of any word. At present *nice* means—whatever our generation makes it mean; and if our generation uses it in the meaning "pleasant, agreeable", then that is its correct meaning for our generation.

"But, even if we can't get back to the original meaning of any word or form, isn't the meaning set by the great periods of the language? You certainly can't say that our present language is great, in comparison to the English of Shakespeare and the Bible; and it's these latter that ought to serve us as models for our speech." First of all, we had perhaps better clarify the meaning of *great* as applied to periods of a language. Is one stage of a language any greater, any better in itself than any other stage?—in itself, that is, quite apart from any considerations of a non-linguistic nature such as social standing or literature. Were the noises that the Elizabethans made with their faces, and the meanings they gave to those noises, any better, finer, more beautiful, or of greater worth as communication, than those that we make with our faces? There is no reason to believe that they were. No language can be said to be in itself any "better" than any other, or any "worse" than any other. Of course, each language has some distinctions, in sounds, forms, words, that others lack; but positive and negative balance each other, by and large, in all languages. As for beauty, that is of course a matter of individual preference; to some people, Italian or Swedish or French seems more pleasing than any other language, whereas it does not to others, and in language preference (as in every other aesthetic matter) one man's meat is another man's poison. And for efficiency of communication, the available evidence seems to show that the Elizabethans—or people at any other stage of the language we care to mention—got

along with each other just about as well and just about
as badly as we do. Elizabethan English was not a better or more beautiful or more efficient stage of the language than our own—nor was it worse, less beautiful
or less efficient.

But people do often speak of, say, Elizabethan
English as one of the "great" stages of the language.
What do they mean by this? Since they cannot be
referring, except erroneously, to the merits of the
language itself, they must have something else in
mind. What they have in mind is quite clear: the
literature of the period. From a literary viewpoint,
Elizabethan England was very great; and we often
carry over our notion about this literary merit into our
views on the merits of the language. What justification
is there for such a carry-over? None. Literature and
language are two separate things, and the study and
judgment of the two is quite independent. Of course,
literature does not exist without language, since language is the medium of literary expression, just as
paint is the medium of oil painting, or stone or clay
is the medium of sculpture. But nobody would dream
of applying to the chemistry and optics of paint, or the
geology of stone and clay, the same measuring-sticks,
the same judgments of value, that we apply to the
artistic merits of oil painting or sculpture. Nobody
would say "They had much better stone in the Middle
Ages—look at all the beautiful cathedrals they built."
Likewise, the study and evaluation of language is a
thing that has quite different approaches, techniques
and conclusions from the judgment of literature as an
art. To say that some word or form is better than some
other, because Shakespeare or Milton or the King
James Bible used it, is like saying that a particular color
of red is better because Titian or Rubens used it. It

may perhaps be better for getting a particular aesthetic or artistic effect—that is the creative artist's or critic's concern, not ours; but it is obviously not better from a scientific or practical point of view.

The same type of professor who objects to the Italian word for "when" being written as *KWAN-do* (see Chapter 3) also often objects to leaving literary values out of consideration in studying languages. One of them asked "Is it quite fair to treat a language like French, which is the vehicle of a great culture and civilization, exactly as we treat some little-known tongue of central Africa that has no literary, cultural, or esthetic values, or even a written form?". This question shows the same confusion between language and writing that we noticed before; and it shows the confusion between language and literature that we have just been discussing. It obviously makes no difference in the merit of a language, *as a language,* whether it has a writing system connected with it (a "written language") or not. Just as obviously, it makes no difference in the merit of a language, *as a language,* whether it has a literature connected with it or not. When we speak of the literary or cultural "values" of a language, we are really not talking about the language itself at all; we are talking about the social standing, the prestige, of non-linguistic things such as culture and literature. Literature has no priority over language, and no relevance in determining our approach to language, from the scientific point of view; a worker in linguistics is not merely a kind of crow-baited student of literature, but a scientist working independently and in his own right. To paraphrase a sentence of Bernard DeVoto's, it is a fallacy to assume "that a language may be understood and judged solely by means of its literature, that literature is the highest expression of a language, that

literature is the measure of language, and finally that
language is subordinate to literature". Literature, in
itself a very valuable thing, is nevertheless not all of
life; literature and language both derive from life as
a whole, not life or language from literature.

In short, what the earlier state of a language may
have been, what a word may have meant or sounded
like at any earlier time, or what literature or culture
may have been expressed in a language at any time,
is quite beside the point when it comes to deciding
whether any particular sound, spelling, form, or word
is good at present. Purists have always been com-
plaining of change in language, and have never ac-
complished anything by their complaints. One such
purist, in the earlier part of the seventeenth century,
complained bitterly and railed against those who no
longer used *thou* and *thee* in speaking to one person:

> "Do not they speak false English, false Latine,
> false Greek . . . and false to the other Tongues . . .
> that doth not speak *thou* to *one*, what ever he be,
> Father, Mother, King, or Judge; is he not a Novice
> and unmannerly, and an Ideot and a Fool, that
> speaks *You* to *one*, which is not to be spoken to a
> *singular*, but to *many?* O Vulgar Professors and
> Teachers, that speaks Plural, when they should Sin-
> gular. . . . Come you Priests and Professors, have
> you not learnt your Accidence?"

Of course it did him no good. We now use *you* to
speak to one person or more than one person, and we
understand each other just as well and just as badly
now as people did in the old times when they distinguished between *thee, thou* and *ye, you*. To insist
on a language standing still, to complain because
people no longer obey the rules of the "goode olde

tymes", and to object to supposed "corruption" of the language, is to act like King Canute ordering the waves to recede—without the good sense of Canute, who (as the story tells) knew full well that his orders were futile and silly.

PART II: HOW LANGUAGE IS BUILT

5. Language Has System

In Part I, we've been criticizing existing attitudes and ideas about language fairly strongly, and suggesting that they are not as accurate as they might be, and that because of this inaccuracy of our notions our society not only wastes much effort, but does much actual harm. At this point in the discussion, if anyone makes criticisms like these, there are at least two main questions we ought to ask: 1) "By what right do you make these criticisms?" and 2) "What do you propose we should do about our language?". These are both very important questions, and the rest of this book will be devoted to answering them, in the order we have just asked them.

There are very good reasons, moreover, for taking them up in this order. The second question, what to do about our language, is of a practical order, it is true, and is immediate and pressing, whereas the first is theoretical, and deals with underlying facts and their analysis rather than with the solution of our problems. Yet we must always, before we try to solve a problem, have the necessary facts at our command, and understand how to go about arranging those facts and analyzing them scientifically; otherwise we can have no guarantee that our solution will be anything other than guess-work. Therefore we should first find out specifically what linguistic science has to tell us with regard to language, and then see how we can apply this new knowledge to the problems that worry us.

There is a further reason, in addition to the logical consideration of priority just mentioned, why we should first have a glance at the basis for the linguistic analyst's pronouncements. Up to now, in general, grammarians and teachers and those who have told others how to talk and what to do about their language, have done so on a purely *normative* basis—that is, setting up rules or norms and insisting that people follow them. Sometimes the normative grammarian has justified his dicta by appealing to "logic", sometimes to tradition, and sometimes to just the weight of his own say-so; but his attitude has always been authoritarian, i.e. depending on the force of authority and not on accurate observation and reasoning. The scientific attitude, on the other hand, rejects normative commands, and tries to base its conclusions on the greatest possible accuracy in observing facts, with the greatest possible objectivity, and on as careful reasoning and analysis as we can apply to the facts at our command. A true scientist also wants others to know as much of the truth as he can find out and make known, so that others also can follow his line of argument and, where possible, carry on up to and beyond whatever point he has reached. Now if we were to proceed immediately to the linguistic analyst's recommendations for changing our current ideas and behavior connected with language, we would be skipping an essential step in the process; and the linguist, by presenting his findings and his advice without first giving his reasons for so doing, would be converting himself from a scientist into simply another normative grammarian. In this process, there would be no gain; there is no use of substituting Language Authoritarian No. 2 for Language Authoritarian No. 1. What we need to do is rather to find out how we can escape entirely from the clutches of authoritarianism of any kind in language, and how we can ourselves acquire the essentials of a scientific attitude, and if we need to or want to, go ahead on our own in studying and thinking about language without being dependent on "authority".

When we want to imagine how things would seem to somebody who could look at us in a wholly objective, scientific way, we often put our reasoning in terms of a "man from Mars" coming to observe the earth and its inhabitants, living among men and studying their existence dispassionately and in its entirety. Such a "man from Mars," or some equally impartial observer, would notice, among the first things he saw in any human group, that its members cooperate by means of signals. They lend each other a hand, literally, in many undertakings, and they are able to exchange the use of all their faculties. We can build skyscrapers and bridges, manoeuver airplanes and battleships, warn each other of coming dangers and tell each other of past happenings, by means of signals. Theoretically, of course, any one of the five senses—touch, smell, taste, sight or hearing—could be used to make such signals. But our senses of touch, smell, and taste do not distinguish very clearly or sharply between various feelings, smells or tastes, and our memories for these senses are not as exact as they are for sight or hearing. These last two senses are more nearly on a par with each other, so far as clearness and sharpness of distinction and memory go: we can distinguish a signal that we see, and can remember it, just about as clearly as one that we hear. But hearing has certain advantages over sight, for signalling purposes: we can hear sounds coming from any direction, whereas we can see only things that are more or less in front of us; and we have, built into our bodies from birth, a pretty complex group of organs that we can use for making sounds, and a wide range of sounds that we can make—

whereas the range of visible signals we can make un-
aided is quite limited. Furthermore, we can make
sounds with the organs of our respiratory tract (what
cigarette advertisements call the "T-zone") without
interfering with what we are doing with the rest of
our body—working, resting, etc.—but any visible signals we might try to make (say, with arm signals) necessarily involve major disturbance to whatever else we
might be trying to do at the same time.

So our "man from Mars" would observe that humans
communicate by means of signals, and that these signals are primarily *oral* and *aural*—made with the
mouth and other "organs of speech", and heard with
the ear. He would observe this in any community he
was in, from the Australian Bushmen to the tribes of
the Congo, from the Navaho sheep-herders to the aris-
tocracy of Buckingham Palace. In fact, this is the
major, basic characteristic that he would find differentiating humans from other living beings: humans
talk, and talk extensively. They are not, by any means,
the only living beings to communicate by means of
auditory signals; but in the various animals that communicate with each other, the range and extent of
communication is much less.

Furthermore, our "man from Mars" or our ideal linguistic analyst would see that when humans talk, their
talk is not just a continual succession of babble, of
sounds no two of which are alike or ever come in a
given order. That is the way that monkeys gabble and
jabber, or that babies prattle; but in grown people's
speech, the world over, the same sounds and the same
combinations of sounds keep recurring more or less frequently. In short, there are *partial resemblances* in the
utterances that people make; and, because people's utterances have partial resemblances, we can say that all
language has *system*—in its sounds and in the way

these sounds are put together. If anything has system, we can describe it, by saying briefly and compactly what are the partial resemblances of the elements of the system; our "man from Mars" or our ideal analyst could make a series of statements about these systems of auditory signalling, about these *languages*, he observed among humans, and thus could make a description of their speech. If he were to do this, he would be engaging in the most fundamental type of scientific analysis as applied to language, in *descriptive linguistics*.

Another very important thing that our observer would see is that these signals always occur in connection with other things—in the last analysis, in connection (direct or indirect) with something in the world around us, with reality. (Let's leave aside all philosophical discussion as to the nature of reality, and simply assume reality as something we take as fact, in the way we all do in normal living.) That is to say, when the word *book* occurs in our speech, it normally occurs in connection, direct or indirect, with an object of the general type that might be described as "a series of sheets of paper in some way fastened together, or a composition or part of a composition that might be written on such a series of sheets of paper or other writing materials". The connections in which a word occurs, the situations with respect to which we use it, are the word's *meaning*. If a child has just learned some new word, say *grass*, and uses it to refer to some object that we normally call by some other name, such as a person's hair or the fur on a coat, we simply say that the child "doesn't know what *grass* means"—he hasn't yet learned in what situations it is and is not used. That is one of the basic features of a linguistic signal—it has to have meaning; if it has no meaning, it is not a signal, and does not come under the subject-matter of linguistics.

On the other hand, the meaning of a word is not by any means fixed, not so much as its sound; for instance, the sound of the word *book* is reasonably definite and always predictable throughout the English-speaking world, but it has many different meanings, as in *a big book* (referring to the actual tome), *a long book* (the composition contained in a book, even before it's printed and bound), or *Book I of the poem* (referring to a part of the composition). The word *book* also has many special uses in phrases such as "to throw the book at someone", "to speak by the book", in England "to book a ticket", and so forth. The meanings and uses of even such a simple word as *book* are much less easily definable and predictable, and change much more rapidly, than the sounds and grammatical form of the word. Hence the linguistic scientist considers it better to study language first from the point of view of its *form* (sounds and combinations of sounds), and tries to avoid, as much as possible, basing his analysis on the shifting sands of meaning.

In so doing, the linguistic analyst gets away at the outset from the approach to language that we find in a considerable part of the Latin and English grammar we learn in our schools—the approach based on meaning rather than form. Even our traditional definitions of the "parts of speech" like nouns, adjectives, verbs and so on, are based on meaning more than on anything else. Most of us probably were taught that a noun was supposed to be "the name of a person, place, or thing"; an adjective, "the name of a quality or accidence"; and a verb, "the name of an action or state of being". Unfortunately, however, this approach is inefficient and keeps us from getting an accurate idea of the way the system of signalling, the language itself, as opposed to its meanings, is built. Meanings vary not only from one dialect to another, but from one person to another, or even in one person's usage: how many of us use the words *Communist* or *Fascist* in exactly the same meaning as the next man does, or are absolutely sure of the exact meaning of every word we use? For that matter, some meanings just will not fit into the definitions that grammarians give for linguistic classes such as the "parts of speech". Take the word *reflection*. In English, the word *reflection* is certainly a noun, just as much as *book, typewriter, ribbon, hat* or any of the other thousands of nouns of the language; but is *reflection* the name of a person, place or thing? It is hardly any of these; a reflection always involves motion, whether that of a light-wave or of a sound-wave or of anything else being reflected off something. It is more of an action, a happening, than a thing. Yet the word *reflection*, as any speaker of English who has learned a little grammatical terminology will tell us, is most certainly a noun.

The reason we say that *reflection* is a noun is, not that it refers to a person, place or thing (for *reflection, light, matter* and many other nouns do not), but that it fits into the system of the English language in the same way as do other words which we call nouns. The word *reflection* can take the suffix -'s (*reflection's*); it can, if necessary, be used in the plural (*reflections*); it can have the word *the* used before it (*the reflection*). Those things are true of all English nouns; and they are all features, not of the nouns' meaning, but of their form. At this stage of our work, the only use we make of a word's meaning is to determine whether the word is a true linguistic signal or not, and whether it belongs together in our analysis with other signals that have the same meaning (as when we classify *went* as the past of *go*); otherwise, it is much safer to keep to the form, which is constant, and can be identified and described with much less trouble than the meaning.

Our analysis has to be *formal* first of all; this implies that it will also be somewhat on an abstract plane, and that we will be analyzing language itself before we come to examine the situations in which it is used. Language naturally does not exist in a void, nor yet in a lifeless world of logic or abstraction. People talk, and use language in all their activities, from the most everyday, commonplace contacts to the most intellectual type of reasoning; that is, language is above all social in the way it works, and we shall have occasion to take up its social function later on. But we must first find out *what* language is, before we examine *how* it functions in the wider context of human affairs. Similarly the chemist, even though he may ultimately be interested in the function and use of some fertilizer or dyestuff, first analyzes it and studies its formal characteristics in terms of the frame of reference which has been worked out for chemical analysis.

Our study of language, in addition to being formal, needs to be *descriptive* at the outset, before we proceed to further more advanced analyses. What we need, first of all, is to get as clear and complete an idea as we can get of the structure of any language we're working on, as it exists or existed at a particular point of time, without letting our picture of the language be distorted by extraneous considerations. There are two types of undesirable approach which we are especially likely to introduce, and which can easily distract our attention from the work of pure description: the *prescriptive* approach, and the historical. On this first point, the analyst's task is not to prescribe what "should" or "should not" be said; his job is to describe what actually *is* said, with as completely scientific and objective an approach as a human is capable of. He is interested in noting down factors of meaning such as the social connotations of "incorrect" forms, but considerations of "correctness" should never induce him to omit from his study or analysis such forms as *ain't, he done*. From the scientific point of view, the truly sub-standard *it ain't*, the supposedly sub-standard *it's me*, the standard *I'm tired*, and all other types of speech (literary, dialectal, rustic, slang, criminal argot, etc.) are of absolutely equal merit. That is to say, questions of merit or value just do not enter into the picture of linguistic analysis, however important they may be in the study of literature. Matters of "correctness", of standard versus non-standard, are socially determined and are relevant only from the point of view of meaning, not of linguistic form. In the same way, the chemist or the biologist studies all chemical or biological phenomena with an impersonal, scientific attitude. Our culture has come to accept this situation with regard to the physical sciences, before it has extended the same recognition to the social sciences such as anthropology, of which linguistics is a branch. No one would now say to a biologist working on *spirochaeta pallida:* "That organism is the cause of syphilis, and venereal diseases must not even be discussed; therefore you must stop working in your laboratory and reporting your findings on spirochetes."

Likewise, the scientific linguist approaches all linguistic systems with what he hopes is an equally unprejudiced eye, no matter what is the level of culture or civilization of the people who use them. Whether we consider American, West European, Bush Negro African, aboriginal Australian, or American Indian civilization to be the highest and "best", we must use the same approach and the same methods for analyzing their languages. This is true even for such lowly and usually despised media of communication such as

Pidgin English; and, when we study Pidgin English with a serious intent and go at it without preconceived notions as to its merit or fitness for use, we find that even Pidgin has a structure and a value of its own.

The other distortion we mentioned, that which comes from a premature introduction of the historical viewpoint, is not basically anti-scientific, as is the prescriptive approach; but its bad effects are just as great, and lead to just as faulty a picture of the state of affairs. At present, in English, the Romance languages, and other languages of the Indo-European family, nouns are definitely distinct from adjectives: among other things, nouns in English have their plural in -s, adjectives do not have a plural formation; adjectives can have adverbs in -ly formed on them, nouns cannot. The present state of affairs, however, seems to have developed out of an earlier condition in which, some thousands of years ago, there was no distinction between the two parts of speech. So far, so good; if we state these two situations separately, and then tell the historical relation between the two, no harm is done. But definite harm is done if we do as one scholar did, and make the statement "Grammatically, nouns and adjectives are identical; their functional differentiation . . . was a later development." Identical at what point of time?—in Indo-European, yes; in modern English, Romance, etc., or even Latin and Greek, no; and the statement, as it stands, is inaccurate and confusing. It is as if we were to say "Maine is really a part of Massachusetts, and Vermont a section of New York; their functional differentiation was a later development," just because that was the situation in earlier times. Historical considerations should not be allowed to obscure our first aim, which is to find out the facts as they are or were at whatever given point of time we are studying; then, if we want to study historical development, we can do so by comparing two or more sets of descriptive data.

What the linguistic analyst does, therefore, when he begins to work on any particular language or on any feature of language in general, is to get rid of any preconceptions he may have concerning the social standing or "merit" of language. Then he has to get a clear idea of the language's structure, of what "makes it tick", at the specific point of time and space he's interested in—whether it be the present or some time in the past—and make an accurate description of it, at least for his own use and preferably published for others' use as well. Such a work is called a *descriptive grammar*. He can then go ahead and study the variations from any particular dialect which are found either in space (*linguistic geography*) or in time (*historical grammar*). In any of these kinds of study, the analyst adopts certain divisions which fit his subject-matter. Just as the chemist, say, classes certain phenomena under organic chemistry and others under inorganic chemistry, so the linguistic analyst divides his work into three main branches: the study of 1) sound, 2) form, and 3) meaning. How he studies these branches of his science, we shall see in the next three chapters.

6. Language Has Sound

One of the very first things that our "man from Mars" would notice, as we have already mentioned, is that human language is primarily an oral-aural system of signalling. In other words, all speech is made up of sounds. Sounds serve more or less as the building-blocks out of which our speech is put together. So, before he can go any farther in understanding how language is built and functions, our linguistic analyst has to have a working knowledge of sounds—how they are made by our organs of speech, how to classify them, and how they are used in any particular language he wants to work on. Sounds, of course, *not* letters; all languages have sounds, only very few have letters or any other system of writing used in connection with them; and, as we saw briefly in Chapter 3, writing is secondary in origin and importance, compared to speech.

This brings us up against a fundamental difficulty at the outset: we have to get a new basis for our work. If we want to study the *letters* with which a language is written, we have little difficulty deciding how to study them: we take them in the order of the Roman alphabet, *a b c d e f g h* and so on; or, if we are dealing with some other alphabet or system of writing, we take them in the conventional order that its users have established. But an alphabetical order, or any approach based on letters alone, will be of no use for studying sounds as such. We all know that our present alphabet is by no means sufficient to represent, with its meager twenty-six letters, all the sounds of the English language; and, in all the other languages of the world, there occur hundreds of different kinds of sounds that we do not have in English. Any kind of approach based on the letters of our alphabet or any other kind of writing is doomed from the start to be inadequate.

We have to study the sounds themselves; but how? One way that immediately comes to mind, and that is quite widespread in our everyday talk about language, is to take the effect that the sounds make on our ears. If we want to describe a sound, and are not quite sure on what basis to do so, one of the easiest things to do is to say "It's—well, I don't know exactly, but something of a *flat* sound" (or a "broad" sound, or "smooth", or "harsh", "soft" or "hard", "bright" or "dark"). Kipling's humorous story "How The Alphabet Was Made" gives several beautiful examples of this way of classifying sounds:

> ". . . because it was a nasty, nosy noise, they just drew noses for the N-sound . . . and they drew a picture of the big lake-pike's mouth for the greedy Ga-sound; and they drew the pike's mouth again with a spear behind it for the scratchy, hurty Ka-sound; and they drew pictures of a little bit of the winding Wagai river for the nice windy-windy Wa-sound. . . ."*

But it is immediately evident that using the impressions of our own ears, our *auditory* impressions, in this way, will not be satisfactory; if for no other reason, simply because the terms "flat", "broad", "soft", "hard", and so on, are purely impressionistic and do not neces-

* From *Just So Stories*, by Rudyard Kipling, copyright 1902 by Rudyard Kipling, reprinted by permission of Doubleday & Company, Inc.

sarily mean the same thing to one person as they do to another. Speaking of a "broad *a*" may suggest one sound to me (the sound of *ah*) and another to you (the sound of *flat*, perhaps). In French, the word *grasseyer*, meaning literally "to fatten", has been used of a great many different kinds of *r*-like sounds, so that in the end there was no way of knowing what was meant by it; the phonetician Kr. Nyrop suggested that the best definition for *grasseyer* would be "a term, generally contemptuous, which people apply to other people's pronunciation; those who pronounce *r* in any given way, use the word *grasseyer* to describe any other way of pronouncing said consonant." In short, trying to describe sounds in auditory, impressionistic terms is likely to give about as accurate results as would, say, describing chemical elements in terms of their smells. The impressions we get through our senses of hearing and smell cannot be stated in clear and analyzable enough terms to be of any use in scientific work.

But of course, the impressions which we get in our hearing of sounds are produced, as any student of elementary physics can tell us, by certain specific properties of the sound-waves in the air, as they strike our ear-drums. Might we perhaps analyze, not our impressions of the sounds, but the sound-waves themselves, and find some basis in the physics of sound for classifying the sounds we hear? We might indeed; if we did this, we would be trying to study sounds, not from an auditory, but from an *acoustic* point of view. To date, though, there has been one great drawback to the study of acoustic phonetics: we have not had any way of recording and analyzing the sound-waves accurately enough, and up to very recently, the study of acoustic phonetics has not been profitable for linguistics. Such machines as were available, such as the *kymograph* (a recording device for transforming the

movement of sound-waves, or of a part of the vocal
organs, into movements of a pen-point on a strip of
paper), have not been able to give us full or accurate
enough information. In the last few years, machines
have been developed, such as the *sound spectrograph*,
which can record and chart the characteristics of sound-
waves as they occur in speech, and which can analyze
for us the intensity, frequency, and other features of
the sound itself. Undoubtedly, one of the greatest developments of the second half of this century in linguistics will be the analysis of speech-sounds by machines such as the sound spectrograph.

Then have linguistic analysts found some other way
of talking about, analyzing, and describing the sounds
of language, other than in mere meaningless impressionistic terms? They have; and, in the main, it has
proven quite satisfactory. It is to describe the sounds in
terms, not of their auditory impression or of their
acoustic characteristics, but of the organs of the body
used in producing them—classifying the sounds by
which organs are used, and how. This kind of phonetic
study is known as *physiological* or *articulatory* phonetics, from the fact that we analyze the physiology of the
articulation of sound. And it is much more exact to
classify a sound as being made with the top of the
tongue raised against the rear part of the palate, say,
than as "hard" or "scratchy".

The first thing that our linguistic scientist must know,
therefore, in as great detail as he possibly can, is the
organs of the body that are used in making sounds—the
organs of speech. When we know all the organs of
speech, and all the ways in which they are used in talking, we have a universal framework in which we can
classify the sounds of whatever language we happen
to work with. This framework is quite easy to learn:

all human beings, of whatever race they may be, have the same organs of speech, and can make whatever sounds are customary in the language they are brought up speaking. We often hear it said that one sound or another is "impossible to pronounce", or that innate differences of physiological structure make people of a certain race—say, the white race—inherently incapable of pronouncing certain sounds found in languages spoken by people of other races, such as Chinese or Japanese. This idea is quite unfounded. A white child brought up exclusively among native speakers of Japanese or Chinese will speak exactly as he hears them speak, and fully as well—and the same will be true of a Japanese or Chinese child brought up speaking a West European language, as many Americans have undoubtedly observed in the case of the Nisei.

The organs of speech include essentially all the human respiratory tract. Air is drawn into and expelled from the *lungs*, which expand and contract under the influence of the *diaphragm*.

DIAGRAM I
THE ORGANS OF SPEECH

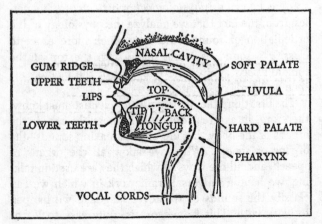

As the breath moves to or from the lungs, it passes through the *mouth, nasal cavity, pharynx,* and *trachea* (or windpipe). These and other closely related parts of the body (such as the *tongue* and *lips*) are the organs customarily used in speech. The air passes in and out of the lungs in a stream or column, called the *breath-stream.* In general, most speech-sounds are made on out-going air, although in some languages (such as Hottentot), there are genuine speech-sounds, often called "clicks", made on in-going air. Diagram I gives a cross-section of the human head and neck, showing the route that the breath-stream follows on its way to and from the lungs, and the main organs of speech.

When we send our breath-stream through the organs of speech, they do not necessarily remain motionless, fixed in one invariable position; if they did, we would not be able to make any sounds at all with them, or would make a continuous, unchanging noise, like that which a jet of steam makes when escaping through a whistle. The human organs of speech can change their position, to a large extent, so as to make a number of different types of sounds—as when we put our tongue low in the mouth to make the "ah" sound, or high to make the "ee" sound; or when we send the breath into the nose to nasalize a sound, or else keep the breath out of the nose and make a non-nasalized sound. It is this mobility of the organs of speech, and the relatively great number of different activities and combinations of activities which they can engage in, that enables us to make a number of different speech-sounds. This is true for all languages; no language has been found in which there are only three or four sounds.

Among all the sounds the human organs of speech can produce, there is a basic division, depending on whether we can produce the sound exclusively by forming resonance chambers in the mouth and nose or by making some kind of obstruction in the stream of breath to produce friction that can be heard, *audible* friction. The sounds we usually write *ah, oh, uh, oo, ee,*

ay, aw are of the kind we make by forming resonance
chambers with the tongue in different positions in the
mouth. Those we usually write with the letters *s, z, t,
k, p, b, f, v* are made by obstructing the breath stream
and producing audible friction in one way or another.
We could, if we wanted, call these two types of sound
the "resonance-chamber" kind and the "obstruction-
and-audible-friction" kind; but, for the sake of brevity
and simplicity, we will use the traditional terms *vowels*
and *consonants,* respectively. Here, incidentally, we
are following a procedure that is very common in scientific discussion: we are using familiar terms in a new
way, and *redefining* our terminology. From now on,
when we speak of vowel sounds, or of vowels pure and
simple, we do *not* mean the letters *a e i o u* "and sometimes *w* and *y*", as they tell us in our school grammars;
and when we speak of consonants, we do *not* mean all
the other letters of the alphabet. We mean vowel
sounds and consonant *sounds* as such, as we have just
defined them, and without reference to any kind of
letters (marks you make with your fist!) at all. From
time to time we shall redefine familiar terms and use
them with special meanings, often rather different from
those they popularly have. This is the same kind of
thing that an economist does, for instance, when he re-
defines *supply* and *demand,* or when a chemist uses
the words *suspension* or *sediment,* or a physicist the
words *force* or *mass,* in a special meaning.

In making both vowel and consonant sounds, we
utilize the variations in position of the organs of speech
from the vocal cords upwards. The phonetician isolates
three main factors as being responsible for differences
in sounds: the activity of the vocal cords, the place or
position in which a sound is articulated, and the *manner* in which it is articulated. For every sound, we also
distinguish three stages in its pronunciation: the *onset,*

or time in which the organs of speech assume the position for its pronunciation; the *hold*, or time during which they are in that position; and the *release*, or time in which they leave the position. Often, a sound may be similar to another in all respects except that of onset, hold, or release: for instance, the *tt* of Italian *fatto* "done" is held twice as long as the *t* of *fato* "fate"; the *t*-sound of English *tin* has a different kind of release from the *ch*-sound of *chin*.

In its passage out of the lungs, the breath-stream goes upward through the windpipe, in which there is a box-like structure of cartilage, that we usually call the larynx or "Adam's apple", and that contains the vocal cords.

The *vocal cords* are two movable membranes—not really cords like the strings of a piano or a violin, but mucous membranes, attached to the sides of the larynx. They can either lie along the side of the larynx without making any sound; or be brought together completely to shut off the passage of the breath; or be brought together partially, letting the breath-stream pass but vibrating as it passes and thus setting up sound-waves. A complete stoppage of the breath-stream by the vocal cords is called a *glottal stop*. The sound-waves resulting from the vibration of the vocal cords are known as *voice*; a sound accompanied by voice (usually all vowels and many consonants, like English *b, d, v, z*) is called a *voiced* sound; one not accompanied by voice (like English *p, t, f, s*) is termed *unvoiced*.

Once it has passed the vocal cords on its way out of the lungs, the breath-stream passes various points in the pharynx, nose, and mouth, at which the column of air can be modified and sound-waves can be set up, either by the formation of resonance-chambers or by specific obstructions of one kind or another.

In the nasal cavity there are no points at which an obstruction or other change in the breath-stream can be made, but the whole nasal cavity can be brought into play as a resonance-chamber (producing *nasalization*) or else shut off from the course of the breath-stream, by the *velum*, a flap of flesh which hangs down at the back of the mouth, between mouth and nasal cavity, and whose movable tip is known as the *uvula*. When we have a cold and can't let the breath into the nose because the uvula is inflamed or the nasal passages are blocked by mucus, we can't use the nasal cavity as a resonance chamber even in such sounds as *n* and *m*, and we have to say, for instance, *sprig is cubbig* instead of *spring is coming*. On the other hand, when we have the habit of not closing the nasal cavity off completely with the velum, as when we've just had adenoids removed, or like the stock comedy figures of Farmer Hayseed or Uncle Josh, we give a certain amount of nasalization to all our speech, or "talk through the nose".

In the mouth or *oral cavity* there are a number of ways in which the breath-stream can be modified. Inside the mouth we have an extremely mobile fleshy organ, the tongue, which can be raised and lowered; we can raise and lower either the front or the middle or the back of the tongue, and we can do this either in the center of the tongue or on its sides. The tongue, being attached to the bottom of the mouth, normally moves toward the roof or makes contact with it, somewhere between the very rear (on the velum) and the extreme front (between the teeth). Outside of the mouth, furthermore, the two lips can be brought together, or the teeth can be put in contact with the lips (normally, the upper teeth with the lower lip).

For vowel sounds, the tongue does not come directly in contact with the roof of the mouth, but assumes various positions inside the mouth to form cavities that serve as resonance chambers, conditioning the specific quality of the vowel sound. There are two main factors that produce the characteristic sound of a vowel: the position of the tongue in the front or back of the mouth, and the height to which it is raised in the mouth. To these are, on occasion, added the two further factors of lip-rounding (puckering out of the lips, as in the "oo" sound) and nasalization.

Vowels are therefore usually classified by phoneticians according to two main categories: tongue-position and tongue-height. In tongue-position, three main varieties are distinguished: *front, central,* and *back;* and in tongue-height, *high, mid,* and *low.* Further sub-divisions can be made if necessary, as in distinguishing *high-mid* and *low-mid.* The *tension* or *laxity* of the tongue and other muscles are also often important. A vowel can always be classified in terms of these features of its pronunciation: for instance, our "ee" sound is high front and tense; our "ah" sound is low central and lax; our "oo" sound is high back and tense. The "eh" sound is low-mid front and lax; the "aw" sound is low-mid back and lax; the "uh" sound is low-mid central and lax. Similarly for the other vowel sounds of English.

In English vowels, we make no use of nasalization, and lip-rounding is always automatic, our front vowels having the lips drawn back (as in the "ee", "ay" and "eh" sounds), and our back vowels having them puckered out (as in "oo", "oh" and some varieties of "aw"). But in other languages, the situation is different: for instance, French and Portuguese have *nasalized* vowels, and French and German have sounds in whose pronunciation the tongue is in the front of the mouth and the lips are rounded at the same time (*front-rounded* vowels, like the sounds spelled *ü* and *ö* in German). Russian has a vowel-sound, named *yeri,* usually called "obscure", but actually a high central vowel with lips unrounded.

In consonants, the breath-stream is obstructed and audible friction is produced by one or more of the organs of speech being placed very close to or in contact with another. The tongue is the main factor in the pronunciation of consonants as it is in that of vowels; but other organs of speech, including the vocal cords, the uvula, and the lips, may also be involved. The phonetician classes all consonant sounds as either *voiced* or *unvoiced,* according to whether the vocal cords are vibrating during their articulation or not (see p. 75); in some instances, the muscular tension of the vocal organs seems to be more important than presence or absence of voice, and the consonant sound is either tense (*fortis*), or lax (*lenis*). Every consonant sound is made in some specific position.

There is of course an infinity of separate locations at which the tongue can make contact with the roof of the mouth. The main regions of the roof of the mouth are, from back to front, the *velum*, the *palate*, the *gum-ridge*, and the *teeth*. The palate has three main sub-divisions: the rear part or *soft palate*, the middle part, and the front part or *hard palate*.

There are a number of special adjectives which are often applied to sounds articulated at these various points:

TERM	REFERS TO	EXAMPLE
glottal	vocal cords	"catch in the throat"
uvular	uvula	Parisian French *r*
velar	velum	Arabic *k*
palatal	palate, especially the front or hard palate	English *sh*
guttural	soft palate	Eng. *k* as in *kodak*
medio-palatal	middle part of the palate	Eng. *k* as in *kick*
alveolar	gum-ridge	Eng. *t, d, n*
dental	teeth	French *t, d, n*
labio-dental	lips and teeth	Eng. *f, v*
labial, bilabial	lips	Eng. *p, b, m*

We make consonant sounds, not only in various positions, but also in different *manners*. There are a number of different ways in which the vocal cords, tongue, or lips can obstruct the breath-stream, either shutting it off completely or directing its passage through one kind of channel or another.

The stream of breath may be *stopped* entirely, as in English *p, t, k;* or it may be forced through a channel. This channel may take the form of a narrow *slit*, as in English *f, v;* or of a trough or depression (a *rill*) in the center of the tongue, as in English *s*. The air may also pass over the depressed sides of the tongue, as in some kinds of *l*. It may be modified by a single or repeated flap of some movable organ, like the lips (in the interjection usually written *brrr* and in the "Bronx cheer"), the tongue (in

Italian and Spanish *r*) or the uvula (in Parisian French *r*). Or the breath-stream may be checked entirely and held while the nasal cavity is used as a resonance-chamber, as in English *m*, *n* and the sound we write with the letters *ng* (e.g. in the word *singing*). Types of release may differ: a sound may be released with a little explosion (like English *p*, *t*, *k*), with the tongue assuming position to form a rill (as in English *ch*) or to make a slit (as in German *pf*).

A number of adjectives are used to refer to the various manners of articulation, such as the following:

TERM	REFERS TO SOUND PRONOUNCED WITH:	EXAMPLE
stop	complete stoppage of breath-stream	Eng. *p*, *b*, "hard" *g*
continuant or spirant	no complete stoppage of breath-stream	Eng. *f*, *s*, *m*
fricative	slit-type channel	Eng. *f*, *v*, both types of *th*
sibilant	rill-type channel	Eng. *s*, *z*, *sh*, *zh*
lateral	channel(s) over sides of tongue	Eng. *l*
trill(ed)	one or more flaps of movable organ	Various types of *r*; "brrr"; "Bronx cheer"
nasal	nose used as resonance-chamber	Eng. *m*, *n*, *ng*
plosive	release involving explosion	Eng. *p*, *b*, "hard" *g*
assibilate	release involving sibilant (rill-type) channel	Eng. *ch*, "soft" *g*
affricate	release involving fricative (slit-type) channel	German *pf*, as in *Pfund* "pound"

While the stream of breath is being modified at a given point and in a given manner, still other things may be happening at the same time. The vocal cords may be suddenly drawn together and released explosively, in which case we call the sound *glottalized;* a puff of air, or *aspiration,* may be sent out immediately after a consonant, which we then term *aspirated.* The breath-stream may be sent into the nose for a fraction of a second before a consonant is articulated, coinciding with the onset of the sound, which we then call a *pre-nasalized* consonant (often found in African languages, in such names as *Mbanga*). If the tongue is raised close to the palate at the same time as the consonant is pronounced, the consonant is *palatalized* as in many Russian and other Slavic words.

Furthermore, sounds are pronounced with different degrees of intensity of the air being expelled from the lungs: this intensity is termed *stress*, and in English (as in most other languages) is quite important—consider the difference between English *cóntract* (noun, stressed on first syllable) and *contráct* (verb, stressed on second syllable). Sounds are also pronounced with varying pitch, from *high* to *low*; in English, variations in pitch help us to distinguish various types of sentence which otherwise have the same elements, such as *You're going home?* (question) from *You're going home.* (statement); but in many languages, such as Chinese, differences in pitch make a difference in the meaning of individual words, such as Chinese *ma* (with high, level tone) "mother", *ma* (with high rising tone) "hemp", *ma* (with low rising tone) "horse" and *ma* (with low falling tone) "scold".

Given this type of frame of reference, a phonetician can, by establishing sufficient categories, take the sounds of any language and describe and classify them. The names he gives to sounds are often rather formidable, such as "high tense front unrounded vowel" for the sound we usually write *ee*, or "unvoiced dental fricative" for what we normally spell *th*, as in *thing*. But a moment's reflection will show that, in the long run, a classification of this type is not only more accurate and exact, but more helpful to our understanding of sounds' nature and relation to each other. An elementary knowledge of phonetics helps us to see, for instance, that our *th*-sounds contain an *h* only in spelling, and that they are actually single sounds—both dental fricatives, i.e. pronounced with a slit-like passage and with the tip of the tongue against the teeth; they differ only in that the initial sound of *thing* is unvoiced and the initial sound of *this* is voiced. We also can see more clearly that, if I say *writin'* instead of *writing*, I am not really "dropping" any sort of *g*: what I am doing is substituting the voiced dental nasal continuant *n* for the voiced guttural nasal continuant which, although it is one sound, we write as *ng*.

Our traditional system of writing, and the way in which phoneticians usually analyze individual sounds, predisposes us to think that sounds in the stream of speech, like letters in a line of writing, come one after the other and are quite distinct from each other. This supposition has had such a strong influence that purists often tell us "Be sure to pronounce all the letters, and don't slur your sounds into each other, else you can't be understood." Many phoneticians, however, have long suspected that this was not so. The onset of one sound often extends far back into the release, or even into the hold, of the preceding sound, and its release lasts into the onset of the following sound. This intermingling of various sounds is known technically as *slur* (without, however, the unfavorable connotation often given the word). Our hearing, likewise, is so constructed that there is, in our nervous system, an inevitable blending, over several hundredths of a second, in our perception of sounds; this is technically termed *smear*. Due to the existence of smear in our perception of sounds, the presence of a certain amount of slur in our pronunciation serves an essential purpose, that of modifying sounds so as to let us know what is coming next or what has gone before. This is especially true of vowel sounds, which are modified by the surrounding consonants. Consonant sounds are often so short in duration, that the actual perception of consonants is lost in the smear of a few hundredths of a second; and if we did not have the special quality of the consonant slurred into preceding or following vowels, we would not be able to know which consonant had been pronounced. In his important book *Acoustic Phonetics* (1948), Prof. Martin Joos says:

> "Such identification of consonants by their effects on contiguous resonants is apparently depended on by listeners to a far greater extent than commonly supposed. It is not only a voiceless-stop hold that is inaudible to a listener; the majority of consonants make such faint impressions on spectrograms that we must suppose them to be either absolutely inaudible or at any rate so faintly inaudible as to be separately imperceptible. . . . If the speaker trained himself to reduce his slur to, say, one third the customary extent . . . there would be very little profit in this 'improvement' because the listener's smear would still blend the segments together nearly as thoroughly as ever, but there could easily be a considerable loss in it because then the vowels would perhaps not furnish enough evidence to identify the consonants properly."

The purists, therefore, in advising us to separate our sounds and articulate each apart from the others, are giving us advice which, if followed, would render speech not more, but less intelligible!

To date, we have been referring to sounds in three ways: either by circumlocution, often long-winded and clumsy, as when we say "the initial sound of *thing*" or "the sound spelled with the letters *ng*"; or by abbreviated references involving English letters, such as "the *ee*-sound" or "the *oo*-sound"; or, in the most recent part of our discussion, by more complicated technical terms like "unvoiced dental fricative" or "voiced guttural nasal continuant". But for sustained and at the same time efficient discussion, the linguistic analyst finds all three of these ways of referring to sounds quite unsatisfactory. The first is long-winded, and it describes sounds in terms of letters of the English alphabet, an inexact and ambiguous procedure at best (what is the sound of *ei*?). The second is shorter, but likewise depends too much on conventional spelling; and the third, although scientifically more exact, is still too consuming of time and space. Can't we find something simpler, clearer, and more consistent, to represent sounds on paper? Of course we can. All we need to do is to devise a set of *symbols*, in one-to-one correspondence with each sound we want to represent; we can then use these symbols to make marks on paper, so as to recall the sounds to our memory or help us to keep them in mind for further discussion. This is, of course, the same type of procedure, using rigorously defined symbols, that we find, say, in mathematics or in chemistry, where certain letters or other marks are assigned specific meanings (Fe = iron; a lowered numeral after a chemical symbol = the number of atoms of an element present in a molecule of a compound, as in H_2O = "two atoms of hydrogen and one of oxygen"; etc.).

Such a set of symbols, used to represent the sounds of human speech, is—as we have mentioned already (p. 40)—called a *phonetic transcription*. To be wholly accurate and useful, a transcription should fulfill two requirements: each symbol should stand for only one sound, and each sound should be represented by only one symbol. Of course, our traditional English spelling is quite inadequate to serve as a phonetic transcription; the twenty-six letters of the Roman alphabet will not even begin to represent all the possible sounds of human speech. To make up for the deficiencies of our alphabet, many people have devised systems of phonetic transcription. A few systems, such as Bell's "Visible Speech" and Pike's "Functional Analphabetic Symbolism", abandon all use of the Roman alphabet, insofar as it represents sounds; if they use letters at all, they use them to stand for organs of speech involved in pronunciation, place or manner of articulation, etc. Most phonetic transcriptions, however, use our traditional Roman alphabet as a base; but, in the first place, they use each letter only in one fixed value. So for instance, in a phonetic transcription, the letter [g] always stands for a voiced guttural plosive stop—the first sound of the word *get*, never the first sound of *gem*. Then, to provide extra symbols where the Roman alphabet proves insufficient, new letters are introduced, or alterations are made in the shape of familiar letters.

Letters can be taken over from other alphabets, such as the Greek or the Old English: for instance, we may use the Greek theta [θ] to stand for the first sound of *thin*, and the Old English letter [ð] for the first sound of *this*. We can turn a letter upside down or on its side: for the last sound of *sofa*, phonetic transcriptions often use the letter *e* turned upside down, thus: [ə], and for the vowel sound of *law*, we use an upside down *c*, thus: [ɔ]. Small capital or italic letters may be assigned special values, as when we write [ɪ] for the vowel sound of *bit*. We can change some part of a letter's shape: for instance, lengthening the right-hand leg of the letter *n* to make a special symbol for the sound usually spelled *ng*, thus: [ŋ]; or curving the bottom part of the letter *z* down and around to make a symbol for the middle consonant sound of *measure*, the *zh*-sound: [ʒ].

We can put various small marks (often called "diacritics" or "diacritical marks") such as accent marks, dots, small straight or curved lines, either above, below, alongside or through a letter, as when we use the letter *c* with an inverted circumflex accent ˇ above it to stand for the first sound of *cheat*: [č]; or the letter *o* with two dots over it to stand for the vowel sound of French *peur* "fear": [ö]. Sometimes a line is written through a letter to indicate some special kind of sound, as in the symbol [ɫ] to stand for an *l*-sound pronounced in the back of the mouth, as we usually do in American English *full*.

Phonetic transcriptions are usually set off in square brackets, [ ], to make it clear that they do not represent conventional spelling or any other kind of transcription.

There have been many phonetic transcriptions devised in the last hundred or so years, such as Lepsius' alphabet, designed in Germany in the middle 19th century and used very widely for recording native languages in former German colonies; the alphabet of the American Anthropological Association, used for American Indian languages; the International Phonetic Alphabet (often abbreviated IPA); and others, including quite a number of partial modifications of IPA, such as Kenyon's version adapted to American English, or Trager and Smith's. The designers of IPA originally intended it to be full enough to cover all the possible sounds of human speech; at the end of the last century and the beginning of this, it attained very wide currency among phoneticians and language teachers, and is used in most beginning language books, in a great many foreign-language dictionaries, and in a few English-English dictionaries, such as the Kenyon-Knott *Pronouncing Dictionary of American English*. (Most ordinary dictionaries, however, do not use a true phonetic transcription, but resort to the makeshift expedient of simply putting one kind of mark or another over conventional spelling.) But IPA is not the only possible or permissible phonetic alphabet, as some phoneticians seem to think. Any symbol, any letter, is as good as any other for the purpose of representing a sound—provided you first define each symbol in terms of the sound it is to represent, and then stick to it.

The following list gives the most common phonetic symbols used for transcribing English, together with definitions in articulatory terms and examples for each. Most, but not all, are taken from IPA. Those who are interested will find a supplementary list of phonetic symbols used for other languages, in the Appendix (p. 264).

Phoneticians often arrange symbols in the form of charts, using dimensions on paper to stand for position and height of vowel articulation, or for position, manner, and voicing in the pronunciation of consonants. Here, for reasons of space, we give the symbols in alphabetical order, except that vowels are given first, then consonants, then other symbols.

SYMBOL	ARTICULATORY DEFINITION	EXAMPLE
Vowels:		
a	Low central unrounded	*far* [far]
æ	Low front unrounded	*hat* [hæt]
ɑ	Low back, slightly rounded	*pot* [pɑt]
e	High-mid tense front unrounded	*say* [se]
ɛ	Low-mid lax front unrounded	*bet* [bɛt]
ə	Low-mid lax central unrounded	*sofa* [sofə]
i	High tense front unrounded	*beet, beat* [bit]
ɪ	High lax front unrounded	*bit* [bɪt]
o	High-mid tense back rounded	*boat* [bot]
ɔ	Low-mid lax back rounded	*bought* [bɔt]
u	High tense back rounded	*boot* [but]
ʊ	High lax back rounded	*book* [bʊk]
ʌ	Low-mid tense central unrounded	*but* [bʌt]
Consonants:		
b	Voiced bilabial plosive stop	*bib* [bɪb]
č	Unvoiced palatal assibilate stop	*church* [čʌrč]
d	Voiced alveolar plosive stop	*did* [dɪd]
ð or δ or đ	Voiced dental fricative	*either* [iðər, iδər, iđər]
f	Unvoiced labio-dental fricative	*fief* [fif]
g	Voiced guttural plosive stop	*gag* [gæg]
ǧ or ǰ	Voiced palatal assibilate stop	*judge* [ǧʌǧ, ǰʌǰ]
h	Voiced glottal aspirate	*hat* [hæt]
j	Voiced palatal glide	*yes* [jɛs]

SYMBOL	ARTICULATORY DEFINITION	EXAMPLE
k	Unvoiced guttural plosive stop	*kick* [kɪk]
l	Voiced dental lateral	*lea* [li]
ł	Voiced guttural lateral	*full* [fʊł]
m	Voiced bilabial nasal continuant	*madam* [mædəm]
n	Voiced alveolar nasal continuant	*no* [no]
ŋ	Voiced guttural nasal continuant	*singing* [sɪŋɪŋ]
p	Unvoiced bilabial plosive stop	*pipe* [pajp]
r	Voiced velar spirant	*roar* [ror]
s	Unvoiced dental sibilant	*sauce* [sɔs]
š or ʃ	Unvoiced palatal sibilant	*shush* [šʌš, ʃʌʃ]
t	Unvoiced alveolar plosive stop	*tight* [tajt]
θ or ƥ	Unvoiced dental fricative	*ether* [iθər, iƥər]
v	Voiced labio-dental fricative	*valve* [væłv]
w	Voiced labio-velar glide	*wow* [waw]
z	Voiced dental sibilant	*zebra* [zibrə]
ž or ʒ	Voiced palatal sibilant	*measure* [mežər, meʒər]

Other symbols:

Heavy stress is indicated by a superior vertical tick ['], and stress intermediate between heavy and weak by an inferior vertical tick [ˌ], whereas weak stress is usually left unmarked: e.g. *procrastination* [proˌkræstɪ'nešən], *procrastinate* [pro'kræstɪˌnet].

Length of vowels or consonants is indicated by a colon [:] or a raised dot [·]: e.g. *bead* [bi:d, bi·d].

A puff of breath (aspiration) after a consonant is indicated by an apostrophe written after the consonant symbol: e.g. *puff* [p'ʌf].

Not only the specialist in phonetics, but the general linguistic analyst as well, finds a phonetic transcription absolutely essential as a basis for further work of any kind. The slight initial effort of learning some new characters and getting accustomed to using others in

strange or unusually consistent values, is far out-
weighed by the ultimate gain in reliability and ease in
use. The linguistic analyst trying to work without a
transcription is as hampered as would be a chemist,
say, or a mathematician deprived of all his chemical
or mathematical symbols.

The great period of the careful and detailed study of
phonetics, on an articulatory basis, was from about
1870 to 1920; in those fifty years, phoneticians amassed
a great body of knowledge for describing the pronunciation of sounds and for symbolizing them in transcription. We still use all this knowledge as our basis for
further work. But, after a while, linguistic analysts began to see that phonetics alone, although an immense
step in advance as compared with the unwieldy and
(in some cases) utterly unworkable study of a language through its ordinary spelling, was still not the
last word in the analysis of speech-sounds. It came to
be a mark of virtuosity in a phonetician to distinguish,
by ear or by mechanical means, as many different
sounds as possible, and to devise special symbols to
represent them; it is said that Daniel Jones could hear
120 different vowel sounds in English. A transcription
representing every minute difference in sound is called
a *narrow* transcription, and is very useful in the first
stage of phonetic analysis. But some workers in phonetics, reacting against this excessive complexity, began to simplify their transcription by omitting distinctions that did not seem great to their ears, and thus
evolved a somewhat less complex type of phonetic
writing called *broad* transcription.

For instance, in a narrow transcription, the sentence *The
pool was empty, and the mill on the lea was idle,* would be given
as [ðə 'p'uʷɫ wəz 'ɛmptiʲ ən ðə 'mɪɫ ən ðə 'liʲ wəz 'ajdəɫ] in a
narrow transcription representing my own speech. A broad
transcription would omit notation of the aspirated [p] in *pool*

and of the upward glide following the vowels in *pool* and *lea,* but would still mark the difference between the alveolar [l] in *lea* and the velar [ɫ] in *pool, mill, idle,* and the same sentence would be given in broad transcription as [ðə 'puɫ wəz 'ɛmpti ən ðə 'mɪɫ ən ðə 'li wəz 'ajdəɫ].

Yet, although it was clear that phonetic transcription needed to be simplified and used only for marking essentials, the "broad transcription" principle did not wholly meet this need. Phoneticians tended to omit details that seemed to them unessential, without explicit and rigorous criteria for their procedure, and on the basis of their own impression of what was essential and what was not. From about 1920 on, and chiefly through the efforts of such men as Edward Sapir and Leonard Bloomfield in this country, and Prince Nicholas Trubetzkoy and his group in Prague, advanced linguistic analysts began to see that sounds are important only as they perform a specific *function* in language; and this they do by differentiating the *meaning* of words. So linguists began to concentrate on discovering and symbolizing, not only speech-sounds as such, but those functional units of speech-sound that are *significant,* i.e. that make a difference in meaning. For such significant functional units of sound, the term *phoneme* is generally used (as we mentioned on p. 37); and for an individual sound functioning as part of such a unit, the terms *positional variant* and *allophone* are both in use. This further stage of analysis, which builds on phonetics and is known as *phonemics,* has by now been accepted by all scholars as an essential part of linguistic analysis.

When the linguist sets about working over his phonetic data in order to determine the phonemes of a given language, he first tries to find all the contrasts between sounds that establish differences of meaning between words. In English, for instance, he finds that the sounds spelled *p* and *b* occur in different words that have different meanings, such as *pit* and *bit, pat* and *bat, pike* and *bike;* he says, therefore, that these two sounds belong to two different phonemes. Similarly for the two sounds that are spelled *th;* that they belong to two different phonemes is shown by such contrasts as those between *either* and *ether,* between *this* and *thick.* Having found all the possible contrasts between sounds, the linguistic analyst then examines the sounds which do not contrast with each other, to see which sounds he can group together.

This he does by applying certain technical criteria, asking: 1) Which sounds are most similar? 2) Which sounds complement each other, each occurring where the other does not? 3) Which groups of sounds fit the pattern of the other sounds of the language? Those groups of sounds which fulfill these criteria and which behave as single units of significant sound, are classed as individual phonemes. (It is possible, of course, for some phonemes to consist of only one allophone, whereas others are made up of two or more allophones or positional variants that meet the requirements just set forth.)

In many types of American English, there are two sounds normally written as *l,* but phonetically quite distinct: the alveolar variety which we find at the beginning of a syllable, in such words as *lead* ['lid], *look* ['lʊk], *light* ['lajt]; and the velar variety at the end of a syllable, in words like *mill* ['mɪɫ], *fool* ['fuʷɫ], *wool* ['wʊɫ]. The first is transcribed with the phonetic symbol [l], the second with [ɫ]; the difference is easily audible and also observable by mechanical means. But these two sounds never make a difference in meaning between two words in English. They are distinct, but phonetically similar, in that both are voiced laterals. They complement each other, or occur in *complementary distribution,* in that [l] occurs only at the beginning of a syllable, and [ɫ] only at the end of a syllable. They fit the pattern of the other sounds of the language, in that the [l]-[ɫ] group together are found in the same kind of position (beginning and end of syllable) as single consonant sounds like [r]. Hence, by our criteria, the two sounds [l] and [ɫ] are, in these varieties of American English, positional variants or allophones of the same phoneme, which for convenience' sake we may transcribe as /I/. The sentence given on p. 88 would be transcribed phonemically as /ðə 'pul wəz 'ɛmpti ən ðə 'mɪl ən ðə 'li wəz 'ajdəl/.

Phonemic transcriptions are usually placed between slant lines: / /, to distinguish them from phonetic transcriptions or from ordinary spelling.

A parallel from the detective story may help to explain our criteria. When a given character (say, the butler) is always off the scene when the murderer is on, and the murderer always off when the butler is on, we begin to suspect that the butler and the murderer are the same (they are in *complementary distribution*). But they must also have a certain degree of *physical similarity* (in sex, height, size, etc.) to be identified as the same person. Moreover, if there is a choice among several possibilities for the murderer, in order for the butler to be the murderer he must fit into the *pattern* of the story (in a detective story, have some motive to commit the crime).

Phonemics does not in any way supplant phonetics, but simply builds further on the results obtained in phonetics, with a change in emphasis. Likewise, a phonemic transcription represents a shift in the aim of our notation—from that of representing every identifiable sound, to that of representing only functionally significant units of sound. It differs from a narrow phonetic transcription basically in being simplified and "essentialized", and from a broad phonetic transcription in being based on a rigorous procedure of analysis. It has the advantage of not being cluttered up with non-significant features, and of representing only essentials.

On an even more advanced level of analysis, much present-day work in phonemics is directed towards isolating and symbolizing the features of sound which compose phonemes, their *components;* this study is called *componential analysis*. Thus, in the English vowel sound [i] (the vowel of *beet*), its components are front tongue position (as opposed to [u]), high tongue position (as opposed to [e] or [a]), and tenseness of articulation (as opposed to [ɪ]). The components of [ɪ], on the other hand, are frontness and height of tongue position, and laxness of articulation. If we choose, we can symbolize any high front vowel by /i/ and add a special symbol, say /ʌ/, to represent tense articulation; or, going one step further, we can identify /ʌ/ with the palatal semi-consonantal glide /j/, and then add /j/ instead of /ʌ/ for tenseness of articulation. We then write [ɪ] as /i/, and [i] as /ij/; *bit* becomes /bit/, and *beet* is transcribed /bijt/, in such a partially componential transcription. And likewise for the other English tense vowels: /e/, /u/ and /o/, which we now take as /ej/, /uw/ and /ow/.

At present, the merits and demerits of this procedure (often called *re-phonemicization*) are a matter of debate. It permits us to reduce the number of unit phonemes we set up, and to make our transcriptions typographically simpler; often, a semi-componential re-phonemicization seems to give a neater analytical pattern. But much recent work of this type is open to doubt on theoretical grounds (e.g. the theories of Trager and Smith on English vowels). The basic necessity of phonemic analysis is now agreed on by all; how far it is to be carried in the direction of componential analysis and re-phonemicization, is still a matter of personal preference rather than of scientific method.

When we are dealing with a language for which there exists no traditional system of writing, phonemic analysis serves as the best basis for devising an orthography for the language. Where there is a conventional orthography that has become petrified and no longer represents the actual phonemes of modern speech (as in English, French, Spanish, etc.), phonemic analysis and transcription helps to point up the true situation and the relation between writing and speech, and to help measure the accuracy of traditional doctrines of pronunciation and grammar. Often the spelling of a language distinguishes phonemes which are no longer separate in modern speech (as in the case of Spanish *b* and *v*); or, even more often, fails to make distinctions which are phonemically significant (as between the two sounds represented by *th* in English *either* and *ether*).

In early 16th century Spanish, the letters *b* and *v* stood for two different phonemes, probably pronounced like English *b* and *v*. Spanish grammarians of that period describe *b* and *v* as having separate sounds, and later grammarians copy the statements of the earlier ones on this point. These statements, and the belief that *b* and *v*, being separate letters, *must* somehow be pronounced differently, have persisted in school grammars of Spanish down to the present. Yet, in normal speech, the situation is quite different. Modern Spanish has indeed two sounds, the voiced bilabial plosive stop [b], and the voiced bilabial fricative [β]. These two sounds are phonetically similar—both bilabial, both voiced. They are in complementary distribution, since the plosive sound [b] occurs only at the beginning of a breath-group or after [l] or [m], and the fricative sound [β] occurs only in other positions. The contrast between [b] and [β] never makes any difference in the meaning of words, and hence is not significant. We can therefore group these two sounds in Spanish under the same phoneme, which we may transcribe /b/ for choice.

The letters *b* and *v*, on the other hand, in modern Spanish orthography both stand for the same phoneme /b/: for instance, it is the phoneme /b/ which we have in Spanish /bíbe/ "he lives" (spelled *vive*) and in /bébe/ "he drinks" (spelled *bebe*). The use of *b* or *v* in Spanish spelling is purely arbitrary, the choice depending usually (though not always) on the spelling of the Latin word from which the Spanish has developed. The use of *b* and *v* in Spanish spelling can therefore be stated as follows: Spanish has a phoneme /b/, under which are grouped two sounds [b] and [β], the former occurring initially in a breath-group and after [l] and [m], and the latter occurring elsewhere; and this phoneme is represented in conventional orthography by the letters *b* and *v* arbitrarily, the choice depending usually on etymological criteria.

Since each language has its own organization, its own economy, the phonemes of one language are not the same as those of another. We find that the sounds of each language fall into a distinctive pattern, and we have no right to expect the language to have the same pattern as another. Any feature of sound may be highly significant in one language and completely without phonemic significance in another. For instance, the little puff of breath or aspiration after a consonant in English does not make any difference in meaning, and we can pronounce *pooh!* with or without aspiration after the initial *p*-sound without changing its meaning. In Chinese, however, aspiration makes a great deal of difference in meaning, and *pu* without aspiration means "not", whereas *p'u-dz* with aspirated *p* means "store". English, on the other hand, makes such distinctions as that between the vowel of *bad* and the vowel of *bed*, which speakers of most European languages do not make and hence have a hard time making in English. In general, adult speakers of any language can hear and imitate without special training only those phonemic distinctions which their own language has taught them to be attentive to; in order to hear and make unfamiliar phonemic distinctions, we normally need to have our attention specially called to them and often have to be carefully instructed in the means of producing them. On the other hand, we often have great difficulty in perceiving differences between sounds in our own language which are present on the phonetic level but which are not significant phonemically, like the difference between the two *l*-sounds in *lea* and *full*.

We also find that, when we treat the phonemes of each language, each dialect, each individual variety of speech, in a completely objective way, there is no justification for saying that the pronunciation of one dialect is "careless" or "sloppy" in comparison with another. On the contrary, we find that each and every language or dialect has its own phonemic distinctions—different, perhaps, from those of some other language or dialect, but none the less real and valid, and of equal value with all others. Sometimes people make statements like the following:

"Some thirty years ago an English poet said that 'the Cockney in speaking with as little speech as possible had reduced speech as near as may be to a stream of uniform vowels bespattered with slurred consonants.' Since then this speech has spread with its characteristics developed so much that you may hear whole sentences without a definite consonant, and this gradual atrophy of the powers of articulation goes on unheeded by the educational powers that be."

—J. G. Anderson, *Le Mot Juste* (New York, 1932), p. viii.

But all we have to do is to analyze Cockney (or any other sub-standard) pronunciation scientifically and accurately, in order to see that the Cockney's speech shows, not a "gradual atrophy of the powers of articulation", but simply a different type of articulation from what is socially accepted as standard. The educated person, through the very fact of being educated to accept only one type of speech as standard, is without the scientific equipment and training necessary to analyze other speech than his own, and without the objectivity necessary to recognize its equal validity even when it differs from his own.

The study of sounds, in phonetics and phonemics, serves as an indispensable base for further linguistic analysis. Unless we are sure what sounds the speakers of a language make, and how those sounds are grouped into functional units or phonemes, we have no assurance that our more advanced analysis, either of form or of meaning, is accurate. Every worker in linguistics has had the experience of doing a certain amount of work on a language, then analyzing his results and realizing he must have failed to hear some significant distinction in sound, and finally returning to check up by listening some more and hearing what he had previously missed. We suspect the same kind of thing must have happened in the writing down of many languages no longer spoken, and that is what makes work on (say) Latin or Greek so tantalizing—we can no longer go back to native speakers and check up. In such a situation, the conscientious linguist is forced to rely on indirect evidence—such as the statements of grammarians, rhymes or other features of versification, and inconsistencies of spelling—to do the best he can in establishing at least an approximative and reasonably plausible idea of what the dead language's sounds and phonemes must have been. Then, when he has gotten the best phonetic and phonemic analysis possible for the language he is working on, the linguist is ready to go ahead and analyze its grammatical structure.

7. Language Has Form

Phonemes, naturally, do not occur in isolation, but only joined together as the elements, the building-blocks, of continuous speech. In our school discussions of grammar, we are usually taught to think of combinations of letters into words, and of words into sentences; with, often, the further injunction that "every true sentence must contain a subject or a predicate" (like *I see* or *The man runs*), and that any combination of words not containing a subject and a predicate (like *Yes, John* or *How much?*) must be simply a mutilated form of a complete sentence with some part left out. The linguistic analyst tries to avoid this approach, as it is incomplete and over-simplified. As we have just seen, the linguist thinks in terms of phonemes, not of letters; and he also finds that the term *word* is often inaccurate or misleading. In some languages, like Eskimo or French, it is hard to tell whether such a thing as a word, in our sense of the term, exists at all. So we avoid the term *word*, and speak rather of greater or lesser parts of an utterance. (Whenever any person has said something with meaning, he has *uttered* something, and each meaningful act of speech is an *utterance*.)

Furthermore, the linguist wants to have a convenient term for any part of an utterance; he uses the word *form* in this sense. Whenever we speak of a linguistic form, we mean an utterance or any of its parts, long or short, that has meaning (*is meaningful*). In the light of this definition, the following are all linguistic forms:

*John!; How much?; Please don't; The man I saw yester-
day; Who was the man I saw you with yesterday?* Our
task is now this: for any language we are dealing with,
to find out what the forms of the language are, to discover the patterns they fall into, and to classify them,
so that we can make a series of statements about them
that will 1) be accurate; 2) be concise; 3) show the
patterns of the language. A good descriptive grammar
will give us such a series of statements, telling us all
the facts and the system of a language and nothing but
the facts and system concerned.

One thing the linguistic analyst notices at the very
outset is that in many languages, not all forms can be
spoken as separate utterances. In English, for instance,
we can say *boy* (singular), and we can say *boys* (plural); but we can't say *-s* meaning "plural, more than
one" alone. We can say *walk, lash,* or *wash,* and we can
say *walked, lashed* or *washed;* but we can't say *-ed*
(pronounced in these verb forms as *-t*) meaning "action in time past" alone. We need to make a distinction,
which proves very fruitful in further work, between
linguistic forms that can occur alone, calling them *free
forms,* and those that can't occur alone, calling them
bound forms. When we look at the forms of English
and other languages to determine whether they are
free or bound, we may get some surprises. We are usually taught that *the* and *a, an* are separate words on a
par with such forms as *good, book, run,* etc.; this is because our grammars use writing, not language, as their
point of departure, and call anything a "word" that is
written with space before and after it. But in speech
itself, there are no spaces before and after "words" in
normal rapid utterances; and we find that *the* and *a,
an* never occur alone or separated from other forms in
normal speech (except when we quote them artificially as linguistic examples, for instance speaking of

"the definite article *the*"). So we find that among the bound forms of English we must count, not only those that we might at first consider bound—like prefixes and suffixes—but also some forms like the definite article *the* and the indefinite article *a, an*. In French, the bondage of individual forms has gone so far that most of the "words" of the language are really bound forms —not only prefixes and suffixes, articles, prepositions and conjunctions, but also many of the pronouns, almost all verb and noun forms, and many adverbs. This makes a difference in practice as well as in theory, too, as we find when we start to learn French; if we try to speak each French "word" separately, treating it as if it were like our words in English, our listeners simply won't understand us.

Then, when we have determined which forms are free and which are bound in the language we are working on, our next job is to find into what sets we can divide them, into what classes they fall. The resulting divisions we naturally call *form-classes*. We are all familiar with the form-classes of English, Latin, etc., under the name of "parts of speech", which is the name the traditional grammars give to classes like nouns, adjectives, pronouns, verbs, etc. The structure of the forms of a language is called its *morphology;* and analyzing a language with a view to finding out its morphology is called *morphological analysis*. The first step is to find out what are all the minimum forms (both free and bound) in the material we have at our disposal, and then to observe carefully which forms always occur in connection with which others. In all the languages that have been studied as yet, linguists have always found more than one class of forms—in other words, there has not yet been found a language without any distinct form-classes or "parts of speech" determined by one criterion or another.

Working with English, for example, we soon find out that there is one class of forms that occur before the ending which is written -*ed* (a spelling that stands for the three pronunciations /-əd -d -t/, such as *added* /'ædəd/, *organized* /'ɔrgə,najzd/ *walked* /'wɔkt/. We also find that there are other forms which never occur before this ending; for instance, we never say *directoried* /də'rɛktərid/. This is a valid reason for putting forms like *add, organize, walk* into a separate form-class in the language and giving them a special label; in this case, the traditional term *weak verb* will do perfectly well.

We have to carry out this procedure for all the forms in the language, and we come out in the end with a set of classes into which all the forms will fit. By definition, we have to keep up this work until we've devised enough classifications to cover all the forms of the language; otherwise our description is incomplete.

Most of us know already, from our school training, the classification of English forms into "parts of speech": nouns, adjectives, pronouns, verbs, adverbs, prepositions, conjunctions, interjections. It is worth realizing that these "parts of speech", these form-classes were set up originally over two thousand years ago, and not in connection with English or any other Germanic language. The Greek grammarians of the Alexandrian period first worked them out for their own language, and the grammarians of the time of the Roman Empire then applied them to Latin. As we might expect, the "parts of speech" fitted the structure of Greek very well; and, as the structure of Latin was pretty similar to that of Greek, they fitted Latin form-classes with only a few minor difficulties and necessary adaptations. When we try to interpret English in terms of Latin and Greek form-classes, it is still not too hard (English is indeed related, though distantly, to Latin and Greek); but it will hardly work as well as it did for Latin. Nouns, adjectives, pronouns, verbs—those we can set up for English with very little difficulty. Adverbs and prepositions, however, give us a certain amount of trouble, and so do conjunctions. These classes overlap to a large extent—for instance, *before* belongs to all three: we can say *before dinner* or *before we go home* or *Why didn't you tell me before?* Their use is rather different from that of their Latin and Greek equivalents (*Never use a preposition to end a sentence with*).

The description of English and other languages of the Indo-European family in terms of Greek and Latin parts of speech is not too bad, though, since that part-of-speech system is common to the Indo-European family of languages. But when we try to force languages which are not Indo-European, which have totally different structures from Indo-European languages, into the mold of Latin, we often get sad results. In the first place, a grammarian who works on some language of alien structure knowing only Latin and no linguistics will end up by giving, not a true picture of the language he is trying to describe, but just a list of equivalents of Latin parts of speech, declensions, and conjugations. When he finds that the native speakers of the alien language use their speech-forms differently from those of Latin, the untrained observer often concludes they must be so stupid that they can't distinguish one part of speech from another, and confuse (say) nouns and adjectives with verbs, and mix up their prepositions with their nouns. In the language of the Marshall Islands, for instance, we find three classes of forms, one of which includes various words whose meaning is like that of some English nouns and of some English prepositions; another Marshallese form-class includes some words corresponding to English nouns, some that are like English adjectives in meaning, and some which translate English verbs; and still another of their form-classes corresponds roughly to our pronouns.

In Columns A, B, and C are given examples of these three form-classes in Marshallese:

A	B

nejü "my child"
  nejim "thy child"
  nejin "his child"
	mädak "pain, suffering; to suffer"

	nuknuk "clothing, clothes"

bara "my head"
  baram "thy head"
  baran "his head"
	bök "to take"

	judak "to stand"

ainigiö "my voice"
  ainigiöm "thy voice"
  ainigien "his voice"
	lap "big; to be big"

	rik "little; to be little"

aö "my property"
  am "thy property"
  an "his property"
	lang "sky"

	bat "slow; to be slow"

ituru "beside me"
  iturum "beside thee"
  iturin "beside him, her, it; beside..."
	til "to burn"

	mij "to die, be dead"

ikijiö "opposite me"
  ikijiöm "opposite thee"
  ikijien "opposite him, her, opposite..."
	jerabal "work; to work"

ibbá "with me"
  ibbám "with thee"
  ibbén "with him, her, it; with..."	

C

ALONE	BEFORE FORMS OF TYPE A OR B	ENGLISH MEANING
nga	i-	"I"
kwe-	ko-	"thou"
e		"he, she, it"
je		"we (you and I)"
kim		"we (he, she, it or they and I)"
kom		"you (more than one)"
ir-	re-	"they"

The forms in Column A all have different suffixes added to them which tell who the possessor is, as in *nej-ü* "my child", *nej-im* "thy child", *nej-in* "his child", etc., and likewise in the other forms given in that column. Such suffixes indicating an owner are called *personal possessive* suffixes; they are found in many languages, such as Hungarian, Hebrew, and so forth. The forms in Column B *cannot* have personal possessive suffixes added to them; if we want to indicate an owner for any one of the forms in this column, we have to make a phrase, consisting of *a-ö* "my property", *a-m* "thy property", *a-n* "his, her or its property" followed by the Column-B-type form: thus, "my suffering" is *aö mädak*, literally "property-my, suffering"; "thy work" is *am jerabal*, literally "property thy, work"; "his clothing" is *an nuknuk*, and so on. Those of Column C are about like French "conjunctive" and "disjunctive" pronouns, in that they substitute for forms of the types shown in columns A and B, and are used either alone (as are *nga* "I", *kwe* "thou", like French *moi* and *toi* respectively) or are limited to occurrence before a form of type A or B, as in *i-jerabal* "I work", *e-bat* "he, she, or it is slow" (like French *je*, *il* respectively). A typically Marshallese sentence is *e-bat am jerabal* "you work slowly", literally "it-is-slow property-your-work".

Now the native speaker of Marshallese is not mixed up in his own language, or confused as to what he means when he talks, just because his form-classes do not correspond to those of Latin or English. The Marshallese have a perfectly good, useful organization of the structure of their language; it just happens not to be the same organization that ours has. In describing Marshallese structure we can, if we wish, use our familiar labels, and call their forms of the first type "nouns", those of the second type "verbs", and those of the third type "pronouns". This is a perfectly permissible procedure, but we must always remember that our terms "noun", "verb" and so on are mere labels, which must be re-defined in terms of the language we are describing. Some of the Marshallese words we call "nouns" are to be translated only with English preposition-plus-pronoun phrases; some of the words which for the Marshallese are "verbs" we would translate with English "nouns", and others with words of the kind we term "adjectives". There is no inherent quality about a meaning or an idea which makes it necessarily a noun or a verb in all languages; which part of speech a word falls into in English or in Marshallese, is determined purely by considerations of linguistic form. Nor is there anything inherently better about the English way of classifying forms than there is about the Marshallese, or vice versa; the two types of classification are simply different, and one type of linguistic organization is as good as another.

The procedure the linguist follows in establishing the forms of a language is that of discovering partial similarities, and peeling out all the combinations of sounds that have the same meaning. For each form he gets in this way, he observes and states under what conditions he finds it—that is to say, before or after which sounds and which forms, and with what meanings. Sometimes we find it convenient to operate with certain algebraic devices in our work. In English, for example, the plural of *sheep* is *sheep*, and the plural of *deer* is *deer*, whereas the normal plural of nouns is formed by adding a suffix, normally those spelled -*s* or -*es*, as in *hats, dishes*. To be able to treat the plural forms *sheep* and *deer* on the same basis as *hats, dishes*, and to consider *sheep* and *deer* as also being made up of noun-plus-suffix, we use the apparently artificial but very convenient book-keeping device of saying that *sheep* and *deer* have a *zero*-suffix. The linguist also tries to make his statements come in the most convenient order, so as to avoid excess verbiage and repetition, especially the complicated statements of "exceptions" which clutter up so many grammars; this often makes our descriptions quite terse, but in the end adds to their efficiency, in addition to saving paper and ink.

Among the plural suffixes which we find added to nouns in English, there are two, zero and *-en*, which are relatively rare, occurring in only a few instances each. In a listing of English noun plural suffixes, these two would be given first, with an exhaustive list of the nouns they occur with. The suffixes spelled *-es* and *-s* stand for three suffixes in speech, the occurrence of which is very extensive and is determined almost wholly by the nature of the preceding phoneme. We would, therefore, make a list like the following for the English plural suffixes added to nouns (with the exception of foreign plurals like *formulae*, *criteria*):

PLURAL ENDING	CONDITIONS OF OCCURRENCE	
-en /ən/	With certain forms to be listed individually and exhaustively	e.g. *ox* /'aks/.
Zero		e.g. *sheep* /'šip/.
-es /z/	After sibilants / s z š ž / as in *dishes* /'dıšəz/.	
-s /s/	After *die* /'daj/ "little cube for gaming", plural *dice* /'dajs/, and after all unvoiced non-sibilant consonants, as in *hats* /'hæts/.	
/z/	Elsewhere (i.e. after voiced non-sibilant consonants and after vowels), as in *mugs* /'mʌgz/, *sofas* /'sofəz/.	

Once the linguistic analyst has discovered all the forms of the language, he goes on to classify them into meaningful units. The individual forms are the raw material of his classification in morphological analysis, just as the individual sounds were his raw material in establishing phonemes. Exactly as we grouped one or more sounds into a phoneme or significant functional unit of sound, so we do with forms, grouping one or more into a functional unit until we have done this for all the forms of the language. For such a unit of form, we have the term *morpheme*, made up out of the Greek root *morph-* meaning "form" and the same ending *-eme* (meaning approximately "distinctive unit of . . .") that we saw in the word *phoneme*. And, just as the sound or sounds which go to make up a phoneme are called its *allophones*, in all modern discussions the form or forms which constitute a morpheme have been called its *allomorphs*. In establishing the morphemes of a language, we follow the same type of technical criteria as we did for its phonemes: all the forms that go to make up a morpheme must have the same meaning, must complement each other, and must together form a group that functions as a unit in the economy of the language. We find in English such morphemes as the noun-plural-suffix, the noun-possessive-suffix, the past-tense-suffix for verbs, etc., as well as thousands of individual "words" (nouns, verbs, adjectives, and so on).

Thus the various suffixes listed just before the preceding paragraph meet the requirements just given, and are to be classed together as allomorphs of the English noun-plural-suffix morpheme. They all occur added to nouns, and have the meaning of "plural, more than one . . .". They occur in complementary distribution, and nowhere is there any contrast between the various plural suffixes. Taken as a group, they fit into the pattern of the other suffixes in English, such as the possessive suffix for nouns or the past tense suffix for verbs.

The linguistic analyst works over his material until he has classified all the forms in the language as allomorphs of one morpheme or another. One of his tasks is to notice and list all the relations between allomorphs and between morphemes: the changes in phonemes—addition, loss or replacement—that he finds when one morpheme is joined with another, and the conditions under which they occur. In English, most nouns do not change before a plural ending; but some do. We can see this by contrasting regular plurals like *hat—hats*, *lass—lasses*, *sofa—sofas* with irregular plurals of the type *wife—wives*, *life—lives*, *loaf—loaves*. In these last-mentioned plurals, the final *f*-sound of the noun is replaced by the *v*-sound before the plural suffix. The same kind of replacement of one phoneme by another, though masked by identical spelling, is found in *house* —*houses, wreath—wreathes,* etc. Another kind of replacement of phonemes is found before the zero suffix of the plural, where the vowel phoneme of the noun changes, as in *goose—geese, mouse—mice, man—men.* Such alternations in phonemes, occurring in connection with morphemes, are called by the portmanteau adjective *morpho-phonemic,* an obvious combination of the Greek root *morph-* "form" with *phonemic.*

Other examples of morphophonemic changes are easily found. We have seen replacements of phonemes in the examples of English nouns just mentioned, and it can also be observed in English "strong verbs" like *sing—sang—sung.* Addition is found in the plurals of certain Spanish nouns; the plural morpheme is /s/, and before it /e/ is added to the end of the noun under certain conditions (after consonants and with certain [not all] nouns ending in stressed vowel), as in the following:

SINGULAR	PLURAL
mar "sea"	*mares* "seas"
piel "skin"	*pieles* "skins"
ciudad "city"	*ciudades* "cities"
rubí "ruby"	*rubíes* "rubies"

Loss of one or more phonemes is nicely shown in the formation of some irregular past participles of French verbs:

VERB-ROOT	PAST PARTICIPLE
dev- "owe"	*d-û* "owed"
voy- "see"	*v-u* "seen"
recev- "receive"	*reç-u* "received"
connaiss- "know"	*conn-u* "known"
mouv- "move"	*m-u* "moved"
pouv- "be able"	*p-u* "been able"
sav- "know"	*s-u* "known"
buv- "drink"	*b-u* "drunk"
lis- "read"	*l-u* "read"
av- "have"	*eu* /y/ "had"

Here, the past participle ending is -*u* (pronounced /y/, cf. p. 264); and, as we can see by comparing the column of verb-roots with the column of participles, each root loses some part of itself before the participle suffix. We can best state the relationship in a single formula by saying that "each root in the left-hand column is modified by losing the last vowel or diphthong and all that follows it"; thus *dev-* "owe" is reduced to *d-*, to which the past participle ending *-u* /y/ is added, giving *d-û* "owed". (The circumflex accent mark here and the cedilla under the *c* in *reçu* are mere peculiarities of spelling.) In the root *av-* "have", moreover, the entire root is lost in speech, and the past participle consists of the single phoneme /y/, which represents the participle ending added to zero root; but in spelling, the zero root is represented by the letter *e*, and the past participle is spelled *eu*, though pronounced simply /y/.

Sometimes, liguistic analysts set up special symbols for morphophonemic alternations, and use these symbols in their transcriptions. Thus, it's convenient to symbolize, for English, an /f/ which changes to /v/, with a capital /F/, and hence to transcribe *wife, life, loaf* morphophonemically as /'wajF/, /'lajF/, /'loF/ respectively. Such symbols are convenient in saving repetitious verbiage, as are all algebraic short-cuts of this type.

After the morphemes of a language have been determined, and all the morphophonemic alternations stated, the linguistic analyst now passes to finding out in what combinations the morphemes occur, and how he can class them as a result. This work is one which has to be undertaken separately for each language, and which cannot be described in the abstract except in a very general way. Each language has different combinations in which its morphemes occur, and different meanings for the morphemes and their combinations. In some languages, such as those of the Romance or the Algonquian families, we find that many or most of the morphemes are bound; in others, like English and Ewe (a language of the west coast of Africa), many or most of the morphemes are free. In some, like Latin, Greek, and Sanskrit, there is a great deal of irregularity in the alternation of phonemes within morphemes, and great complexity in the way bound morphemes are

added to each other (for instance, in Latin noun declensions or verb conjugations); whereas in others,
such as Hungarian or Turkish, there is little morphophonemic irregularity, and morphemes are added to
each other in a very clear and transparent fashion. A good example from Hungarian is the word
láthatatlanul "invisibly", whose elements are all quite
distinct: *lát-* "see" is a verb-root, a free form; *-hat-*
means "be able" and can occur as a free form, but com-
pounded with other verbs makes forms that mean "be
able to . . .", as in *láthat-* "be able to see"; *-atlan* is a
suffix which makes negative adjectives on verbs or
adjectives, so that *láthatatlan* means "invisible"; and
-ul is an adverb-forming suffix equivalent to English
-ly. Most other Hungarian words are as transparent as
this.

For over a century, it has been the fashion to make
a rough classification of languages by types, distinguishing three main supposed types: "isolating", "agglutinative", "synthetic". "Isolating" languages were
said to be those in which most of the morphemes are
free and have meaning when standing alone, as in the
case of English words. "Agglutinative" referred to
those whose morphemes are strung along one after the
other, with individuality and meanings apparent at the
first glance, as in Hungarian *láthatatlanul* "invisibly".
A "synthetic" language was supposed to be one of the
kind in which many morphemes are bound and there
is a great deal of irregularity in the alternations of
phonemes within morphemes, as in such Latin noun-
declensions as *homō* "a man", *hominis* "of a man",
hominī "to a man", etc. For some American Indian languages that seemed to show extreme complexity, and
that have long "words" which contain in themselves as
much meaning as a whole English sentence, the term
"polysynthetic" has been invented: a good example of

such a language is Eskimo. But all these terms are only approximative and inexact, and the term "polysynthetic" is particularly unsuitable; many familiar languages, such as French, are fully as polysynthetic as Eskimo in having long phrases consisting almost wholly of bound forms.

In Eskimo we can find such utterances as /aːwlisa-ut-issʔarsi-niarpu-ŋa/ "I am looking for something suitable for a fishline". But such a sentence as this is almost exactly paralleled by such a French utterance as /žə-n-i-e-paz-y-boku-d-travaj-a-fɛr/ "I didn't have much work to do there". The fact that we write the bound forms in French as separate words (*je n'y ai pas eu beaucoup de travail à faire*) disguises the fact that they are indissolubly linked in speech, nearly as much so as the elements of the Eskimo utterance.

What morphemes we will find cannot be predicted for any language. Individual "words", of which each language has many thousands, vary markedly in their meaning from one language to another, and so do those morphemes that show what are usually termed "categories of inflection". We usually think that such familiar categories as number, gender, tense or person must be universal in human speech, and we tend to look down on any language that does not show them. When we look at the evidence, however, we see that those categories are anything but universal. Many languages make no distinction in linguistic form between singular and plural, or between past, present, and future. On the other hand, we may find distinctions that are unknown to us, such as the classification of nouns according to the size or shape of the object referred to, or whether it is animate or inanimate; or a distinction in verb forms according to whether the action is complete or incomplete.

After determining all the morphemes of a language, we pass to a more advanced level of analysis, that of *syntax*, in which we analyze the structure of the larger combinations of forms. Here we find it useful to distinguish between *phrases* and *clauses*, at least for English and West European languages in general. A phrase is a group of forms which can take the place of a single form in an utterance. For instance, we can take such a very simple English sentence as *boys run*, and expand the form *boys* by adding other elements, as follows:

                    boys
                  the boys
                 good boys
               the good boys
                  five boys
               five good boys
             the five good boys
                 these boys
              these good boys
            these five good boys
                   all boys
                all good boys
              all five good boys
           all these five good boys
         all these five good boys here
  all these five good boys here who have eaten their supper

and so forth. In all these phrases, a speaker of English will consider, even without conscious analysis, that the noun *boys* is the most important element, no matter how far we expand the phrase—even beyond the limits of the last expansion. This is not only because of the meaning involved, but also because of factors of linguistic form: if we use any of these phrases as the subject of the verb, the verb must be in the plural, as in *the boys have come* (in standard English, never *the boys has come*); and the verb being in the plural is determined by the fact that the noun *boys* is in the plural. In each of these expressions, the form *boy* is the one which determines the function of the whole phrase, and so we call it the *center* or *head* of the phrase; the parts of the phrase other than the head, we call *attributes*. Thus, in the phrases given in the preceding paragraph, *boys* is the head, and *the, good, five, these, all, here,* and *who have eaten their supper* are attributes. Most phrases in English are of this type, consisting of a head with one or more attributes; they have their center inside themselves, and are referred to in technical language as *endocentric* (a term formed from Greek *endo-* "inside" and *centr-* "center", with the ending *-ic*). Some phrases, like those introduced in English by prepositions (e.g. *in the book, for me, by looking, to go*), do not have this structure, and have no head or attribute; since what determines their function, their center, is not inside themselves, they are termed exocentric (Greek *exo-* "outside" + *centr-* + *-ic*). The linguistic analyst's task is to find and tell what types of phrases occur and what their structure is, in terms of the form-classes and morphemes permissible.

Then, finally, we come to the structure of utterances taken as wholes. In every language, we notice that there is a certain type of single form or phrase, or combination of forms or phrases, which occurs normally as the largest usual unit of utterance: this the linguist terms a *clause*. There is, in general, more than one type of clause in any given language: in English, we have clauses which consist of a noun or pronoun plus a verb (or an equivalent phrase in each instance), like *John runs* or *The six fat boys sat eating apples.* We also have clauses that do not have that structure, such as *Yes. No. Why? Why not? Not at all. Where? In the garden. Eating apples.* For English, the type of clause that has the structure: noun or pronoun + verb, is statistically the most common of all, and is the most consistent in its structure, whereas other types of clauses in English have various structures (endocentric phrases, exocen-

tric phrases, or special words like *yes, no,* or *hey!*).
Whatever type of clause is the most common and the
most consistent in any given language, the linguistic
analyst calls a *major* clause; all others are *minor* clauses.
In English, therefore, a major clause is one of those
whose structure is noun or pronoun + verb, and the
others (including those usually called "elliptical") are
minor. Minor clauses are just as legitimate, linguistically, as major clauses; they are not "incomplete" and
have nothing "left out" except in comparison with major clauses (whose definition is, after all, a matter of
statistical frequency). Most ordinary conversation contains, in the give-and-take of speech, a large proportion
of minor clauses, which is quite correct and as it should
be for clear understanding: *Hello! Where're you going?—To eat.—What for? It's not time yet.—How so?
It's noon.—No kidding?* In that brief dialogue, there is
a total of eight clauses, three major and five minor.
Traditional grammars often speak slightingly of "elliptical" sentences, and imply that they are in some way
incomplete or fail to convey meaning accurately;
which is not true, as a minor clause has just as definite
and accurate a meaning as a major clause.

In other languages, we find other types of major clause.
Whereas in English a noun or pronoun is one of the basic elements of a major clause, in many languages a verb alone suffices
as basic element; for instance, in Italian the verb *corre* alone
means "he (she, it) runs", *canto* is "I sing", *dormiamo* is "we
sleep". Traditional grammar would say in this connection that
these Italian verbs have subjects which are "implicit but unexpressed"—somewhat of a contradiction in terms, since if something is unexpressed in a linguistic utterance, it simply is not
there.

In Russian, Hungarian, and other languages, there is a type
of major clause which consists just of a noun or pronoun combined with a noun or adjective, the meaning of the clause being
"identity" or "equality". For example, the Hungarian sentence
ez a könyv jó means "this book is good"; it is a combination of

the noun-phrase *ez a könyv* "this book" plus *jó* "good". Other types of clauses may be found in other languages, until we get radically different combinations of elements in American Indian languages such as those of the Algonquian, Iroquoian, or Siouan families.

The determination of phrase-structure and clause-structure is carried out in accordance with essentially the same criteria as those applied to the analysis of phonemic and morphemic structure. The linguistic analyst's chief task is to discover what are the smaller combinations of morphemes that can be substituted for single morphemes, and then what larger combinations can be substituted on higher levels, on the basis of functional equivalence, as in the examples we gave in expanding the single noun *boys* to a long phrase. The significant relationships in syntax, that is, how phrases and clauses are constructed, are then stated in terms of functional units, just as are those of phonology and morphology. In recent years, especially by Zellig S. Harris and his followers, techniques have been worked out for an algebraic, quasi-mathematical symbolization of all grammatical relationships, involving the establishment of formulae and equations, and their ultimate reduction to a very few formulae for a language's basic clause types; for English, Harris arrives, after many complicated operations, at a clause formula: N^4V^4 with certain pitch patterns; in this formula, N and V stand for "noun" and "verb" respectively, and the superior numerals indicate levels on which forms or combinations of forms may be substituted by other combinations. Most present-day linguistic analysts, however, have not attained this degree of concentration or of abstract symbolism; nevertheless, we try to be as concise and economical as possible.

In this very brief outline of the linguistic analyst's methods in analyzing sounds and linguistic forms, we have necessarily had to be extremely sketchy, and to concentrate more on bald statements of basic aims and concepts rather than on specific techniques or examples. To expand this outline and to put flesh on the bare skeleton of our discussion, would require a separate book, with much fuller detail both as to the linguistic analyst's procedures and as to concrete exemplification. The chief lesson we need to learn from modern descriptive linguistics at this point is that the analysis of language is like that of any other systematic structure—an operation to be carried on with a scientific approach and with objective, rigorously applied criteria. We base our observations on facts as they are and we draw our own conclusions from those facts, not what somebody says the facts or the conclusions ought to be. We must be especially careful not to let our own language or the traditional notions of Anglo-Latin grammar we learn in school lead us astray. Applied to English, our customary Latinizing grammar is not only a distortion of the facts of the language, it is downright wasteful. Up to a relatively recent time, English grammar books used to follow their Latin models so closely that they gave whole sets of forms (*paradigms*) which were nothing but slavish translations of Latin paradigms, such as

Nominative	a table
Genitive	of a table
Dative	to a table
Accusative	a table
Ablative	from or by a table
Vocative	O table!

Even our grammarians have by now seen that such a procedure tells us nothing about the structure of the English noun, since, as we can see, the English noun *table* does not change in such a paradigm, and such a

Latinizing list as this obviously just does not fit the English language. But our English grammars still give us, all too often, such paradigms as this:

I can	we can	I do	we do
you can	you can	you do	you do
he can	they can	he does	they do

I am	we are
you are	you are
he is	they are

A paradigm like this, too, is wasteful and uninforming, since only the one verb *be* has more than two forms in the present (*am, is, are*), most verbs have only two forms (*do, does*), and some have only one (*can*); and the difference in person and number is, in general, made clear by the pronoun or noun used together with the verb in the clause, and not by the verb form itself. It would be much simpler, clearer, and more informative to list these English verb forms in some such way as this:

3. sg.	is	does	
1. sg.	am ⎫	do ⎫	can
all others	are ⎭		

A scientific linguist attempting to make a complete description of a language will, of course, do as thorough a job as possible in the various types of analysis we have discussed—phonological, morphological, and syntactical. Naturally, the completeness of his description will depend on two things: the extent and the accuracy of his information. If he has only meager materials, or if what he has to work on is not very reliable, his description will of course suffer, in completeness, trustworthiness, or both. The ideal situation is that in which a trained linguist devotes all his time and attention to describing his own language; he can then be his own source of information (or *informant*) and can, over the years, note down all the forms, all the types of utterances, of which he normally makes use, and then analyze, classify, and describe them completely. No one has ever wholly measured up to this ideal, and perhaps it is an ideal impossible of complete attainment; the closest that anyone has ever come to it was in the description which the Hindu grammarian Pānini wrote of Sanskrit, the language of the Old Indian hymns of the Vedas. Next to this ideal situation, the best possible thing is a trained linguist working in close collaboration with an intelligent and reliable (*not* necessarily educated!) speaker of the language under analysis. Some good descriptions of languages have been produced in this way, in recent years notably Mary Haas's grammar of Tunica and Stanley Newman's grammar of Yokuts (two American Indian languages).

A trained linguist working with a not so intelligent or reliable informant is the next best choice; certainly such a combination is preferable to having a person without training in linguistic analysis attempting to work on a language, no matter how good a source of information that person may have. Informants are by no means always intelligent or reliable. If an informant is educated in the traditional grammar and folk-lore about his own language, he may try to tell the analyst, not what he really says, but what he thinks he ought to be saying—exactly as Miss Fidditch told her class to say *it is I* and then when talking naturally said *it's me*. If the informant is ignorant or stupid, he may not understand what the linguist is trying to get at and hence may give him misleading information; or the informant may develop an inferiority complex, or think he is being put through some kind of an intelligence test, or become antagonistic in some way, if he is not handled properly. But the point is that a trained linguist can see where the difficulty lies and take steps to straighten it out, and can analyze even imperfect material and make at least some sense out of it, whereas, on the contrary, one not trained in linguistics is very likely to bungle any analysis he undertakes, even of the best material.

This latter danger is especially present if the untrained would-be analyst has been exposed to the traditional grammar of English or Latin, for then he is likely to interpret everything he meets in terms of English or Latin structure, as expounded in the orthodox text-books. The classical examples of this kind of mis-analysis are the descriptions of "exotic" languages of America, Africa and Asia made by well-meaning but linguistically naive persons such as missionaries, who discovered the categories of Latin in every language they met. As a result, it is very hard to make any sense out of many missionary grammars forced into the Procrustean bed of Latin categories. Some of the most frequent misinterpretations of linguistic structure fall into three main types, which have been facetiously termed:

1. The "Barmecide" or "St. Patrick" school of linguistics, in which the analyst tells, not what is present in a language, but what features familiar to him are absent ("Japanese has no grammatical gender and no distinction of number").

2. The "Ripley" school, in which the analyst selects only features which are strange or unusual to him, listing idly jotted oddities ("Ainu has a curious duplication of the French-Celtic expression for 'eighty' ['four twenties']").

3. The "Bullamacow" school, in which the analyst says that a language makes up for some lack or other by using separate words where *we* might have ex-

pected merely different grammatical forms ("The gender of Japanese nouns is determined by sex" in that Japanese has separate words for "bull" and "cow", "uncle" and "aunt", etc.").

Interestingly enough, scientifically accurate and reasonably complete descriptions—quite rare for any language—have been made, up to the present (1960), for more "queer" or "unusual" languages than for "familiar" tongues such as those of Western Europe. The reason for this is not far to seek. Modern scientific linguistics has developed fastest in those fields where it was least hampered and restricted by the influence of traditional grammar, that is to say, in the fields where little grammatical work had been done before. The great anthropologist Franz Boas was one of the leaders in this type of work, insisting (by example and by teaching, especially in the *Introduction* to the *Handbook of American Indian Languages*) that the linguistic analyst, when approaching an American Indian language or any other, had to take it on its own merits and on its own terms, seeking to discover its own system rather than that of some different language, Latin or any other. Following Boas, Edward Sapir and Leonard Bloomfield applied this same criterion, as have their more recent disciples.

But in work on languages like English, French, Italian, German, etc., where there is a strong tradition of grammar modeled on that of Latin, most people who are at all interested in grammar have had a strong attachment to traditional grammatical terms and analysis, and have reacted strongly against any attempted change in the tradition. For instance, some recent discussions of French have used a somewhat different approach than the usual one in describing adjectives, and it has been pointed out that it is more convenient and concise, in dealing with the language itself as spoken, to start from the feminine as basic and derive the masculine from the feminine (rather than to start from the masculine, as is usually done). From the outcry that was raised against this innovation, one would have thought the very foundations of grammar were being shaken. And yet this approach is not especially new, since it goes back at least to the time of the great French phonetician Paul Passy in the 1880's. The Lord did not create the masculine grammatical gender before the feminine in the garden of Eden, nor did St. Paul declare the feminine grammatical gender to be the "weaker vessel". The protests against the unwelcome innovation were due simply to the fact that it went counter to tradition and to custom—a fact which was apparently to outweigh all possible convenience and usefulness the new approach might have.

However, progress is gradually being made to applying to familiar European languages the type of linguistic analysis—phonemic, morphological, syntactical —that has already given such excellent results when applied to unfamiliar or "exotic" languages. There is still a great deal of work to be done in this field, and new recruits to the field of linguistics could do no better than to apply their talents to the description of a European language. If progress continues to be made, we should have, by the end of the century, at least adequately accurate and complete descriptions of European languages, as well as of many others.

PART III: LANGUAGE IN THE WORLD AROUND US

8. Language Has Meaning

Language does not exist in a vacuum. Language is used in human society, for purposes of communication, and hence has *meaning*. Our discussion in the previous two chapters has been based on form and concerned with the analysis and description of linguistic structure, and we have paid relatively little attention to matters of meaning as such. Yet we must always keep the factor of meaning in mind, as a decisive criterion for determining whether a sound or a form has functional significance or not. And, of course, meaning is what gives language its usefulness, and is its very reason for existence: no one would care to juggle with so complicated a system of vocal habits, unless they were able to convey meaning by it and thus profit by their use of it. We have said several times that language exists by virtue of its use among human beings as a system of signalling; and the meaning of any linguistic signal is the situations in respect to which we use it, as we saw in Chapter 5.

We have just used a somewhat complicated way of defining meaning, especially by speaking of "the situations in respect to which" we use linguistic signals. Why couldn't we have made it simpler, by saying "the situations in which" we use linguistic signals? There is a very good reason: because linguistic signals are often used when what they refer to is not present in the actual situation between speaker and hearer. If I am at a lunch counter, see a piece of pie, and ask the waitress "May I have that pie, please?", the pie is present in the situation itself—both the waitress and I can see it, and she can get it for me then and there. But if there is no pie on the lunch counter, I can still ask "May I have some pie, please?", and the word *pie* has the same meaning, even though no pie is present in the speaker's and hearer's situation. There may be some pie out in the kitchen, and the waitress may bring it to me; or there may be none available, in which case I go without pie; but in either case, I can refer to pie, and the word *pie* can have a relatively definite meaning ("a certain kind of pastry with one kind of filling or another") whether there is any pie around at the given moment or not. This second type of situation is extremely frequent. The use of language in such a situation—to refer to something that is not present—is termed *displaced speech;* and the fact that we can use displaced speech is what gives language its tremendous effectiveness as a means of achieving most intricate social coordination. We can relay messages from one person to another, almost indefinitely, until in the end we attain some desired goal, such as receiving a shipment of rails from a country halfway around the globe—and almost wholly by the use of displaced speech.

One basic assumption in linguistic analysis is that in every language (or dialect), some utterances are alike as to form and meaning. Otherwise, of course, if the speakers of a language could never depend on similarity of form and meaning for any given combination of sounds, from one moment to the next, communication would be impossible. But we have already noted that linguistic form is far more nearly constant, and more easily identifiable, than linguistic meaning. This is because of the relatively limited range—of phonemes, morphemes, syntactical features—which linguistic forms cover, and because of the immense range which is covered by the situations with respect to which almost any form is used. That is to say, when we analyze all the factors in any human situation, even the simplest, in which language serves as a means of communication, we find that their ramifications are enormous. Even such an apparently clear meaning as that of the word *pie* is much more complicated than we might think at first sight. There are quite a number of different kinds of pie (e.g. apple, blueberry, chicken, "Eskimo pie"; shallow, deep-dish; covered, open-top; and so on), and not the same in the various parts of the English-speaking world. The chemical and physical constituents of pie, simple though they may seem, are very complex, and even, in the present state of our scientific knowledge, not wholly definable. Moreover, the meaning of the word *pie*, like that of every other word, differs for each situation in which it occurs—depending on the state of mind, attitude, and so on, of the speaker and the hearer—and no two situations are ever alike; the term *pie*, for instance, may cause me pleasure or disgust, or leave me indifferent, according to how I am feeling, how hungry I am, the previous experiences I may have had with pie, and so forth. Emotional factors such as these last are usually left out of dictionary definitions (it would be hard to include them), but they are very real factors in the total meaning of any linguistic signal in each specific situation in which it is used. To give a complete definition even of *pie* would be a tremendous task, and it would be much harder in the case of admittedly more elusive terms such as *justice, love* (noun and verb), or *matter*.

But the meaning of any specific linguistic form is purely arbitrary. There is no underlying connection, no inherent and inescapable relationship, between any linguistic form and what it signifies. The same animal is referred to in English as *dog,* in French as *chien,* in German as *Hund,* in Hungarian as *kutya,* in Russian as *sobáka,* in Armenian as *šun,* and so on. From the point of view of pure logic, there is no relationship between any of these combinations of sounds and the animal "canis familiaris" to which they all refer. It is wholly a matter of social convention; the meaning of words is something determined by the usage of the speakers of a language, not by some divine fiat; and the only reason we make the word *dog* refer to an animal of the species "canis familiaris" and the word *cat* refer to one of the species "felis Lybica domestica", rather than vice versa, is that we, as speakers of modern English, are in the habit of doing so, and have learned this habit from other speakers of English. On the other hand, different languages use the same combinations of sounds with entirely different meanings: the English word *do* means "perform, act" and is a verb, whereas French *doux* (pronounced almost exactly like English *do*) is an adjective meaning "sweet", and German *du* is the second person singular pronoun meaning "thou, you".

All meaning reflects our experience of the universe we live in. It is a commonplace to say that if we have had no experience of something, then we do not know what it means—not only linguistically, but also emotionally and in our social adjustment. Yet our experience of the universe is something which, in itself, is indivisible, and any division we set up in our experience—as the meanings of our language inevitably lead us to do—is of necessity conventional. The spectrum, for instance, is a continuous scale of light-waves, whose length ranges from 40 to 72 hundred-thousandths of a millimeter; but our language and its meanings cut the spectrum for us into various shades, from *violet* through *indigo, blue, green, yellow, orange* to *red,* thus segmenting our experience for us into quite arbitrary divisions. For colors which the human eye cannot perceive and hence experience directly, our language simply offers no terms—and hence physicists had to coin the new terms ultra-violet and infra-red. Terminology referring to kinship ought, theoretically, to be quite easy and simple, and yet even in English our kinship terminology shows surprising quirks and gaps. We have, for instance, the words *brother* and *sister,* but no popular term for "person born of the same parents" without reference to sex. The anthropologist uses the term *sibling* in this meaning, but it still remains a learnèd term.

When we go from one language to another, it is immediately obvious that the segmentation of experience differs, in the meanings which different languages ascribe to forms. This is true even (and especially) in what we might think the most simple and self-evident words and meanings: *be, get, have, do.* No two languages have exactly the same range of meanings, covered by comparable forms. In Spanish, the meaning of English *be* is covered by three verbs: *estar* and *haber,* referring to "being" in a given location or not adhering to a fixed norm, and *ser* referring to identity or "being" that adheres to a fixed norm. To translate our word *get* into any other language, we have to resort to half a dozen or more different equivalents, as we can see from the various meanings of *get* in such expressions as *to get* ("obtain") *some money, I got* ("became") *sick, he got* ("arrived") *home after midnight, he got* ("received") *a prize, I've got to* ("must") *go home,* or *do you get* ("understand") *me?* For the speaker of French, the verb *se promener* (literally "to promenade oneself") covers all that segment of experience involving making an excursion or short pleasure trip, no matter by what means; if he looks for a single, simple English equivalent, he'll be disappointed, and will have to resort to various expressions like *take a walk*, *go for a ride*, etc., which force him to specify what means of locomotion are involved, whether he wants to or not. When we get to "exotic" languages (e.g. Japanese or some American Indian language), the entire classification of experience, even in the grammatical categories of the language, is totally different from what we are accustomed to.

Yet, despite all the difficulties in the way of analyzing meaning, the study of meaning (*semantics*) has made considerable progress, and linguistic analysts have been able to note certain facts of considerable importance. One is that a great many linguistic forms have more than one meaning, that is, are used in more than one type of situation. The word *book* can have several different meanings, as we pointed out earlier (p. 62); and we could cite a great many other examples, such as these chosen at random: *try* (*I'll try to do it; I'll try it* meaning "I'll sample it"; *they're going to try him for murder; it's enough to try anybody's patience; I'll try out the fat*), or *party* (*a wild party; the Republican party; a party line* on the telephone; *he was party to the crime; the party of the first part; this party* meaning "this person"). Whenever a form has two or more meanings, its users almost always regard one of them as the *central* meaning (also called the "literal" meaning) and the others are considered *marginal* (or "transferred" or "metaphorical") meanings. Sometimes it is hard to tell whether a given combination of phonemes represents a single form with two or more widely divergent meanings, or two or more distinct forms, as in the case of *ear* (*the human ear* vs. *an ear of corn*). In general, the central meaning of a form is the meaning in which we use it most consistently, and which we assume it has unless there is some special reason to look for a transferred or marginal meaning. As Leonard Bloomfield says (*Language*, p. 149):

> "Sometimes the practical feature that forces us to take a form in a transferred meaning, has been given by speech: *Old Mr. Smith is a fox* is bound to be taken in transferred meaning, because we do not call real foxes 'Mr.' or give them family-names. *He married a lemon* forces us to the transferred meaning only because we know that men do not go through a marriage ceremony with a piece of fruit."

The existence of transferred meanings and their relation to the central meaning of any given form is a thing which of course varies from one language to another and also, within the same language, in the course of time. Many metaphors which we think are normal and self-explanatory seem quite foreign to speakers of other languages; no speaker of French would ever use *oiseau* "bird" in such transferred meanings as "fellow, guy" (*He's a queer old bird*) or "a Bronx cheer, or other kind of derisive or unfavorable reception" (*He gave me the bird*). Some metaphors common in earlier English seem out-of-date to us now, like Mark Twain's frequent use of *party* as a facetious term for "person"; and some which are very common now, like *off the beam* or *in the groove*, would have been incomprehensible in Mark Twain's time—partly because the practical situations on which they are based (radio, phonograph records) did not exist.

In addition to transferred meanings, there's another kind of supplementary value that forms can have. Analysts of meaning distinguish between *denotation*, or the meaning a form has for all those who use it, and *connotation*, or the special additional meaning the same form may have for some one speaker or for certain speakers. In general, our dictionaries give us only the denotation of a form—as much of its meaning as can be stated objectively and for all the speakers of the language. Mathematicians and scientists strive to avoid all connotations in the meaning of their terms, a perfectly valid and attainable goal in the specific and carefully delimited type of work they are doing. Sometimes purists tell us we should do likewise in everyday speech, but such an aim is hardly realistic or to be achieved in view of the complexity of any human being's life and environment—and, even if it could be attained, it would remove from our speech much that makes it interesting and living, including all poetry and imaginative use of language.

Connotations may be individual in their extent— that is, only one speaker may have a special connotation for a form—or they may extend to whole groups of speakers or even the majority of those who use a form. Each of us has some words which convey a special flavor, for us alone. The word *swerve*, for example, has for me a very unpleasant connotation, due to its use in connection with a childhood accident; whereas, on the other hand, because I happen to be an electric railway enthusiast, the words *street-car, elevated, subway* fill me with a much warmer glow of pleasure than they give to the majority of their users. An individual or private connotation of this type is just as real as a more widespread one, but, because it's restricted to one speaker, it has little or no communicative value.

Of the more widespread connotations, perhaps the most common are those which ascribe words to cultural (social) levels and to functional varieties. A form like *ain't* or *I seen* has the same denotation as *isn't* or *I saw*, but quite a different connotation: many people think that the first pair connote undesirable characteristics on the part of the speaker, such as ignorance or illiteracy or carelessness, whereas the second pair carry a connotation of desirable characteristics. We have already seen, in Chapter 2, that these connotations are primarily a matter of social or cultural standing, and hence we may speak of *cultural levels* in the connotation of forms; linguists distinguish primarily between *standard* (socially acceptable) and *non-standard,* which includes *sub-standard* (not socially acceptable). Among non-standard types of speech there are a number of different levels, including urban sub-standard (*T'oity-t'oid Street*) and rural dialect (Scottish *a hae nane* for "I haven't got any").

Often confused with cultural levels, but in reality quite separate, are *functional varieties* of speech—determined, not by the cultural standing of the speaker, but by their use in speaking or writing, and differing according to the degree of familiarity they connote. There are some words or turns of speech that we would use only in a formal situation, such as the "subjunctive" *be* in *unless this be so,* or the expression *busy though he may be,* or such items of vocabulary as *vociferation* for "yelling", *contingency* for "chance", *enumeration* for "listing", and so on. Most of our formal vocabulary has been taken over from Greek or Latin by men of letters or others with special learning, and hence is called *learnèd* vocabulary. There is a whole range of different situations, from the purely formal through the semi-formal (as in a university lecture) to the wholly informal (private correspondence or familiar conversation); and, to a certain extent, we feel that some forms are suited to one type of situations and not to another. *Unless this be so* sounds very stilted outside of a speech from the platform or the pulpit; *he has bats in his belfry* is extremely informal;

and most of our vocabulary and usage falls in between these two extremes.

These two contrasts—that between standard and sub-standard, and that between formal and familiar—combine to produce four main types of usage (given here with examples):

Familiar standard: *He did it too soon*
Formal standard: *He did it prematurely; am I not?*
Familiar sub-standard: *He done it too soon; ain't I?*
Formal sub-standard: *Between you and I; aren't I?*

The last-mentioned category is the kind of speech we often hear from sub-standard speakers who try unsuccessfully to use formal standard language on occasions which they feel demand it. Prof. John Kenyon cites, as further examples of semi-literate or sub-standard formal usage, a radio speaker's announcement "Sunday will be Mother's Day" (which many hearers misunderstood, thinking he had said *Some day will be Mother's Day*), and "This program will be heard again tomorrow from one two three" (= *from one to three*).

Other types of connotation, often on the formal or learnèd side, are those of *archaisms, foreignisms,* and *technical terminology.* It sounds either Biblical or Shakespearean to use the *-th* ending in the third person singular of a verb: *he goeth, she cometh;* and even more archaic to use *ye* (as in *Hear ye!*) or the second person singular pronouns *thou, thee* and the corresponding verb forms in *-(e)st: thou singest,* or *I tell thee.* If we use a sprinkling of foreign words or phrases in our speech or writing, we convey to our hearers the impression that we know more than one language, and also (often) the idea that we are seeking the exact term to refer to some strange thing or concept, as when we speak of *Panzer* divisions, of the *Politburo,* of Indian aspirations towards *svaraj* (self-government), or of Puerto Rican *jíbaros* (hillbillies). Borrowings from other dialects of our own language also convey special connotations, especially that of slight affectation in the use of specifically British vocabulary such as *cove* for "guy, fellow", *lift* for "elevator" or *tram* for "street-car". Technical terms have all kinds of different connotations, which depend essentially on the social standing of the calling they are associated with, such as *bebop* and *gut-bucket* from jazz, *stick 'em up!* and *scram!* from criminals' vocabulary, or *schistosomiasis* and *beta-haemolytic streptococcus* from medical terminology.

We can also give a humorous twist to our speech, by making use of *mock*-forms, which have a purposely ridiculous connotation. We make fun of learnèd or formal vocabulary by inventing and using such words as *discombobulate, busticate, ruction, rambunctious* (and the verb formed on the last-mentioned, *rambunct*). Students plowing their way through Shakespeare or Milton often intentionally add the ending *-est* where it doesn't belong, together with humorous use of *thou* and *thee*: in high school we used to say such things as *Wiltest thou comest to the officest with me-est?*. We can make fun of foreign languages, or of foreign speakers' accent in English, as in the following quotation:

> "Pugsy . . . appeared to have a fixed idea that the Italian language was one easily mastered by the simple method of saying 'da' instead of 'the', and tacking on a final 'a' to any word that seemed to him to need one.
> "'Say, kid,' he began, 'has da rent-a man come yet-a?'."

> P. G. Wodehouse, *Psmith, Journalist*.

Slang is distinguished as such by its connotations, which are those of extreme familiarity (sometimes substandard, sometimes not) and of very recent introduction. On the margin of the standard language, there are always new words or new meanings for old words being introduced, which at the time of their introduction have a strongly slangy flavor. Very often these new usages do not become permanent, or they linger in the speech-habits of only one age-group; when I was a child, my parents would often tell me to *skidoo!*, but persons of my generation rarely use that word, preferring to tell someone to *scram!*. I later found that *skidoo!* and *twenty-three!*, both in the meaning of "get out!", were slang usages current in the early 1900's; the first of them I remember from my childhood in the 1910's and 20's, and the second I never heard in normal speech. Similarly, the expressions *funny ha-ha* and *funny peculiar*, as slightly jocular ways of distinguishing the two meanings of *funny*, were current in the 1930's and still are in my own usage; they seem out-of-date to younger persons. On the other hand, some slang expressions "catch on" and we soon forget that they began as slang; we now speak of *jazz* music, eating a *sandwich* at a *snack bar*, or riding in a *jeep*, without realizing that *jazz, snack, sandwich, bar* in the sense of "eating or drinking place" and *jeep* were slang at one time or another. In fact, all neologisms (new words or meanings introduced into the language) begin as slang, except in those branches of terminology where (as in scientific and philosophical study) there is an established tradition of word-coinage or re-definition.

Also coming under the head of connotations are the factors of taboo on sex and other obscene terms, which we discussed in Chapter 2 (pp. 20–22). Here, too, there are various degrees of taboo or impropriety; I can, under certain circumstances, speak or write the word *whore*, whereas there are some other words which I know, but which I would rarely speak and never write. Of this same type, essentially, are the connotations of *ominous* meaning that we attach to some words, so that we replace them by other, less strongly connotative expressions (*euphemisms*): in our society, with our intense fear of death, we're often afraid to say *if I should die*, and instead we say *if anything should happen to me*; some people are afraid to mention such words as *syphilis* or *venereal disease*, and substitute them by *social disease* or similar less meaningful terms. To a certain extent, these ominous connotations are unreasoning survivals of older superstitions to the effect that a name has some magical power of its own, and that hence naming some evil thing or spirit might bring its evil workings upon us; this was why, for example, the Greek goddesses of revenge, the Furies or *Erinnyes* ("Furious Ones"), were called by the Greeks, not by their real names, but *Eumenides* ("Gracious Ones").

And yet, despite such observations as these, the linguistic analyst cannot at present say very much about meaning, because meaning lies largely outside his field of analysis. The linguist can simply define linguistic forms and their approximate meaning, but he cannot do the work of the chemist, the physicist, the anthropologist, etc., in analyzing and defining the further ramifications of ultimate physical and social structure involved. To define meaning completely and exactly, even that of the simplest linguistic form, we should have to have a complete knowledge of the structure of the universe, and also of everything going on inside the body and head of every speaker and every hearer. This is manifestly impossible. Meaning remains something approximate and indefinite, much more so than linguistic form; and yet we are left with the paradox that meaning, even with the difficulties it presents us (both the analyst and the unreflecting speaker of a languate), is what makes language effective in human society. Perhaps future scholars will discover a way in which linguistic analysts can state meaning as precisely and as concisely as they can do for form; when this is done, we shall be able to correlate form and meaning without running the risk, as we do at present, of losing sight of the simple essentials of form in the maze of meaning.

9. Language Covers Territory

Not everybody talks the same way; this is a common-place whose truth we can all observe. People of different social classes, of different occupations, of different cultural groups in the same community, will show variations in their speech even from one individual to another, from one family to another. And people show variations in their speech from one place to another: variations in sounds, in forms, in arrangements of forms, and in vocabulary and meaning. If you go into a drug store east of the Alleghenies and ask for a *milk shake*, you are likely not to get ice cream in the mixture of milk and syrup; west of the Alleghenies, you will get ice cream, in greater quantity the farther west you go. If you ask for *tonic* outside of Eastern New England, you are likely to get some kind of hair restorative or other liquid for improving your health or bodily condition; but in an area whose center is Boston and which extends outward for about fifty to a hundred miles, a request for *tonic* will get you a bottle of ginger ale, root beer, or some other drink of the kind that elsewhere is called "soda pop". If you're from south of the 40th parallel, you are likely to have the z-phoneme in your normal pronunciation of the third consonant of *greasy*; if from north of the 40th parallel, you are likely to have the s-phoneme.

This kind of variation is so widespread that we all recognize its existence, and we can normally tell by a person's speech at least what general part of the country he comes from (New England, the Southeast, the Midwest, etc.). Those who have special training in the study of regional variation in speech can often come much closer to placing people's geographical origins by the way they speak. Dr. Henry Lee Smith, Jr., in his radio program "Where Are You From?" from 1940 to 1942, would undertake, on the basis of a person's pronunciation of certain key words, to guess that person's home and not be more than fifty miles off—and he was correct in over eighty percent of the guesses he made.

Such a performance as Dr. Smith's is made possible by the fact that not only the social and occupational variations of speech, but also the geographical variations, follow definite patterns and can be determined and analyzed. The linguist, when he wants to find out about geographical variations in language, first of all goes to as many places as he can in the region he's interested in, and finds out how people talk in those places. If we are interested in tracing the regional variations of only one or two features of speech in pronunciation, forms, or vocabulary—such as the meanings of *milk shake*, or the terms for "earthworm", or the pronunciation of the word *on*—we can listen to the speech of many informants from many points. If, on the other hand, we want information on a great many matters, or have only a relatively short time at our disposal, we must of necessity restrict our investigation to a smaller number of speakers and places. The places whose speech we investigate are often called the *network* of points we cover, and we study material gathered from a *wide-meshed* or *fine-meshed* network in an area according as there are few or many points and/ or speakers we have been able to observe; naturally, the finer mesh our network has, the more detailed our observations can be. We have to be sure, too, that the speakers we have as informants represent the normal speech of their localities; for instance, a person (like the present writer) born in North Carolina and brought up in Minnesota, New York City, New Jersey and Illinois would not be a very trustworthy source for information on the speech-patterns of Ithaca, N. Y. (where he now resides).

The linguistic analyst makes just as close and accurate observation of his informants' speech as he can. Ordinary spelling is, for all topics but those of vocabulary, far too uncertain and inaccurate to serve our needs for careful registration of the sounds we hear; therefore, we use the narrowest of phonetic transcriptions to record what our informants say. (The phonemic pattern of each local dialect may be different from that of others, and so we must take care not to let phonemic interpretations or simplifications creep into our phonetic transcriptions at this point; for geographical study of language, non-phonemic distinctions of sound are fully as important or more so than phonemic distinctions.) We start out our investigation into regional variations of speech with a *questionnaire*, determined by preliminary study, and containing a list of the words and expressions we want our informants to give us their customary equivalents for. We ask each informant for the same items, so that we'll have comparable material for each point when we're through: "What do you call this? [pointing to a table, a pen, a hat, etc.]"; "What do you call the serenade they gave a newly-married couple?" "How do people call pigs (cows, etc.)?". As the informant gives us the answers, we take them down in careful phonetic notation, usually with one or more carbon copies to minimize the risk of loss. Here, as in working with an informant in general, the investigator has to be careful, in the first place not to offend or frighten the informant, and also to avoid (as far as

possible) misunderstandings or misleading replies. Informants will often intentionally try to trick the investigator, or unintentionally give him "elegant" or "fancy"
forms which it later turns out they themselves never
use in normal situations.

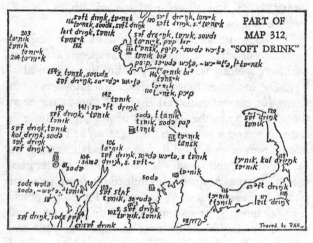

MAP 1

When we have our materials gathered—and, if possible, records or tapes made also—we collect them
all together and edit them. When they have been carefully edited and prepared for publication, they can be
published in any one of various ways: we can print our
transcriptions on an ordinary page, in columns, like a
set of logarithmic or similar tables, with, say, a single
column for each informant whose speech we investi-
gated, and all the responses to a single question printed
across the page on the same line; or we can have our
page arranged in the shape of a map, with the informants' responses placed on the map in the relative positions of their localities, as shown in the sample map
above. This latter way of reproducing the material is

perhaps the best, and certainly the easiest to use and to interpret at a glance, but it is quite costly, since the lettering usually has to be done by hand and the printing costs are very high. A collection of such tables or maps, each one giving us the geographical distribution of informants' responses for a single item (word or phrase), is called a *linguistic atlas,* and is an extremely valuable source of information for our knowledge of present-day speech and of its past history. There are linguistic atlases either completed or in process of planning or completion for many countries (Germany, France, Italy, Corsica, Rumania, Catalonia, Spain and Portugal, the Mediterranean basin, etc.). For the United States, a three-volume atlas of New England (over 600 maps) was published in 1940–43, and gathering and editing of the materials is well in hand for the remaining parts of the country.

When the geographical distribution of words and phrases has been gathered and recorded in maps and tables, the linguistic analyst can then set to work studying the material thus recorded. The most important single thing we do is to mark the divisions between features of speech (pronunciation, forms, syntactical combinations, vocabulary); such a linguistic division or boundary, setting off one linguistic area against another, is called an isogloss. If we take such a map as the one reproduced on p. 141, we can draw a line around the area, say, in which the word *tonic* is used in the meaning of "soda pop", thus marking the isogloss dividing the *tonic* area from other areas. (Note well that an isogloss such as this, drawn on the basis of a map which represents only a sampling of localities and informants, is of necessity approximate, and is not to be taken as an absolute.) Since it would be in general undesirable to mark up the maps of the original atlas we are working on—after all, a linguistic atlas is an expensive thing, which very few people can own for themselves and which an individual would not like to spoil even if it were his own property—we usually make our marks on blank maps or *base maps,* which are outline maps of the region covered by the atlas we are working on, with numbers to correspond to each of the atlas's numbered localities. We can simply draw isoglosses on the base map as we look at the materials contained in the atlas, or we can make conventional marks (squares, circles, triangles, plus-marks, x's, etc., in various colors) to represent whatever features we want to—contrasting sounds, word types, etc.—of the map we are studying. The map for *tonic* shows various kinds of conventional marks; that reproduced on p. 142 gives isoglosses, in this case for the area within which Latin *-rj-* changed into *-j-* in Tuscany.

Once the mechanical aspect of transferring and abstracting the content of the atlas maps or tables is taken care of, we can proceed to making deductions about the various areas and their relation to each other. We find three main types of area, according to the prevalence of the feature we are studying and according to the size and position of the areas. In some areas, a given sound or form—like *tonic* in the area around Boston—is universally prevalent, in a compact region centering around a specific point or focus: this type of area is called a *focal* area. In others, such a feature as *tonic* for "soda pop" is present only sporadically and at certain points; or, if we are comparing more than one isogloss (as in the map on p. 142, which shows the extent of the sound *j* coming from Latin *-rj-* in Tuscany and nearby regions of Italy), we find that there is considerable spread between the various isoglosses and that they flare out or cross and re-cross each other. This indicates that we find whatever feature we are studying only partially, and not in all words; an area showing sporadic distribution or spreading, flaring isoglosses is called a *graded* area. Finally, we often discover some features only in areas which are outlying or cut off from frequent communication with other areas (such as peninsulas, islands, or mountain regions); such areas we term *marginal,* as in the map on p. 144.

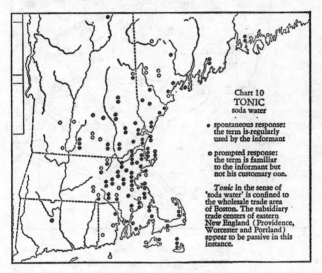

Chart 10
TONIC
soda water

● spontaneous response: the term is regularly used by the informant

○ prompted response: the term is familiar to the informant but not his customary one.

Tonic in the sense of 'soda water' is confined to the wholesale trade area of Boston. The subsidiary trade centers of eastern New England (Providence, Worcester and Portland) appear to be passive in this instance.

MAP 2
Tonic in New England

In general, we can place a historical interpretation on the geographical distribution of a linguistic feature. In the simplest cases, the presence of a word (sound, form, etc.) in a focal area like that of *tonic* around Boston or of *-j-* from Latin *-rj-* in Tuscany, tells us that it has been there for a long time, long enough to have become thoroughly customary in the whole area and to have edged out all competitors. Its presence in a graded area (like the outer edges of the *tonic* area or that of Tuscan *-j-*) tells us that there is a spread taking

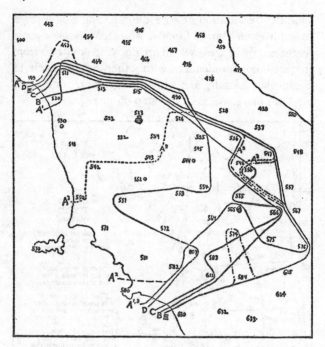

MAP 3

-rį in Tuscany and Surrounding Regions

A[1] outer limit of *-aio* in *mugnaio* 251 ——
A[2]   "   "   " *-aio* in *carbonaio* 211 —— ——
A[3]   "   "   " *-aio* in *macellaio* 244 – – –
B   "   "   " *-į-* in *cuoio* 1568
C   "   "   " *-į-* in *acciaio* 401
D   "   "   " *-į-* in *cucchiaio* 982
E   "   "   " *-į-* in *aia* 1468
     ara within outer limits of *aio* —·—

place or that there has been one in recent times; but
we cannot tell simply from the map alone in which
direction the spread is taking place, and whether, say,
tonic or Tuscan *-į-* from Latin *-rį-* is gaining or losing
ground. But if we find a feature only in marginal areas,

with some other competing word or sound in all the rest of the territory we're dealing with, the conclusion is usually that a feature now evident only in the marginal areas was once more widespread, and used to cover a much larger territory.

The study of the geographical distribution of language, *linguistic geography,* is of great importance for our understanding both of linguistic history and of present-day linguistic facts. It has taught us, above all, that language *covers territory*—not only in the static meaning of that expression, but more especially in its dynamic meaning. Language is constantly *on the move:* features of speech are spreading from one place to another. The instance of *tonic* in New England is instructive: we can see from the map that its extent, in the meaning "soda pop", correlates closely with the wholesale trade area centering on Boston. When this type of drink was introduced in Boston, it was termed *tonic water,* presumably to induce customers to favor it because of supposed medicinal values, or else to avoid restrictions of one type or another; and, along with its distribution to wholesale dealers who bought from Boston jobbers, the term *tonic* spread. Together with this type of drink, customers in the Boston wholesale trade area became familiar with the name *tonic,* both the drink and the name being at first importations from Boston. Importations of this kind are known as *borrowings;* and linguistic geography teaches us that a very great many features of language originate in a given place—usually a cultural center such as Boston or New York in America, or London, Paris, Madrid, Florence in Europe—and then are borrowed from the cultural and linguistic focus of diffusion by other, outlying areas. A feature which originates in a given place is at first an *innovation* in contrast to whatever preceded it, as was *tonic* meaning "soda pop" at one time in Boston,

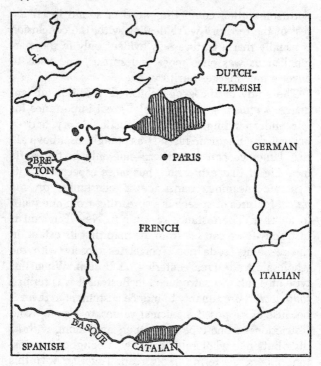

MAP 4

Marginal Areas

The shaded areas show those parts of the French speech-area in which /k/ has not been shifted to /č/ or /ts/, or later developments thereof, in *cheval* "horse" from Proto-Romance /kabállu/. After map 269 of the *Atlas Linguistique de la France*.

or -*j*- taking the place of -*rj*- in the speech of Tuscany. The innovation is then borrowed, i.e. imitated by the speakers of the surrounding territory—usually, though not always, because an innovation coming from such a cultural center as Boston or Florence enjoys prestige, higher social standing. As the innovation spreads, the outer edge of its area presents the appearance of a graded area, and in the inner core of the area it eventually replaces all its competitors so that the central part of its territory comes to be a focal area. Finally, the defeated competitors survive only in marginal areas; and eventually, if the process of spread is carried through to its conclusion, even the marginal areas are wiped out and the innovation is solidly evidenced throughout the entire territory.

This process takes place, not only with individual sounds and forms, but with entire complexes of linguistic features, i.e. with entire dialects. In this way, the dialect of a given region which is politically, economically, or culturally dominant in a country comes to be the standard language of the country as a whole. For instance, in the early Middle Ages in Europe, national states were almost non-existent or very weak, and the largest effective political unit was the duchy or province, or in some countries (such as Italy) the city-state. Correspondingly, the largest linguistic unity was the regional dialect, and before about 1200 or 1300 most writings in the vernacular were specifically identifiable, not as "French" or "Italian" or "Spanish", but as Norman, Picard, Leonese, Asturian, Milanese, Genoese, Venetian, Neapolitan, and so forth. But during the following three or four hundred years the various national states (France, Spain, England) became essentially unified politically and economically; and in each, one particular region (normally that of the capital: Paris, Madrid, London) set the pattern for the rest of the country, its language going along with its political, economic and cultural dominance. Significantly enough, Italy was not unified politically until 1870, considerably later than the rest of the countries of Western Europe. Up to 1870, Italy was divided into small fragmentary city-states, duchies and minor kingdoms; and its linguistic development went along with its political history—a single national standard language did not find universal acceptance until after political unification in 1870. Even the economic importance of Florence from about 1250 on, and its cultural supremacy from about 1350 on, were not able to bring about the unquestioned dominance of its language—on which modern Italian is based—as the political sway of Madrid, Paris, and London did in their respective countries.

Before a single standard language has arisen in any given country, the local dialects are of equal social standing: in the early Middle Ages, the speech of Northeastern England, of Scotland, of Southern England were all equally acceptable, and each person spoke and wrote without hesitation in his own dialect. Likewise in France, Spain, Italy and the other countries of Europe; in Italy, for instance, thirteenth- and fourteenth-century writers used their own local speech, very little modified under the influence of other Italian dialects: Bonvesin da Riva of Milan wrote in Milanese, Jacopone da Todi of Umbria wrote in Umbrian, the anonymous Roman author of the famous Life of Cola di Rienzo (the fourteenth-century republican rebel) used his native Roman dialect, and so forth. But as soon as the dialect of any particular place or region comes to acquire special prestige for non-linguistic reasons such as political, economic or cultural dominance, then speakers of other dialects begin to have an inferiority complex concerning their normal native speech, and want to use instead the dialect whose use carries greater prestige. This situation then forces the local types of speech into an unfavorable position vis-à-vis the standard language, and use of a local dialect comes to have the connotation of lower social or cultural standing. In the European countries in general, this happened by stages: there first arose regional standard languages—in France, those of the region around Paris (the so-called Ile de France, whose language is termed *Francien*), of Picardy, of Normandy, of Champagne, of Southern France (*Provençal,* itself based on the speech of several sub-regions); in Italy, those of Sicily, of Tuscany, of Lombardy, etc. Then a single region acquired political, economic, or cultural dominance over the others, and consequently linguistic dominance as well, so that the various regional standards were in their turn relegated to the status of inferior social acceptability: Francien became the basis of modern standard French, because Paris became the capital of France; Castilian became the basis of standard Spanish, because Madrid became the capital of Spain; the English of London and Middlesex became likewise the basis of standard English. Finally, with the development of literature in the standard language, a split occurs in the standard language itself, a more formal or literary variety being distinguished from the less formal, everyday, colloquial variety; and for some whose ideal is that of static perfection defined as a set of rigid norms, the literary language (or, in some instances, even a particular sub-dialect of the literary language, such as poetic usage) becomes the exclusive standard, in contrast to which even colloquial standard is unacceptable.

In the meanwhile, especially in large urban areas such as those of Paris or London, innovations have gone on arising, as they always do—but they have arisen too late to be included in the standard language as it was at the time of its rise to dominance. So, for instance, the cockney of London "drops his *h*'s", that is, no longer has the *h*-phoneme at the beginning of a word, saying *'ouse* instead of *house, 'Arry* instead of *Harry, 'eat* instead of *heat,* and so forth. The lower-class speaker of Parisian French merges the phonemes represented in spelling by *a* and *â* (front and back low vowels, respectively) and generalizes the latter in all positions. He converts the element *-t-il* (roughly equivalent to *does he . . . ?*, in such a question as *donne-t-il?* "does he give?") into an interrogative particle, usually written *-t'y*, which he adds to all statements to turn them into questions, as in *tu vas-t'y?* "are you going?". The Florentine develops, in place of the single unvoiced plosive stops *p t k* between vowels, the corresponding fricative sounds, and says *la hasa* "the house" instead of *la casa*. Other speakers of the standard language—from the dominant center or from other regions—then feel that these later, obviously lower-class innovations are not socially acceptable, and reject them as "vulgarisms"; witness the attitude of the ordinary speaker of British English towards "dropping one's aitches", or of the ordinary American towards the New Yorker's pronunciation of, say, *bird*.

The conflict that then arises has two further consequences: 1) misunderstanding of the nature or condition of the unwelcome innovation; 2) over-correction. For instance, the non-Tuscan speaker of standard Italian often misunderstands the conditions under which the Tuscan substitutes a fricative for a plosive stop, and thinks that the Tuscan would say also *a hasa* "to (the) house" where standard Italian would write *a casa* but pronounce *accasa*; actually, the Tuscan speaker would say *la hasa* "the house", but *accasa* "to (the) house". Likewise, the ordinary American thinks that lower-class New Yorkers say *boid* for *bird*, *oil* for *earl*, etc., and, taking his cue from the approximate spelling *boid*, *oil*, thinks that the New Yorker uses the vowel sound of *for* in such words. Actually, the New Yorker shares this particular feature of pronunciation with a good part of the Eastern seaboard, and does not use the vowel sound of *for* at all, but that of *but*; I have heard this pronunciation from natives of Princeton (New Jersey), Virginia, Tennessee, and Texas, as well as from many upper-class New Yorkers.

In more concise, technical language, the difference is this: the New Yorker, etc., pronounces *bird* as ['bʌid], with a very short [ʌ] sound, and with the tongue somewhat to the rear in the mouth; his naive hearer equates this back [ʌ] with his own [ɔ] sound, and thinks, wrongly, that the New Yorker is saying ['bɔid], without understanding the New Yorker's phonemic pattern.

People are also often likely to misunderstand the social extent and acceptability of such a later innovation in the regional dialect on which the standard language is based. The supposedly "vulgar" pronunciation written *boid, oil* for "earl", etc., is normal in all of New York City and wide areas on the Eastern seaboard, and I have heard it from such obviously acceptable speakers as heads of departments in Hunter College and Princeton University. Many Frenchmen will tell you that the merging (they call it "confusion") of the two phonemes usually spelled *in* and *un,* or of the two phonemes usually spelled *é* and *è,* is vulgar, and characteristic of extremely low-class speech in Paris; but in fact, all we need do is to keep our ears open, to realize that these phonemic mergers are to be heard from all Parisians of whatever class, even from such as will insist vehemently that they never merge the phonemes in question.

Then, the speakers of non-acceptable regional or social dialects try (naturally) to acquire more acceptable speech patterns. But neither they nor their critics have the requisite linguistic training to analyze the situation objectively and accurately, and all the non-standard speaker has to go by is a blanket condemnation—often based on misunderstandings such as those we have just been discussing—of some particular feature of his speech. The cockney who has been told he must not "drop his aitches" comes to the conclusion that he ought to put an *h*-sound at the beginning of every word where he pronounces only a vowel: since he has been condemned for saying *'Arry, 'Erbert, 'Ounslow* for standard *Harry, Herbert, Hounslow,* he puts in an *h* in such words as *Alice, Anna,* or *Ealing,* and makes them into *Halice, Hanna, Healing.* This process is known as *over-correction* or *hyper-urbanism.* Catullus, the Roman poet, made fun of a man who over-corrected on his aitches, a certain Arrius who pronounced *chommoda* for *commoda* and *hinsidias* for *insidias;* finally he left Rome for Syria, and everybody's ears had a rest, until the frightful news came from the East that the Ionian sea was now the *Hionian* sea. Catullus implies that Arrius was a social parvenu, whose ancestors had been slaves; and, in fact, over-correction is a thing we find very often among people who are insecure about their normal speech and go too far in imitating what they take to be "better" usage. In the same way, a person from the country who said *Marthy* for *Martha,* or *Ameriky* for *America* in his native dialect, once he had been taught that the final vowel in his pronunciation of those words was "incorrect", would easily go too far, and say *Cincinnata* for the standard form *Cincinnati,* or *Missoura* for *Missouri,* substituting in such words the final vowel of *sofa* for an actually quite normal and correct *-i.* In some instances, as in the local pronunciations of *Cincinnati* and *Missouri,* such an over-correction becomes established as the regional standard.

When a standard language has been established, it often borrows forms from other dialects (regional, social, or occupational), for various reasons: distinctive meanings, humorous connotations, or to establish or avoid pleasant or unpleasant connotations of one sort or another. The Northerner who has come in some contact with the social structure of the Southern states may use the term *po' white trash*, with an approximation of the Southern pronunciation *po'*, although in all other situations he will use his normal pronunciation for *poor*. Such expressions as *thar she blows!* (originally from whalers' jargon), *hoot mon* (Scotch), or *petrol* or *tram* (British English) have the flavor of the regional or social types of speech from which they were taken. A good example of dialect borrowing for favorable connotation is French *amour* "love". As this word goes back to the Latin stem *amōr-*, we should normally expect *ameur* just as *hōra* "hour" gave *heure* and *dolōr-* "pain, sorrow" gave *douleur;* but we actually find *ameur* only in rustic dialects and with the meaning "rut (period of sexual excitement in animals)". The French form has the vowel normally spelled *ou*, not that normally spelled *eu* as we would expect; it is clearly a borrowing from Provençal (Southern French), in which the development to *ou* is to be expected in this word. We know that in the Middle Ages Provençal was the prime literary language of love, and that the Provençal poets formulated and expressed doctrines of courtly love which found widespread acceptance throughout the European upper classes; we conclude that Northern French (on which modern standard French is based) took over the form *amour* from Provençal because of the literary and social prestige of the form, and that the indigenous *ameur* was then relegated to the meaning of "animal love, rut".

Borrowings of this type are not limited, of course, to the relations between one dialect and another, or between standard language and dialect. Borrowings between mutually unintelligible languages are also very frequent; we are all familiar with such foreign words in English as *blitzkrieg, kamikaze, sputnik, spaghetti, smörgasbord, chile con carne, fortissimo, au revoir.* We are perhaps less aware of the fact that many other words, which to us seem completely familiar and form part of our everyday usage, are of foreign origin: of the words in the first part of this sentence, for instance, the following are wholly or partly of Latin origin: *fact, completely, familiar, form, part, usage, foreign,* and *origin.* Every language has foreign borrowings of one sort or another, even German or Finnish or Hungarian, or the language of the most untutored savage tribes. Often, indeed, the borrowings have taken place so long ago or have become so familiar that the speakers of the language no longer recognize them as borrowings, as in the case of our *chair* (from Latin *cathedra*) or *table* (from Latin *tabula*), or of German *Kaiser* "emperor" from Latin *Caesar, Strasse* "street" from Latin (*via*) *strata* "paved (way)", or *Kreide* "chalk" from Latin *crēta.* From more remote languages, we have in English such words as *sugar,* from Arabic, and ultimately from Sanskrit *çarkara* "gritty substance"; *thug,* from an East Indian word; or *squash,* from an American Indian language. There is not and has not been for thousands of years a "pure" language, in the sense of one without any borrowings from a foreign language. Sometimes purists want us to avoid all words that are not of "pure Anglo-Saxon origin", not realizing that if we were to do so, we would deprive ourselves of considerably more than half of our vocabulary, and indeed of the part that is most useful in its analytical and technical function.

Borrowing between languages normally occurs in connection with cultural contact (here we are using the term *culture* in its broadest sense referring to all activities which men learn, from their birth on). Where a cultural borrowing is made, that is, where people take over a certain custom or thing from others, the word referring to it often goes along with it, as in many instances we can all call to mind, such as *spaghetti, opera, pianoforte, sonata* from Italian; *frankfurter, wiener, hamburger, sauerkraut* from German; or English terms in other languages, like Spanish *béisbol* "baseball", *fútbol* "football", *nócaut* "knockout". These are instances of words which travelled along with the institutions or things which they referred to—which had previously been unknown in the countries to which they were introduced. In other cases, the foreign word gave a particular flavor, served to distinguish in one way or another the special variety of meaning to which it referred: there were lightning-like campaigns conducted long before 1940, but the term *Blitzkrieg* referred to the particular style in which the German *Panzer* divisions, aided by the *Luftwaffe,* especially its *Stuka* dive-bombers, conducted that type of warfare. Americans living in Puerto Rico have the normal English word *bus* at their disposal, but nevertheless often refer to the local vehicles (which have characteristics all their own) by the Puerto Rican Spanish term *guagua,* and to a station wagon as a "little bus" or *guagüita.* All such borrowed words are often called *loan*-words.

A special type of borrowing is that in which words themselves are not borrowed, but direct translations are made from one language into another, so-called *loan-translations.* Strong emotion was regarded by Greek Stoic philosophers as something morbid, and was called by them *pathos* "suffering, disease"; the Romans translated this by *passiō* "suffering", from which our word *passion* was later borrowed. We use the term *passion* in the meaning "suffering" only in connection with the *passion* of Jesus Christ, and otherwise use it in the meaning of the Latin loan-translation *passiō* "deep emotion". In French *ça va sans dire* means literally "that goes without saying", and figuratively "that's obvious"; in English we often use the loan-translation *that goes without saying,* and likewise *a marriage of convenience* for French *un mariage de convenance,* or *a superman* for German *Übermensch* (given currency by the philosopher Nietzsche). Only a few loan-translations achieve acceptance in any given language, and other literal translations of foreign idiomatic expressions sound strange or ridiculous; such an expression as *I'm in train of writing* makes no sense in English unless the hearer is familiar with French *je suis en train d'écrire* "I'm in the process, the act of writing".

Single words are most easily borrowed from one language to another; and when they are borrowed, they are normally adapted to the structure of the borrowing language, in sound and in form.

Thus, the word *garage* is pronounced in French fashion as /ɡəˈraž/ only by some who know a certain amount of French; most speakers of American English say /ɡəˈradž/; in England, the stress has—in accordance with normal English patterns—been shifted to the first syllable, and the word is pronounced by upper-class speakers as /ˈgæraž/ with a French-type ending, but by lower-class speakers it is wholly Anglicized into /ˈgærɪdž/.

Loan-words, once assimilated into the body of a language, serve as bases for further formations just like all other words: for instance, on the noun *chauffeur,* borrowed from French, we now have the verb *to chauffe* (as in *I had to chauffe my mother around all day*); and a suffix like *-able,* originally used only in Latin or French loan-words like *inevitable, amiable,* has now become so general that it can be added to any English verb, as in such forms as *eatable, seeable, lovable.*

Not only individual words, however, but sounds, phonemic distinctions, and even structural patterns may spread across language boundaries and be borrowed from one language into another of different origin. In most of the Romance languages, the *r*-sound is a tap made with the tip of the tongue against the inside upper front teeth (a voiced dental flap); but since the seventeenth century, a different kind of *r*, made by allowing the uvula to hang freely and vibrate in the breath-stream, has become fashionable, first of all in French, originating in Paris and spreading from there to other urban centers. It was imitated in languages other than French, spreading along with French courtly behavior in the seventeenth and eighteenth centuries: it has become the normal urban representative of the *r*-phoneme in German, and is widespread in Spanish and Portuguese as a variant of the long *rr* phoneme. The suffix *-able*, which we just discussed, was first abstracted from French loan-words in English and has now become one of our most widespread and productive English formative elements. The suffix *-(e)teria* was present originally in the one word *cafeteria* (a borrowing from Italian *caffetería* "coffee-shop") and then generalized from that word, with the meaning—peculiar to English—of "place where one serves oneself", as in *groceteria, hatteteria*. Even the whole structural pattern of a language may be affected in this way; for instance, Armenian, originally a language related to English and the other Indo-European languages, has gradually favored more and more those regularized structural patterns which resemble those of the neighboring Turkish, until Armenian is now far more similar in pattern to Turkish than it was formerly.

All these different types of borrowing—dialect and interlanguage, in vocabulary, phonemes, or structure—are of course not made in a void; as the Italian scholar P. Goidànich once said sarcastically, they are not "packed up in boxes and shipped across country by rail," to be opened and distributed impersonally at the receiving end of the line. The intermediary in all cases of borrowing is someone who is bi-lingual, to the extent of having at least some slight knowledge of both the source from which the borrowing is made (standard or foreign language, etc.) and the language into which the borrowing is made (regional dialect or borrowing language). The New England farmer who goes to town and hears a new pronunciation for *road* and takes that new-fashioned pronunciation back home with him; the soft drink salesman who travels out from Boston and sells *tonic* to the country stores in Massachusetts, New Hampshire or Maine; the scholar who reads German, and not finding a good English equivalent for German *Leitmotif* (literally "leading theme"), takes the word over into his speaking or writing in English; the journalist or radio commentator who similarly knows and uses such words as French *maquis* "underground resistance movement" or German *heil* "hail" and *Führer* "leader", because of their special connotations and even make further English formations such as *heiling the Führer*—all these are active helpers in the borrowing and transmission of loan-words to the speech-community at large. And this is a process which will always go on as long as cultural interchange between groups takes place, and which no amount of puristic protest or condemnation can ever put a stop to.

10. Language Doesn't Stay the Same

In Chapter 9, we examined instances of linguistic borrowing, that is, of features of language (sounds, forms, structural patterns) being taken over by one dialect from another, or by one language from another; and we saw some of the things we can learn from the study of linguistic geography. This is one way in which a language can change—by importation of features from some source outside itself, from some external source; and we can therefore call this kind of change in language *external* change. All external change is, by its nature, borrowing, whether the source is a dialect closely or distantly related to the dialect which does the borrowing, or an unrelated language. It was to this kind of change—primarily to obsolescence and revival of archaic forms (i.e., borrowing from an earlier stage of the language)—that Horace was referring to when he wrote in his *Art of Poetry:*

Multa renascentur quae iam cecidere, cadentque
Quae nunc sunt in honore vocabula, si volet usus

"Many words which have already gone out of use come back to life again, and words which are now in honor fall into disuse, if usage so wills it."

This observation is quite well-founded and justified. Languages change, over the centuries, so much as to render them completely different in the space of only a thousand years or so. If Horace, for instance, were to come to life today and converse with a speaker of

Modern French, the two would be completely unable to understand each other. Imagine a speaker of Old French (of, say, around the year 1000) added to the conversation, and the situation would not be much better. The speaker of Old French would not be able to act as interpreter, but instead would have great difficulty in understanding either his linguistic ancestor (Horace) or his linguistic descendant (the present-day speaker of French). They would have in common a great many words that were related historically, but which would be too different from each other to be understood—such as the word for "August", which Horace would pronounce *augustum,* the speaker of Old French *aúst,* and the modern Frenchman with just one phoneme, a vowel similar to our "oo" sound. The entire linguistic systems of Latin, Old French, and Modern French differ so greatly that speakers of the three languages would each have to learn two other languages in order to grasp what the others were saying. The same would hold true for a speaker of the English of King Alfred's time, one of Chaucer's time, and one of our own time, if they could try to converse together.

However, when Horace discusses borrowing of archaic forms, he is seeing and presenting only a part of linguistic change; and so would we, if we took into account only the results of external borrowing, such as we study in linguistic geography. Theoretically, it might be possible to keep an otherwise-normal speech-community hermetically sealed off from all outside sources of borrowing (including knowledge of past stages of their language), and maybe even—by extremely detailed supervision like that of a super-police-state—to prevent inter-dialectal borrowing within the speech-community. But even in such a completely isolated, regulated community, the language would still change, no matter how much effort was made to keep it stable. For, in addition to borrowing or external change, there is another force at work to keep language constantly changing, which would work no matter how little external influence were exerted on the language: *internal* change. Internal change is, in its turn, of two subvarieties: *internal borrowing,* and *evolution* or *organic change.* The inner evolution of a language, particularly in its phonemes, goes on gradually, and speakers of the language are often not even aware that it is going on, or else they see only such a small part of the total pattern of change that they don't realize its import. After some hundreds or thousands of years have passed, however, a language comes to be very different from what it was at an earlier stage; and the changes have taken place so gradually and so inevitably that no one could possibly have halted them.

Internal borrowing, or *analogy,* is the kind of change that takes place when a child says *foots* instead of *feet, oxes* instead of *oxen, sticked* instead of *stuck,* or *breaked* instead of *broke.* We usually call such forms as *foots, oxes, sticked, breaked* "mistakes" and all of us—even the most illiterate users of sub-standard English—train our children to say *feet,* not *foots,* and so on. Yet what lies at the root of these "mistakes" is an extremely widespread process, which we call *analogical replacement.* What has happened when the child has said *foots* or *sticked?* Simply this: he has heard and learned a whole host of "regular" formations —plural formations such as *root—roots, hat—hats, book —books, map—maps, box—boxes,* and past formations like *kick—kicked, lick—licked, trick—tricked, rake— raked,* in the hundreds and thousands. He has simply made his new formation of a plural for *foot* or *ox* by abstracting (unconsciously, for the most part) the "regular" ending *-s -es* and adding it to *foot* or *ox.* Likewise, he has taken the "regular" past ending *-ed* or *breaked* "on the analogy" of other pasts like *kicked, raked,* and so on. He is making what we often call an *analogical new-formation,* by borrowing an element of linguistic form or construction (here the noun-plural suffix *-s -es* or the verb past suffix *-ed*) from one part of our linguistic structure (here the "regular" formations) and adding it to another (here the "irregular" forms). This is a kind of borrowing, just like external borrowing; but the source of borrowing is not somewhere outside but within the language itself, and so we call it internal borrowing.

Analogical changes of this kind are often presented in the shape of proportional formulas, with x standing for the new-formation, thus

> *hat* : *hats* = *foot* : x ("*hat* is to *hats* as *foot* is to x")
> *box* : *boxes* = *ox* : x
> *kick* : *kicked* = *stick* : x
> *rake* : *raked* = *break* : x

Sometimes, objections are made to our statement of analogical replacements in a proportional formula, such as those we have just given; critics say that naive speakers would not be capable of exact enough reasoning to make up a formula of this sort and carry it out. There are two answers to this objection: 1) that what we are giving here is a description of what takes place, not a statement of reasoning that we might necessarily expect from a naive speaker, who speaks normally without abstract analysis and who habitually does perfectly many things he could not possibly describe; and 2) that even naive speakers from time to time are perfectly conscious of the basis for their analogical formations. The great Danish linguist Otto Jespersen tells the story of a Danish child who should, according to normal Danish usage, have said *nikkede* "nodded" as the past of *nikker* "nod", but said *nak* instead on the analogy of *stak* "stuck", whose present is *stikker*. When the child was corrected, he immediately retorted "*Stikker—stak, nikker—nak*", showing that he knew perfectly well on what analogy he had made the new past tense form, and stating it in the form of a proportion.

From the point of view of the present language, analogical new-formations like *oxes* or *taked* are "mistakes", forms that would be uttered only by children or others learning the language, or by adults when tired or flustered (that is, as "slips of the tongue"), and that would not be accepted by any native speaker at present. But there are always some forms with regard to which our usage is not fully settled, even that of normal adult native speakers of the language, and for which we may use first one and then another alternative. We have, for instance, the "irregular" plural formation *hoof—hooves*, and the "strong" past tenses *wake—woke, dive—dove;* yet we often hear and make regularized forms for these words: *hoofs, waked, dived.* That is to say, in some respects our usage is *fluctuating;* and in the course of time, we will gradually come to favor one competing form over the other (say, *dived* over *dove*), until at last one is triumphant and drives out the other completely in normal everyday usage.

What we often fail to realize, however, is that some forms which seem fully fixed in our present language were, in earlier times, analogical new-formations, and went through a period of newness, and then of fluctuation, before displacing older forms entirely. Our plurals *days* and *cows* are both analogical replacements of earlier forms which would have sounded quite different if they had developed normally into Modern English. Old English had the singular *dag* "day", plural *dagas,* and *cū* "cow", plural *cȳ* (in which the letter *y* stands for a vowel like that spelled *u* in French or *ü* in German); the Old English plurals, had they developed normally, would have given *dawes* and *kye* (rhyming with *high*) in present-day English. But we do not say *day—dawes* or *cow—kye;* we use the regularized plurals *days* and *cows* instead. This is because around the year 1200, our linguistic ancestors made an analogical new-formation, borrowing the stem *day* from the singular to replace the stem *dawe-* in the plural before the ending *-s*. In the plural of *cow,* there were two successive analogical formations. Around the year 1300, people started to use the plural *kyn,* with the analogical plural ending *-n* (which was then very frequent, but survives now only in *oxen, children, brethren*). The form *kyn* survives at present as an archaism, *kine;* in its turn, it was replaced around 1600 by the plural *cows,* in which the plural ending *-s* was borrowed from the majority of nouns and added to the singular *cow.* There must have been a time when *days* seemed as much of a "mistake" as *foots* does now, and—slightly later—a period when *days* and *dawes* were in competition just as *hoofs* and *hooves* are now. If we extend our time-perspective far enough back, we can see that we use relatively few plural formations which are direct continuations of those in use four or five thousand years ago.

These considerations are of importance when it comes to judging forms like *hisn, hern,* and so forth, or *he done,* of the type we discussed in Chapter 2 (p. 12 and following pages). When an "ignorant" person borrows the ending *-n* from the possessive pronoun *mine* and adds it to the adjectives *his, her, our, your* and *their,* to make the distinctive possessive pronouns *hisn, hern, ourn, yourn, theirn,* this procedure on his part is not due to ignorance or stupidity. It is due to exactly the same process of analogizing, of regularizing the forms of the language, that we saw in the instances of *cows* or *days,* and that has gone on in producing a great many other forms we now use. The analogy in this instance is, of course:

$$my : mine = his : x$$

and so forth. Likewise, such a past tense as *he done* is traceable to some such analogy as this:

$$he\ has\ kicked : he\ kicked = he\ has\ done : x$$

That such forms as *hisn* or *he done* are not accepted as part of the standard language is not due to any defect in the forms themselves—they are perfectly respectable analogical forms, with as much right to existence as *cows* and *days;* the thing that makes them unacceptable is simply the connotation of social disfavor which has been attached to them.

Very often, internal borrowing (analogy) comes into play when linguistic forms become irregular and grammatical relationships are obscured as a result of changes in phonemes. This is what happened in the case of English *day—dawes;* it has happened in recent centuries in such instances as those of the old plurals *eye—eyen, shoe—shoon, brother—brethren,* which have now been replaced by the more transparent and easily understandable formations *eyes, shoes, brothers* respectively; or in such past tenses of verbs as *help —holp, work—wrought,* now regularized by analogy in the new-formations *helped, worked.* In English noun plurals and verb pasts and past participles, the trend of development is slowly but surely towards analogical leveling of irregularities; even though forms like *gooses, mouses* or *drinked, writed* are simply "errors" or "blunders" now, they may perhaps be perfectly normal by two or three hundred years from now. Today's analogical "mistakes" are often tomorrow's competing forms, and day-after-tomorrow's "correct" forms.

In other instances, analogy works rather to restore distinctions that have been lost through phonemic change. The Italian imperfect singular is an excellent example of this. The three forms of the imperfect singular in Latin—first, second, and third persons— ended in *-bam, -bās, -bat* respectively, as in

    1.sg. *cantābam* "I used to sing"
    2.sg. *cantābās* "you (sg.) used to sing"
    3.sg. *cantābat* "he, she, or it used to sing"

During the development of Latin into Italian, final *-m, -s,* and *-t* ceased to be pronounced, and all three of these forms would have developed normally into Italian *cantava*. In other tenses of the verb, however, changes in sound did not obscure the distinction between first, second, and third singular; and hence there was a strong pressure from the pattern of the rest of the language, to re-establish such a distinction where it had been lost through the disappearance of final *-m, -s, -t*. Even before the earliest documents were written in Italian, the second person singular of the imperfect was distinguished from the other two persons by the substitution of the ending *-i,* taken ultimately from the second singular of the present in verbs like *audīs* "you (sg.) hear", whose ending *-īs* developed regularly to *-i*. The second person singular of the imperfect was thus remade analogically into *cantavi;* in Old Italian, the first and third singular both were *cantava,* the normal development of both *cantābam* and *cantābat*. In later times, the ending *-o* was borrowed from the first singular of the present (as in *canto* "I sing") and used instead of *-a* as a distinctive first singular ending in the imperfect also. The following table shows the historical development of the imperfect singular from Latin to Italian, with daggers placed before the forms which are analogical replacements:

	LATIN	LATE LATIN	OLD ITALIAN	MODERN ITALIAN
1.sg.	cantābam	cantaba	cantava	†cantavo
2.sg.	cantābās	cantaba	†cantavi	†cantavi
3.sg.	cantābat	cantaba	cantava	cantava

Analogical change is always at work in language—not only in inflectional forms like *foots* and *taked*, but also on the level of word-formation, syntax and meaning. We are always deriving new words from already existing ones, by extending the use of some prefix, suffix, or other formative element. On the analogy of *Jacobite* "follower of King James", *Adamite* "descendant of Adam", *Hamite* "descendant of Ham", and similar formations in *-ite*, we can coin such terms as *Hicksite* or *Buchmanite*. We take the prefix *de-* from formations like *decode, deface, derail,* and add it to other nouns to make new words such as *delouse, degut.* Sometimes we separate the elements of a word differently from the way earlier speakers did, and thus remodel the word: so, for example, in the Middle English phrases *a naddere* "a certain kind of snake" and *a napron* "a small cloth", the *n* was taken as being part of the indefinite article *an,* and the phrases were redivided as *an addere* (Modern English *an adder*) and *an apron,* respectively. The analogy in these instances was something of this kind:

$$an\ other : other = a\ naddere : x$$

Syntactical constructions are often extended by analogy; as Leonard Bloomfield points out (*Language*, p. 407):

"From the sixteenth century on, we find English subordinate clauses introduced by the word *like*. We can picture the innovation in this way:

to do better than Judith : *to do better than Judith did* = *to do like Judith* : *x*

where the outcome is the construction *to do like Judith did*."

Changes in the meaning of words are also due to analogy: to the extension of the situations with respect to which the words are used. There is a shift in the central meaning of the word, and what was formerly a marginal meaning becomes central, whereas the old central meaning becomes marginal or eventually disappears. In Old English, for example, the word *bede* meant "prayer" (it is ultimately related to German *beten* "to pray"); however, in saying one's prayers, one used a rosary, a succession of little spheres on a string, as part of the process. Counting one's *bedes* gradually came to mean, not so much counting the prayers, as counting the little spheres on the string; and the word *bead* thus came eventually to mean, not "prayer" any longer, but what it does now, "a little sphere" of one kind or another—by now, no longer necessarily connected with a rosary at all and even usable in connection with bead-like, spherical shapes such as *beads* of perspiration. Similarly, Middle High German *kopf* meant "cup, bowl, pot"; during the late Middle Ages, its meaning shifted to that of "head", which it has in Modern German. The word *kopf* was used in the meaning "head", first of all in a special situation; we find it in texts which describe battle scenes, in which a warrior smashes some one else's *kopf*. At first, this usage was probably a loan-translation of Old French *teste*, which had developed the meaning "head" out of an earlier meaning "pot, potsherd"; it was then extended analogically from situations referring to head-smashing in battle to other situations in which heads were referred to. The proportional formulas for developments like those of English *beads* and German *kopf* would be set up more or less like this:

to count pearls : to string pearls = to count beads : x
to smash a head : to nod one's head = to smash a kopf : x

The process of semantic change is an entirely normal one, and is going on all the time, as when someone uses *awfully* in the sense of "very". Here, too, the meaning of *awfully* is being extended from some situation where "fear-inspiring" and "extremely" are very close to one another:

I was very frightened : I was very tired
            = I was awfully frightened : x

When someone uses *terribly, fearfully*, or the like in the same way, it is simply on the analogy of *awfully* in the meaning of "very". There is no more sense in protesting against such an extension of meaning in the case of *awfully* than there is against using *bead* in the meaning of "little spherical object", or Modern German *Kopf* in the meaning "head".

Up to this point, we have been talking about analogical change in language, as a kind of borrowing; we have come beyond Horace's idea of change in language, in that our discussion has dealt with changes within linguistic systems, but we have still been dealing with borrowings. At a couple of points we have hinted at another kind of change without taking it up in detail, as when we said that Old English *dagas* would have developed normally into modern *dawes*, and that final *-s* and *-m* ceased to be pronounced during the transition from Latin to Italian. The kind of change involved here is not one of analogical replacement, but of development in the phonemes of the language: *phonemic* change. As phonemes change, linguistic forms—being composed of phonemes—change also, even without the help of analogical new-formation; for instance, as when Latin *cantābam, cantābās* and *cantābat* all merged into *cantava* through the effects of phonemic change. Phonemic change, and the resultant change of forms and constructions, is what we referred to on p. 159 as organic change. This is the kind of linguistic change that the speakers of a language are least aware of, and which was the last, in fact, that students of language came to realize the existence of. This is because phonemic change and its results take place quite gradually, so much so that the ordinary speaker does not realize its existence. Yet organic change is the most basic type of linguistic change, and is at the base of all other change in language; analogical replacements are normally due to the fact that phonemic change disturbs the pattern of a language, either introducing divergent developments like *day—dawes*, or leveling distinctions as in the case of Italian *cantava*.

When we speak of phonemic change, what we mean is this: that the phonemes of a language, its significant functional units of sound, change in the course of time. They change in their make-up, that is, in the sounds which compose the functional units; they change in their relationships to each other within the language; and they change in the positions in which they can occur. There was a vowel phoneme in Latin which was spelled *u*, and pronounced approximately like our "oo" sound, in such words as *mūrus* "wall", *nūda* "naked", *lūna* "moon", *tū* "you (sg.)". This phoneme is normally continued in Modern French by a phoneme which has a sound different from the one it had in Latin, the tongue being in the front of the mouth instead of in the back, in such words as *mur* "wall", *nue* "naked", *lune* "moon", *tu* "you (sg.)". This *u*-phoneme in Latin belonged to a series which also included the vowels *o* and *a* (pronounced like our "oh" and "ah" respectively), which had in common the feature of being pronounced with the tongue in the back of the mouth; its relation to the other phonemes of the language has changed in French, so that its continuator belongs to a series characterized by the tongue being in the front of the mouth with the lips rounded. In the meanwhile, the older *o*-phoneme has changed also, so that its continuator now has the "oo" sound (spelled *ou*) in some words (like *vouloir* "to wish" from Lat. *volēre*, *pouce* "thumb" from *pollicem*), and a sound spelled *eu* and pronounced with lips rounded and tongue in the front of the mouth, as for German *ö*, in other words (like *soeur* "sister" from Lat. *soror*, *douleur* "grief" from *dolōrem*).

Phonemes can also change, as we said, in respect to the positions in which they occur. For instance, Old High German *b d g* ("hard" *g!*) could occur at the end of a word as well as elsewhere, but in Modern German the occurrence of these phonemes has come to be limited to the beginning or middle of a word, and at the end of a word they are automatically unvoiced (cf. p. 75), that is, replaced by *p t k* respectively. Hence the Old High German words *gab* "(he) gave", *bad* "bath", and *tag* "day", which were pronounced with the final sounds *b*, *d*, and *g*, are continued in Modern German by forms which are spelled the same, but pronounced *gap*, *bat*, and *tak* respectively; on the other hand, the Modern German plurals *gaben* "(they) gave", *Bäder* "baths", and *Tage* "days" have the sounds *b d g* unchanged, since they are not at the end of the words.

In this way, phonemes can change, split, and merge;

and this they are doing ceaselessly. During the course of hundreds and thousands of years, the phonemes of any given language change so much as to alter entirely the building-blocks out of which the speakers of that language make their meaningful utterances. What sounds they can use in their speech and how they can use them, depends wholly on how their habits of pronunciation are patterned at their particular point in the language's evolution. There is no factor of physical heredity involved, nor yet of psychological disposition or the like; nobody has ever been able to make any valid correlation with such factors. Our linguistic ancestors, the speakers of Old English, who were also the physical ancestors of a great many speakers of Modern English, were able to make the sound which they wrote as *y* and which is spelled *u* in French and *ü* in German; we, however, have entirely lost the habit, so much that we have considerable trouble learning this sound when we meet it in French or German. A few centuries ago, Dutch had a sound like that which we spell *th* in, say, *ether;* there has been little change in the population of the Netherlands since then so far as racial, cultural or psychological characteristics are concerned, but Modern Dutch has lost this sound entirely, and the present-day Netherlander has a hard time learning it when he studies English. We could go on and multiply examples *ad infinitum.*

Often, features of sound (such as voicing, vowel length, and so on) lose, acquire, and then lose again their functional significance in any given language, over the centuries. Thus, vowel length was phonemically important in Latin, where the distinction in the length of the final vowel was all that marked the difference between many forms, such as *mēnsa* "a table" (nominative case) and *mēnsā* "from a table" (ablative case). This distinction in vowel length was lost in the

Romance languages, and the later developments of *fātum* "fate" (with long *a*) and of *malum* "bad" (with short *a*) are alike in their treatment of the vowel *a*. But in Middle French, around the year 1400, the consonant *s* ceased to be pronounced at the end of a syllable, and any preceding vowel was lengthened; this lengthening was indicated in spelling by a circumflex accent (^) written over the vowel letter. At this time, therefore, such a word as *paste* "paste" came to be pronounced and spelled *pâte*, differentiated from *pat(t)e* "paw" only by the length of the vowel *a*. This distinction has again been lost since the seventeenth century, and in present-day colloquial French, *pâte* "paste" and *patte* "paw", though still spelled differently, are pronounced alike, both with a short vowel.

Phonemic change does not take place simply at random, however, with one phoneme developing in one direction and another in another direction. Just as the phonemes of a language fall into a certain pattern, so do their changes fall into patterns, which we often call *shifts*. When the long vowels of Middle English changed, for instance, they all shifted in the same direction, towards a higher position of articulation in the mouth. An important change in the vowel system of Old French took place not long before our first literary documents were written, that is to say, not long before 900 A.D.; this shift involved the breaking or splitting of several vowels into diphthongs, or their articulation in a higher position in the mouth, when they were stressed and when no consonant followed in the same syllable.

In the "great English vowel shift", the Middle English long vowels shifted upward in articulation, and in two instances the shifted vowels have given diphthongs in modern pronunciation:

MIDDLE ENGLISH	MODERN ENGLISH
/'na:me/	/'nem/ *name*
/'dɛ:d/	/'did/ *deed*
/'ge:s/	/'gis/ *geese*
/'wi:n/	/'wajn/ *wine*
/'stɔ:n/	/'ston/ *stone*
/'go:s/	/'gus/ *goose*
/'hu:s/	/'haws/ *house*

The following table gives examples of diphthongization and raising of stressed vowels in a "free" syllable (one in which no consonant follows the vowel) in Old French, as opposed to their remaining the same in "checked" syllables (in which a consonant follows the vowel in the same syllable). The stage preceding Old French in linguistic history is usually termed Proto-Gallo-Romance (abbreviated PGRom.). Old French spelling is given in italics following the phonemic transcription.

PGRom.

IN CHECKED SYLLABLE		IN FREE SYLLABLE		OFr.
/'met-to/	"I put"	/'kre-do/	"I believe"	/'met/ *met*
				/'kreiθ/ *creit*
/'fɛs-ta/	"feast"	/'bɛ-ne/	"well"	/'fɛs-tə/ *feste*
				/'biεn/ *bien*
/'pas-ta/	"paste"	/'ta-le/	"such"	/'pas-tə/ *paste*
				/'tæl/ *tel*
/'pɔr-ta/	"door"	/'bɔ-nu/	"good"	/'pɔr-tə/ *porte*
				/'buɔn/ *buon*
/'mo-ltu/	"much"	/'flo-re/	"flower"	/'molt/ *molt*
				/'flour/ *flo(u)r*

Note the symmetry of the developments in free syllable: the high-mid vowels /e/ and /o/ changed into /ei/ and /ou/ respectively, the low-mid vowels /ɛ/ and /ɔ/ into /iɛ/ and /uɔ/; and the low-central vowel /a/ developed into a front, slightly raised vowel which we may write as /æ/, and which was undoubtedly intermediate in sound between /a/ and /ɛ/, with which latter it eventually merged.

We cannot say, however, that there is any specific trend in phonemic change as a whole—either towards reducing or towards multiplying the phonemes of any given language or family of languages. Earlier (especially nineteenth-century) writers often talk about "phonetic decay" as if all sound-change involved only slurring or loss; and this notion has gradually seeped into our folklore about language, as exemplified, say, in the quotation on p. 95. However, this is far from true; some phonemic change does involve loss or merger of phonemes, but other shifts in phonemic structure involve splits in phonemes, the rise of two phonemes where there was only one before—as in the diphthongs which developed out of earlier simple vowels in Modern English and Old French which we have just discussed. Phonemes change, but the result-ant condition is neither better nor worse than what went before; we cannot speak, in general terms, of either impoverishment or enrichment as a result of phonemic change.

How do phonemes change, and why? Both of these questions have worried linguistic analysts and laymen, ever since our science became aware of the fact of pho-nemic change. By now, we are at a stage where we can give a reasonably good answer to the first, but not as yet to the second. As to the "how" of phonemic change, the usual idea of nineteenth-century scholars was that sounds changed more or less by themselves, much as plants or other organisms evolved. The idea of the phoneme had not yet been elaborated, and linguistic analysts tended to think of individual sounds as the building-blocks of language; and sounds were thought of as undergoing a kind of spontaneous evolution in the course of time. Later, when we had arrived at the notion of the phoneme—not an individual sound, but a functional unit comprising one or more sounds—it was evident that the important thing was change in pho-nemes, and that in some way the sounds comprised in a phoneme gradually changed; Bloomfield, in 1933, said "Historically, we picture phonemic change as a gradual favoring of some non-distinctive variants and a disfavoring of others". Recent theoretical discussions have cleared up our idea of the relation between phonetic and phonemic change. Phonemic change involves some displacement, not in pronunciation, but in the function of sounds—whereas phonetic change precedes phonemic change, and involves non-significant, non-functional displacements in the speakers' habits of articulation.

In the instance of the Old French diphthongization and raising of stressed vowels in free syllables, for example, we must assume that at first there took place a non-significant, non-distinctive change in articulation, conditioned by the position of the vowel in a free syllable. As long as the syllable remained free, the difference in pronunciation was determined by and statable wholly in terms of surrounding sounds, and the diphthongs or raised vowels met all the requirements for still being classed as allophones of the simple vowels out of which they had developed. (For convenience, we may refer to this intermediate stage as Pre-French.) But somewhat later, one of the changes which took place was the loss of all final vowels except /a/, which changed to /ə/. This loss of final vowels caused many consonants which had previously been between vowels to come at the end of words, and to belong to the syllable of the preceding vowel (since there no longer was a following vowel). With this change, there now came, in the stage we call Old French, to be a contrast between simple vowel and diphthong, or between low and raised vowel, before a consonant in the same syllable; and since we can no longer state, for Old French, that the diphthongs or raised vowels occur under specific conditions, we have to treat them as functionally distinct, i.e. phonemically different, from the vowels out of which they originally developed.

The following table gives a more detailed picture of the transition, phonetically and phonemically, from Proto-Gallo-Romance to Old French, in the words listed on p. 172. Each word is now given in phonetic and phonemic transcription. Note that in the Pre-French stage, the diphthongization or raising of the vowel has no phonemic significance, and hence is indicated only in the phonetic transcription, between square brackets; in the Old French stage, the phonetic change has acquired phonemic significance, and so is shown between slant lines as well.

PGRom.	Pre-French	OFr.
/'met-to/ ['met-to] "I put"	/'met-to/ ['met-to]	/'met/ ['met]
/'kre-do/ ['kre-do] "I believe"	/'kre-do/ ['krei-do]	/'krei θ/ ['krei θ]
/'fɛs-ta/ ['fɛs-ta] "feast"	/'fɛs-ta/ ['fɛs-ta]	/'fɛs-tə/ ['fɛs-tə]
/'bɛ-ne/ ['bɛ-ne] "well"	/'bɛ-ne/ ['biɛ-ne]	/'biɛn/ ['biɛn]
/'pas-ta/ ['pas-ta] "paste"	/'pas-ta/ ['pas-ta]	/'pas-tə/ ['pas-tə]
/'ta-le/ ['ta-le] "such"	/'ta-le/ ['tæ-le]	/'tæl/ ['tæl]
/'pɔr-ta/ ['pɔr-ta] "door"	/'pɔr-ta/ ['pɔr-ta]	/'pɔr-tə/ ['pɔr-tə]
/'bɔ-nu/ ['bɔ-nu] "good"	/'bɔ-nu/ ['buɔ-nu]	/'buɔn/ ['buɔn]
/'mol-tu/ ['mol-tu] "much"	/'mol-tu/ ['mol-tu]	/'molt/ ['molt]
/'flo-re/ ['flo-re] "flower"	/'flo-re/ ['flou-re]	/'flour/ ['flour]

To the question "Why do phonemes change?", therefore, we can answer "Because habits of articulation change, and then are re-interpreted in a different function from that which they had before." The question then becomes, naturally, "Why do habits of articulation change?", and to this we have as yet found no satisfactory answer. When we say "satisfactory answer", we mean valid correlation between change in habits of articulation and other aspects of human culture or environment. All kinds of suggestions have been made —correlation with climate, with race, with national psychology, and so forth—but none that will hold water. At present, it looks as if we must simply say that habits of articulation are subject to changes in fashion, just like habits of dress, eating, and so forth—

and, just as these latter vary with no apparent reason, so do habits of pronunciation. No linguistic system has a watertight organization; all languages have loopholes for change, possibilities of variation which at first seem to have no importance and hence are subject to the vagaries of fashion. The Italian poet Dante, the first great thinker on the subject of linguistic change, said:

> "Since, therefore, every human language . . . has been remade in accordance with our whims since the confusion of the Tower of Babel . . . and since man is a most unstable and variable being, language cannot be long-lasting nor stable; but like other human things, such as customs and dress, it has to vary in space and time."

This is as good a statement of the situation with regard to phonetic (not phonemic!) change as has yet been made; and the further solution of the problem now merges with the general question of why all human habits, all human culture changes. One thing seems clear: that change in habits and culture is the way in which man adapts himself to his environment, and has done so for a million or so years, substituting cultural change for biological change. But the working out of the theoretical aspects of this problem is a matter for anthropologists—including linguistic analysts—to attack and solve in the future.

Linguistic change has been going on for thousands of years, right under people's noses; and yet, except for a handful of anticipators in preceding centuries, only in the past hundred and fifty years have people made any start in its analysis. Why this delay? In the first place, no one had a satisfactory technique for describing people's linguistic habits, until the Greek grammarians developed a technique for their own language, and the Sanskrit grammarians developed one for theirs. Even then, the Greeks and the Romans, and also the ancient Hindus, were primarily interested in their own language alone, in that of their own times, and from the point of view of "correctness"; they had little sense of historicity, and little interest in things plebeian or barbarian. And, most important of all, even though they had techniques for description of their own language, they had none for comparison of different languages or for analysis of historical change.

This situation was made more or less permanent by people's misunderstanding of a condition that was present from the late period of the Roman Empire onward: the co-existence of Latin, as a fixed form of speech and writing learned in the schools and used in the Church, and the currently-spoken and rapidly developing everyday speech of the common people. Those who, like priests, monks, and lawyers, learned Latin were taught to regard it as the only correct form of language, in fact as "grammar" *par excellence*, and to see in the everyday vernacular nothing but a "corruption" of Latin, which—as Dante put it—was "acquired without any rules, as one sucked one's mother's milk". Both Latin and the vernacular were regarded as having co-existed at all times, and people failed to see any historical relation between them. Intellectual prejudice played a part here, too: the pride of the educated and of the grammarians led them to despise the untutored speech of the illiterate, naive common folk.

During the sixteenth century, however, some people began to see that there was a historical development from Latin to the modern Romance tongues, and that these latter were not mere corruptions due to "ignorance" or "mental laziness" of lower-class speakers, but the result of normal, regular, inevitable change, whereas the apparent correctness of modern Latin was due simply to its being kept artificially alive in Church and schools. The truth of this assumption was made evident in the fifteenth and sixteenth centuries in Italy, when the gap between Latin and vernacular was made even wider by the humanists' reform of Latin writing, and re-introduction of strict adherence to the norms of the Golden Age of Latin literature. To a sixteenth-century Italian, Claudio Tolomei, goes the honor of first stating clearly the basic principle of what we would now call *regular phonemic change,* which he deduced from observing the Italian (Tuscan) words derived from Latin words beginning in *pl-*. He noticed that most Latin words beginning in *pl-* were continued in Italian by words beginning in *pi-*, such as Italian *pieno* "full" from Latin *plēnus,* Italian *piano* "level" from Latin *plānus,* Italian *più* "more" from Latin *plūs,* and many others. On the other hand, some Italian words had *pl-* representing Latin *pl-*, as in *plora* "he implores" from Latin *plōrat.* Tolomei explained this difference in development by assuming that the normal continuation of Latin *pl-* in Italian was *pi-*, saying:

". . . and I would be so bold as to say that in the original and pure speech of Tuscan men, this was a universally valid rule [i.e. that Latin *pl-* gave Italian *pi-*], and that all those words which are now used and written differently, such as *plora* "he weeps", *implora* "he implores", *splende* "it is resplendent", *plebe* "populace" and the like, were not taken from the middle of the town squares of Tuscany [i.e. from everyday speech], but were set up by writers, and by someone who wished to enrich the language, preferring to use them in the form in which he found them written in Latin, without giving them the form of Tuscan speech [i.e. without substituting *pi-* for *pl-*] . . . because without a doubt the common usage of earlier times would, had it inherited these words, have said *piora, impiora, spiende* and *pieve,* and we have manifest evidence of this latter in that in the vernacular we call *pieve* a church devoted to the religious services of the common people."

This passage from Tolomei is very important; it contains, not only in germ, but fully developed, all the essential points of modern historical linguistic analysis. Tolomei starts out by making one basic assumption: that phonemes change regularly, and hence explains the Italian words with initial *pi-* like *pieno* "full", *piano* "level", and *più* "more" as being the normal representatives of Latin *plēnus, plānus,* and *plūs* respectively. That leaves a group of forms, a *residue*, which show, not *pi-* as we would expect according to the formula just set up, but *pl-*, apparently unchanged from Latin. The older approach would have shrugged off the discrepancy as mere happenstance, since there was not supposed to be any historical relation between Latin and Italian anyhow. Tolomei, however, is forced by his basic assumption to find an explanation for exceptions to his rule; and he finds it in a further assumption, that the residue showing the discrepant treatment *pl-* is due to some other factor than phonemic change: in this particular case, to direct borrowing from Latin, of the kind we now call learnèd borrowing. Tolomei thus distinguishes between two kinds of words in modern Italian: those which developed in everyday speech (like *pieno, piano, più*) and those which were not developments in everyday speech but were taken directly from Latin by writers and other learnèd men (words like *plora, implora, splende, plebe*). He notices and comments on the existence of pairs of words, both from the same source, but one of which developed in everyday speech (*pieve*) and the other of which was taken directly from Latin (*plebe*); such pairs of words are now called *historical doublets*.

Tolomei, four hundred years ago, hit on the basic elements of historical linguistic science; unfortunately, after his time, no one continued or improved on his method, and grammarians were too concerned with prescribing "correct" speech and with forcing all languages into the mold of Greek and Latin grammar, to make any real progress in studying languages from a historical point of view. Real, enduring progress towards a scientific approach was not made until about a hundred and fifty years ago, at the end of the eighteenth and the beginning of the nineteenth century. People's horizons had been steadily broadening, so far as their knowledge of the world's languages was concerned, until by 1800 something was known of a number of exotic languages, the most significant of which were Sanskrit (Old Indic, the language of the ancient hymns of India) and Finnish. When these languages became known, it was quite evident that there must be some relationship between them and the better-known languages: between Sanskrit and a number of European languages, and between Finnish and Hungarian (and various Siberian languages, but no others in Europe). For a while, and due to the old confused notions about the relationship of languages, people thought that all the other languages related to Sanskrit must be derived from it; we still come across that notion from time to time, in uninformed quarters. Soon we began to see that, rather, Sanskrit was a sister language to Latin, Greek, the Germanic, Celtic and Slavic languages, and so on. The first person to state this relationship clearly was Sir William Jones, one of the first great Western Sanskritists, in 1786, pointing out that Sanskrit in relation to Greek and Latin

". . . bears a stronger affinity, both in the roots of verbs, and in the forms of grammar, than could possibly have been produced by accident: so strong, indeed, that no philologer could examine them all three without believing them to have sprung from some common source, which, perhaps, no longer exists; there is a similar reason, though not quite so forcible, for supposing that both the Gothick and the Celtick, though blended with a very different idiom, had the same origin with the Sanskrit."

During the first half of the nineteenth century, a great deal of work was done by scholars to reconstruct the parent language from which Sanskrit, Latin, Greek, Germanic, Balto-Slavic (the intermediate ancestral stage of the Slavic languages such as Russian, Polish, etc., and of the Baltic languages like Lithuanian) and Celtic must have originated. Similar reconstructions were made for Finno-Ugric, the ancestral language of Finnish, Hungarian, and a number of languages in Siberia. Between the languages of each of these groups there are a great many correspondences, in sounds, forms, syntax, and vocabulary, which simply cannot be due to mere chance nor yet to borrowing (no matter how widespread), but can be explained only on the hypothesis of differentiation from a single earlier source. Take such sets of words as these, showing correspondences between Sanskrit, Greek, Latin, Old Church Slavonic, Gothic (the earliest attested of the Germanic languages) and Old Irish:

	"brother"	"carry"	"flee, bend"	"split, bite"	"beech"
Lat.	*frātr-*	*fer-*	*fug-*	*find-*	*fāgo-*
Gk.	*phrātr-* "member of a religious brotherhood"	*pher-*	*phug-*	*pheid-* "save, spare"	*phēgo-*
Skt.	*bhrātar-*	*bhar-*	*bhuj-*	*bhind-*	—
OChSl.	*bratr-*	*ber-* "gather, take"	—	—	
Gothic	*brōþar*	*ber-*	*biug-*	*beit-*	OHG *buohha*, OEng. *bōc*
OIr.	*brāthir*	*ber-*	*bocc* "bow (n.)"	—	—

The first scholars to notice these wide-spread correspondences (which run into the thousands) were, for
the Finno-Ugric languages, the Hungarian S. Gyár-
mathi in 1799, and for the languages we now call Indo-
European, Rasmus Rask of Denmark in 1814 and the
German scholar Franz Bopp in 1816. By comparing
related languages, they were able to make statements
concerning correspondences of sounds—not merely
isolated, but in whole sets, which enabled them to reconstruct the phonemic and grammatical systems of
the ancestor language from which the later languages
had developed. Thus, for instance, in the sets of forms
given in the table above, we notice the correspondence
of Latin *f-*, Greek *ph-*, Skt. *bh-*, and Old Church Slavonic, Gothic, and Old Irish *b-*. Because of these and
similar correspondences in all the other sounds in the
forms in the table, we set up for the ancestor language
the hypothetical forms:

bhrātr- "brother" *bher-* "carry" *bhug-* "flee, bend"
  bhi(n)d- "split, bite"

and, with somewhat less certainty (because it is not
found in all the related languages) *bhāg-* "beech".

Note that these reconstructed forms *bhrātr-* etc. are
purely linguistic reconstructions. We set them up on
the basis of correspondences of *phonemes* in the languages which are obviously derived from this common
source, and they tell us nothing at all about either the
kind of people who used them or the place where they
were used. There are certain inferences which we may
perhaps make from the presence of some words in all
of the related languages, e.g. the word for "snow" (reconstructed *sneig^whs*), which leads us to suppose that
the speakers of that language knew of snow and hence
did not live in an extremely hot region; but even those
inferences are tentative. Some scholars, especially in

Germany, under the influence of non-scientific pressures like that of nationalistic ideology, have gone off the deep end in drawing unjustifiable deductions about the physical race (supposedly "Nordic") and the dwelling place (often ascribed to Northern Europe or even specifically Germany) of the speakers of this unrecorded ancestral language which we reconstruct from the evidence of related languages attested later. Even the very name we give to the ancestral language has been misused for non-scientific purposes: of the various names that have been proposed for it, *Aryan* (taken from the Sanskrit term for "noble") was converted by German philologists into a pseudo-racial term to mean first "Nordic" and then (especially in Nazi usage) "non-Jewish"; and the term most commonly used even in scientific German usage, *Indo-Germanic*, is perhaps likely to be misinterpreted as giving undue emphasis to the Germanic element. The term normally used outside of Germany is somewhat more general, being based on the two main areas where we find speech descended from this ancestor language: *Indo-European*.

At one time, people hoped that, by reconstructing the phonemic and grammatical system of Indo-European, we could get appreciably closer to the speech of primitive man, and that it would give us light on the origin of language and the mentality of the earliest men. This hope was nourished by the fact that in the early nineteenth century, the traditional chronology (according to which the world was supposed to have been created only some four thousand years before Christ) still dominated most people's thinking. There was also a certain amount of misunderstanding caused by the name that was given to the parent language: *primitive* Indo-European, which was taken to refer to a truly "primitive" state of affairs, or something approaching the primeval or original condition of human language as a whole. This hope has proven wholly unfounded, although echoes of the misunderstanding are still heard here and there. Indo-European was a language like any other, with phonemes and morphemes and syntactical features. So far as we can tell, the time that Indo-European was spoken as a unified language must have been somewhere between 2000 and 4000 B.C., that is, about six thousand years ago. But six thousand years is a very short time, not in proportion to recorded history, but in proportion to the history of mankind as a whole; man has been man for hundreds of thousands of years, if not a million years or more—and anything we can get by reconstructing one of the languages spoken a mere six thousand years ago, will not get us at all appreciably nearer to the origin of human speech. To avoid this confusion many Americans now prefer to use the term *Proto-Indo-European,* since the Indo-European language as we reconstruct it was the *prototype* of the various modern languages.

After the time of Rask and Bopp, many others worked on the comparative grammar of the Indo-European languages, notably Jacob Grimm (1785–1863), August Pott (1802–1887), and August Schleicher (1821–1868). With the development of the natural sciences, the tendency of the mid-nineteenth-century scholars was of course to ally their work with these latter, especially with the evolutionary doctrines set forth by Darwin and his followers. Since the evolutionists assumed a kind of "family tree" to show the origin and relationship of the different species they studied, Schleicher did likewise for the Indo-European languages. By this technique we might set up a "pedigree"-like table of this kind:

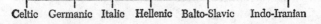

Proto-Indo-European

Celtic   Germanic   Italic   Hellenic   Balto-Slavic   Indo-Iranian

and sub-tables under each one of the main divisions, like the following for the Germanic languages:

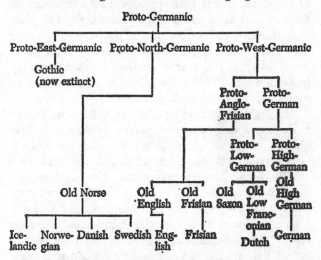

The whole picture would make a "family tree" far too large to reproduce as such without several pages of tables, as you can see from these two samples.

In the 1870's a number of developments took place in Indo-European and general linguistics; in many ways, the 1870's were as exciting a period in historical linguistics as the past twenty or so years have been in descriptive work. A group of scholars centered on the University of Leipzig carried to their normal conclusion the principles on which people had been working since the beginning of the century, and which Tolomei had prefigured so clearly in the passage we cited on p. 178. These scholars—of whom the two most important were the Slavicist August Leskien (1840–1916) and the comparativist Karl Brugmann (1849–1919)— made an overt, categorical statement of the principle that phonemes change regularly, under the form "Phonetic laws admit of no exceptions" (*die Lautge-*

setze kennen keine Ausnahmen, Leskien, 1876). Because of their rigor in procedure, and perhaps because of the brusqueness and apparent over-confidence of their manner in announcing and adhering to this principle, Leskien and Brugmann and their group were not universally liked; they were given the name of *Junggrammatiker* ("young grammarians" or, as it is usually translated into English, *Neo-Grammarians*), at first as a nickname, and the nickname stuck.

Although competent scholars had been using the basic assumption of regular phonemic change as their guiding principle since Tolomei's, and particularly since Rask and Grimm's time, it hadn't been stated explicitly. Immediately it was stated, it aroused opposition, from some older men such as the Hellenist Georg Curtius (1820–1885), and also from younger men like Johannes Schmidt (1843–1901) and the Romance scholar Hugo Schuchardt (1842–1927). To a certain extent, the rigorous assumption that phonemes change, without reference to the meanings of the words in which they occur, and apparently blindly and mechanically, aroused the hostility of people who were emotionally attached to the idea that speech must of necessity "mirror" and follow human thought, not determine it. To a much greater extent, the dispute—which in some instances reached extremes of bitterness and developed into a true quarrel—was due to the poor way in which Leskien made his statement of principle. Furthermore, the term *law* was applied to statements of phonetic developments, on the analogy of such "laws" of physics as "Boyle's law" or "Watt's law". Thus, for instance, the scholar Karl Bartsch (1832–1888) was the first to observe and state the fact that Latin stressed *á* developed, when no consonant followed in the same syllable, into Old French *ié* after a palatal sound but into *é* otherwise; from *mare* "sea" we have OFr. *mer*, but from *carum* "dear" we find *chier* in Old French. This statement is known as "Bartsch's law". But the "laws" of historical linguistics are statements, not of general relationships, but of specific historical developments, each of which took place at a certain time and in a certain language. Thus, "Bartsch's law" is a statement of a phonemic change which took place under certain conditions, and at a certain time—not earlier than the 8th century and not later than the 10th—and in a certain language, the dialect of the region around Paris. It's about as sensible to talk about "Bartsch's *law*" as it would be to talk about "the *law* of Gettysburg" referring to the historic event of the battle of Gettysburg.

The assumption that phonetic "laws" suffer no exceptions, or, better stated, that phonemes change regularly, is an assumption, not a statement of fact; it is a guiding principle which we assume in order to help us discover and explain exceptional developments. So, for instance, in Modern English we find *f-* as the normal representative of Middle English *f-*, as in *fox, full, foot* (from Middle English *fox, ful, foot*) and a host of other words. However, we find *v-* instead of *f-* in the word *vixen* "female fox" (from Middle English *fixen*). Does this invalidate our assumption of regular phonemic change, here of the continuation of Middle English *f-* by Modern English *f-*? By no means. We look for another explanation of the aberrant *v-* of *vixen;* and we find that *vixen* is borrowed from a dialect of Southern English speech in which *f-* regularly became *v-*. But it's only our assumption of regular phonemic change that permits us to isolate exceptions and establish a residue of this kind and which forces us to seek and find explanations for it. The assumption of regular phonemic change is a fruitful one, because it helps us analyze, classify, and explain developments that we would otherwise just regard—as did almost all people before about 1800—as an inexplicable welter of criss-cross and meaningless correspondences, so much so that Voltaire is said to have called etymology "a science in which the vowels count for nothing and the consonants for very little".

It was during the 1870's, also, that the investigation of linguistic geography was begun, which was to prove very fruitful. To prove that the Junggrammatikers' doctrine of "no exceptions to phonetic laws" was literally true, a German named Georg Wenker started to investigate the dialects of Germany, and sent out questionnaires with test sentences to be translated into the local dialect, to over forty thousand schoolteachers throughout Germany. The results of his investigations have been published in a linguistic atlas, the first of the great European atlases. Wenker was expecting to find that the local dialects would show regularity of sound change more clearly than the standard language, by preserving the traits of the mediaeval language more faithfully and more regularly. What he actually found was that the local dialects showed just as much apparent irregularity as did the literary language, due to a great amount of borrowing from one dialect to another and from standard language to dialect, of the kind we saw in Chapter 9. From the results of Wenker's investigations for Germany and those of others for France, Italy, etc., many scholars concluded that, since local dialects showed as much irregularity in phonetic developments as did standard languages, the Neo-Grammarians' principle of regular phonemic change must be unfounded. This conclusion was due to a very superficial kind of reasoning, without realizing that the assumption of regularity in phonemic change is the only thing that gives any foundation to whatever inferences we make concerning dialect borrowing. The principle of regular phonemic change is an assumption of the same type as Newton's "first law of physics", that every body remains in a state of rest or of uniform motion in a straight line unless it is compelled to change that state by force acting upon it. This "law", like the principle of absolutely regular phonemic change, is something we never see in nature, because there are always other factors entering in; but it is, nevertheless, this assumption of regularity that enables us to sort out the various factors that cause irregularity.

Language doesn't stay the same, as we said in the title of this chapter. There are the forces of internal organic change, in phonemic, morphological, and syntactic matters; of internal borrowing (analogy); and of external borrowing, from related dialects, related languages, and non-related languages. All these kinds of change are going on all the time. Their work is like that of geological forces, in erosion and building up: at one place, the structure of the language may be wearing away through phonemic and morphological reduction, while at another place it may be building up through phonemic splitting, analogical new-formation, change of meaning, and borrowing. And, like the work of geological forces, linguistic change is, in the present state of human technology, irresistible. We may try to dam it up at one point, but it's sure to burst forth at another, and where we are least expecting it. We try to teach our children not to say *it's me* but *it is I,* and so they substitute *I* for *me* in other situations as well, and say *between you and I.* It is futile to try to stop linguistic change; to do so, a super-police-state would be necessary, and also a different type of nervous system in the human body, one with much greater capacity for rigorous adherence to fixed norms of behavior. As a matter of fact, for the past million years, the human race has changed linguistically *instead of* biologically—culture and its changes, rather than biological change, are our mechanism of adaptation to environment. We would do better, therefore, to cease objecting to and trying to impede linguistic change; we should accept linguistic change and its results as something entirely natural and normal, and something which we expect to happen as surely as we expect everything else in the world to change, whether it suits our personal tastes or not.

PART IV: WHAT WE CAN DO ABOUT LANGUAGE

11. Learning Your Own Language

So far, we have seen that there are a lot of things we worry about and have conflicts about, with regard to the way we speak—mainly in the way of feeling or being told that there is something wrong with it and that we must make it better. We have also seen that there is a way of finding out the facts of language, and the science of linguistics gives us some positive knowledge that is different from—often the exact opposite of—what we are told, in school or out, about language. The final question is, can't we do something about applying this knowledge to the problems that face us, and resolving these conflicts and ridding ourselves of the worries we have about our language? Of course we can. There are two steps in the process: first, for the general public and especially the teaching profession to become acquainted with linguistics and its results; and second, to change our attitudes and behavior in accordance with what we can learn from linguistics. If we could do these things, there are a great many ways in which everybody would benefit.

The first field in which change is called for is a field in which every one of us is involved and interested: the teaching of our native language—in this country, of American English. A radical improvement is needed in the way English is taught in our schools—a way which at present is wholly unrealistic and out of touch with the facts of language, and hence far more harmful than beneficial. The ordinary schoolroom approach to English makes (tacitly or explicitly) at least four assumptions, all of them without foundation in reality:

UNREALISTIC ASSUMPTIONS

1. That the child who comes to school at the age of six does not know his own language, and that "his own language" is to be defined as equivalent to the standard language in all instances.

2. That the standard language is something which can be set up as an absolute, and taught on the basis of authority (either some dictionary's or grammar-book's, or the teacher's own say-so).

3. That any variation from the standard language, as defined in the preceding paragraph, is "bad English", so that all variations are equally to be condemned.

4. That the standard language is to be taught in terms of spelling (with speech entering in only secondarily, if at all), and in the mold of traditional Latin grammar.

How unrealistic these assumptions are, we have seen in the first three parts of our discussion in this book. Each one of these assumptions needs to be changed, and teaching procedures need to be adjusted to fit the new assumptions, as follows:

REALISTIC ASSUMPTIONS

1. The child who comes to school at the age of six already knows the basic structure of his own language (not all its vocabulary), and his own language is not necessarily the standard language.

2. Standard usage is not an absolute, but something determined by social acceptability; the way to find out whether any given linguistic feature (phoneme, form, word) is socially acceptable is by relying on scientific

observation and investigation, not on authoritarian dogma.

3. There are different kinds of variation from the standard, different in nature and in acceptability.

4. The standard language should be taught in terms of speech, and spelling should be taught in relation to speech; grammar should be taught in terms of the structure of English itself, not of Latin or any other language.

First of all, the level of linguistic achievement of the six-year-old child. We often tend to think that, because there are a lot of words the six-year-old still does not know, and because he still makes slips (like *tooken* for *taken, I don't know where to put down it* for . . . *put it down,* both of which I have heard recently from my own six-year-old) he therefore does not know his own language, and has to have it taught to him in school. For the matter of vocabulary, there is a valid basis for such an assumption, at least with regard to the extent of his vocabulary: there are many words he still needs to learn, and that is one of the things he should be taught in school as well as outside. But we should never confuse vocabulary with linguistic structure; and at six, the child already has as firm a grasp as he ever will have of the structure of his language, with the exception of a few loose ends still to be picked up. Slips like *tooken* for *taken* or . . . *put down it* for . . . *put it down* are simply the tail end of the long process of trial and error by which the child has been learning his native language for years beforehand—ever since he was one or two years old. They are analogical substitutions, perfectly normal in all human speech, which are sure to be ironed out in a year or two more whether he receives formal instruction in grammar or not. For that matter, everyone makes similar analogical formations and will keep on making them from time to time all through their life, just as random "slips of the tongue" (like *foots* for *feet*), which need not worry us at all. Our attitude need only be, if a child in school uses (say) *tooken* for *taken,* to point out to him that we simply do not say it that way—not because *tooken* is "bad English", but just because we do say *taken* and we don't say *tooken*.

For the same reason, there is no point in trying—as is often done—to teach the normal child the sounds of his own language at the age of six or older. He has already learned them, along with the forms and constructions of his language, by the time he comes to school. Here again, some few may be retarded, and still make certain substitutions, such as *v* for the *th*-sound of *this,* or *f* for the *th*-sound of *thing,* and say *vis fing* instead of *this thing.* This calls, naturally, for special remedial treatment in teaching the child normal pronunciation —in terms of the organs of speech used in pronunciation, not in terms of letters. I have known some instances where teachers told normal children, whose pronunciation was already quite regular and well established, to pronounce *th* by first saying a *t* and then an *h* after it. I was one of the children that were told to do so, and I believed for a long time that that was actually the way we pronounce *th*.

Now, of course, the situation is relatively simple where we are dealing with children whose families and playmates speak standard English, and where all the difficulty we may meet is simply that of tying up the last loose ends left over from the period of initial language learning. We run into real difficulty, though, when children come into the schoolroom not speaking standard English to begin with. Here, the usual procedure is to berate the children for speaking in the way that comes natural to them; to condemn their usage as "bad English", without telling them why; to preach at them that they must speak only "good English" (defined in some arbitrary way), and to mark them down when they don't. The models held up to them are, for the most part, impossibly artificial and stilted (like *it is not I* or *am I not?*), and far removed from ordinary everyday usage among people whose English is unquestionably standard. Result: the child who comes in speaking a non-standard variety of English does not really acquire true standard English, but only a half-understood semi-literary jargon of which he never gets a real grasp, the *formal sub-standard* we mentioned earlier (p. 130). Naturally, this gives him no real help or satisfaction, and in the end only makes him more insecure about his usage than he was before. Our present treatment of non-standard speakers serves only to give insecurity instead of security, worry instead of certainty, fear instead of confidence, and makes enemies instead of friends for the standard language.

How can we handle the matter better? The really fundamental problem is to get rid of the undemocratic attitude that underlies the whole situation, that makes us condemn variant speech-forms, and that makes such teaching necessary. This is a question of basic attitude, which it will undoubtedly take generations and centuries to outgrow. From the short-run point of view, we still have with us the fact that standard speech is regarded as desirable and necessary by a dominant portion of our community, and that a sub-standard speaker is going to find certain doors closed against him, certain opportunities denied him, until he acquires standard speech-patterns. This means, first of all, that we have to supply a really good motivation, to make it palatable, to the sub-standard speaker, in order to persuade him to *want* to change and adapt himself to the standard. We can easily make it clear to a child of ten or twelve that his advancement, his getting along, his getting whatever he wants out of life (whether that be personal advancement in any field, or money, or prestige, or intellectual or artistic pleasures) is going to depend to a considerable extent on his use of socially favored instead of disfavored forms. And it is much more realistic, much closer to the facts, and much easier for anyone to understand, to put it on the basis of *getting what you want out of life* than on the basis of some abstract "right" or "wrong", "good" or "bad", or on the basis of being flunked if you don't do as you're told.

To teach standard speech to a child whose linguistic background is non-standard, we need to refine our approach, and to take into account the various facts about standard speech and its relation to sub-standard usage that we have been pointing out. If little Johnny uses some form that is really not standard, we can point it out to him and get him to change, not on an authoritarian basis, but on a basis of actual usage among people whose speech is acceptable. We also need to point out where and within what limits the substitution should be made—otherwise Johnny is sure to over-correct, and come out with things like *I have did it,* because he was told to replace *I done it* by *I did it,* and has carried the analogy too far because the pattern and its limitations weren't thoroughly explained to him. Many teachers, too, would do well to get a clear idea of the real structure of English; otherwise the situation becomes what it all too frequently is, a case of the wholly blind leading the half-blind. Usually, it is not a case of ill-will or evil intentions on the teacher's part, but mostly of ignorance, as in the case of the one who told us children to pronounce *th* as *t* followed by *h*. To a large extent, the teacher is simply doing as he or she has been taught to do; what is needed is to teach the teachers better.

In the classroom situation we must, of course, make clear the difference between the various types of really or supposedly unacceptable usage that we pointed out in Chapter 2. Not with the same words, necessarily— we will use a style suited to whatever age-level and intellectual development we are dealing with, but getting the attitude across. In some instances, say when Johnny has said *it ain't*, the teacher will take the attitude "Sorry, Johnny, I know that *ain't* comes natural to you, and as a matter of fact there's nothing wrong with *ain't* in itself, in fact it would be a rather useful word if only people didn't disapprove of it. Unfortunately, you're going to run into trouble if you keep on using it, and you'd better avoid it and use *am not, isn't* or *aren't* instead, as the case may be." If Johnny has used a taboo word, our attitude will be "Sorry, we simply don't use that word. The action it refers to is a normal and necessary function of the human body, and the word itself is just a word like any other, but, for some reason or other, people are very strongly down on anyone who uses such words and who talks about such things in any way but by using high-brow, scientific words." An alert teacher might teach the students the word *taboo* at this point, and explain the concept as it applies to our society. And, if Johnny has said *it's me*, the teacher will say nothing at all unless the point is brought up. If it does come up, the best attitude might be: "There's nothing wrong with *it's me*, and it's in constant use by people whose usage is unquestioned; you are, however, likely to run into difficulty with some people who *think* that *it's me* is incorrect, and when you're talking with people who are quite puristically inclined, you'd better avoid *it's me* and use *it is I*, even if it does seem somewhat unnatural."

Needless to say, we will not try to set up any single or absolute standard for usage, particularly a standard which differs from the real one that prevails in our town or region. There is no use in trying to teach Boston English in New York, or Eastern Seaboard English in Kansas City. Once, in a Brooklyn school, I had for a whole year a teacher who insisted on making us pronounce *shone* to rhyme with *Don,* rather than with *bone. Shone* rhymed with *bone* in the natural speech of all of us, and it did in hers too—in fact, she would slip back into making *shone* rhyme with *bone* whenever she was not careful about it. At the time, of course, we did not understand it and just thought it something strange, another of those queer things teachers want you to do for no good reason, and of course it did not stick with any of us. Much later, I realized that she must have had some fancy ideal of high-class speech, modeled (dimly and at many removes) on British English, in which *shone* does rhyme with *Don* for many people; but most of my former classmates in that schoolroom have probably forgotten the whole matter, or if they do think of it once in a while, still have no idea of what she was driving at. Variations in speech from region to region are completely natural and normal, as we have already seen, and we should never try to substitute something completely foreign, for our own speech-habits as far as they are socially acceptable.

Furthermore, as we have kept emphasizing all through our discussion, the only way to determine acceptability is through actual observation. Never take anybody's word for anything in matters of usage, if you are in a position to observe for yourself. If you cannot observe for yourself, try to get a source of information whose prime interest is in the facts as they *are*, not as somebody says they *ought* to be. We have already mentioned C. C. Fries's *American English Grammar* as a description of actual usage on certain moot points in American English. We need to have new school grammars, whose statements are based on fact-finding surveys like that which Fries made. But there is a danger, even here, of such a work as Fries's coming in its turn to be taken as an "authority" and treated as a source of dogma, rather than of fact. To be really accurate in whatever we say about standard usage, we should re-examine and re-study the situation at least every fifty years or so, if not more often.

But there's a further pre-supposition for the type of approach we have just been advocating: that both teacher and pupil know the relation between writing and speech. This is a matter which we must make clear from the very beginning, not only in the first grade, but even in kindergarten or at whatever stage the child begins to become familiar with letters. We must make clear from the outset that the reality of language is *sound*, the noises we all make with our faces to communicate with each other, and that letters are simply things which stand for sounds, with much less basic importance than the sounds themselves. That is not an easy notion to get across, because many people's initial impulse is to take the fixity of the printed sign as an indication that it is necessarily more fundamental or more important than the fleeting, evanescent speech-sound; but it is essential to get it across from the very beginning, as all true understanding of language phenomena rests upon it. This is not to deny that writing and reading have their importance, especially in our civilization, which so emphasizes achievements based on use of "the written word"; it is just putting things in their proper perspective, and getting first things first.

English spelling and its teaching present an extremely knotty problem in themselves, and one which needs to be completely re-examined and reformed in our schools. If the spelling of English were wholly or nearly phonemic, like the spelling of Finnish or Hungarian, or even that of standard Italian, there would be practically no problem. The child knows—unreflectingly, of course, and without analysis—the phonemes of his own language by the time he's six, and all the Finnish-speaking or Hungarian-speaking child has to do is to learn the spelling of these phonemes. They do not have any spelling problems in Finnish, say, and extremely few in Hungarian or Italian schools, compared with what we have; such trouble as does arise comes from children whose native language is not the literary standard, but a local dialect whose phonemes are different from those of the standard language. The American institution of the spelling-bee, which depends on the existence of all kinds of tricky spellings and "hard" words, would be completely meaningless for a native speaker and writer of standard Italian or Hungarian. Our problems in the spelling of English come from the unfortunate fact that English orthography is not wholly phonemic, and that its non-phonemic aspects are highly erratic. The folklore about our language recognizes that fact in the widespread saying that "English isn't a phonetic language"—meaning, not that English has no sounds, but that its spelling is inaccurate and unreliable.

The most radical and effective solution to the problem would be to make English spelling completely phonemic. This could be done, by using the alphabet of the IPA or any other set of characters we found most useful and acceptable. Such a radical reform would at first arouse intense hostility in most of us who have painfully and with great difficulty acquired the habits of traditional spelling. But later generations, once they had acquired it from the outset, and without any emotional attachment to an older system, would take to it like ducks to water, and the whole spelling problem would have disappeared.

One problem would have to be recognized and met in one way or another, that of regional variations in standard speech. How would we represent, say, the three words which we now spell *marry, merry,* and *Mary?* People east of the Alleghenies have three different vowel phonemes in these three words, whereas Mid-Western speech uses only one vowel in all three.

In phonemic transcription, the Easterner says /'mæri/ for *marry,* /'mɛri/ for *merry,* and /'meri/ for *Mary;* the Mid-Westerner says /'mɛri/ for all three.

We would have to adopt and teach one of two attitudes: either taking one particular regional variety and basing our new spelling on that—preferably the variety which made the greatest number of distinctions; or allowing for a variation in spelling to correspond to the variation in speech patterns. The latter procedure would definitely be more realistic and more scientific; if we based our completely reformed spelling on one particular variety, people who used a different variety of speech would find such a spelling unrealistic and artificial, and we would be back where we started. Recognizing regional varieties in spelling as well as in speech would, it is true, require more attentiveness to what we read, and would deprive us of the convenience of having a single graphic representation to cover divergent pronunciations. But it would be more in accord with the facts, and would force us to recognize the existence and nature of linguistic differences far more than we do now.

The whole question is somewhat academic, anyhow; such a radically reformed spelling for English

would be highly desirable, but at the present time it
is a quite unattainable goal. The obstacles are not linguistic in nature, but political and economic. To put
such a reform across, and to reduce the transitional
difficulties and dislocations to a minimum, would take
a far more centralized political system than we have
or want to have in the United States. It could be done
by governmental order in some such country as Russia,
or even France or Italy, where the central government's
say-so counts for much more in the school system and
out of it, and where people are willing to follow an
official ukase of this sort. It was done in Turkey in the
1920's, under the dictator Kemal Ataturk, when the
Roman alphabet was substituted for the older Arabic
writing. In the United States, with its loose organization of school systems, with control of the schools in
the hands of individual local boards, and with Americans' normal attitude of distrust and rebellion against
centralized authority and orders coming from above,
it just could not be put across. On the other hand, such
a drastic reform could never be adopted by any other
than authoritarian means; even if people could be
persuaded of its worth (an almost impossible task in
the present state of the English-speaking public's
knowledge concerning linguistic matters), it would
take so long to adopt that the language would have
changed and the reform would be out of date even
before it was fully adopted. There are too many vested
interests, also, standing in the way, quite aside from
the widespread conservatism and inertia of the general public: just to mention one aspect of the matter,
the trouble involved in reprinting all our books would
be enormous, and the expense staggering. A great
many important, but not popular, books might go un-
reprinted and fall into undeserved oblivion; for, within
fifty years, everything that is now in print would be

as obsolete and unreadable as the English of Chaucer's time is to us.

And yet a partial reform would be useless; it would fall between two stools, that of rational and thorough improvment, and that of sticking to what we have, which at least has the virtue of familiarity and ease through long acquaintance and practice. "Simplified spelling" is not a satisfactory goal, because it does not go far enough. Eliminating the "silent" *gh* in *right, night, fight* by spelling them *rite, nite, fite* is all right as far as it goes, but these latter spellings are still inadequate representations of the phonemic structure of these words.

To be accurate, a transcription of the words *right, night, fight* should be something on the order of /'rajt/, /'najt/, and /'fajt/ respectively. It should at least indicate the presence of four phonemes in each of these words, the second phoneme of each being the same phoneme that occurs as the second phoneme in *how* /'haw/ or *wow* /'waw/, and the third phoneme of each being the same one that occurs at the end of *boy* /'bɔj/, *my* /'maj/, and *sigh* /'saj/.

There is no basic gain in spelling *aisle* as *isle* or *aile*, or even in spelling both *aisle* and *isle* as *ile*, as long as the fundamental aberrance of the system as a whole still remains.

But if we keep to the present conventional spelling —can it be taught any better and more effectively than it is now? It certainly can, and years of each child's school life could be saved that are now wasted in an inefficient way of learning to read and spell. The ordinary beginning reader and spelling book has an utterly unscientific choice of material, including both easy and difficult spellings from the very beginning. Picking up and looking at one such book, I find simple and relatively phonemically spelled words like *cat, and, fun* beside such words as *Dick, night, look,* or *door,* that contain "silent letters", conflicting spellings for the same phoneme, and conflicting phonemes for the same spelling. As Leonard Bloomfield has said (*Language,* p. 501):

> "The coordination between letters and phonemes, accordingly, has to be established as an analogic process by practice on graphs [i.e. spellings] in which the symbols have a uniform value, such as *bat, cat, fat, hat, mat, pat, rat—can, Dan, fan, man, pan, ran, tan, van—bib, fib, rib—*and so on. The real factor of difficulty is the host of irregular spellings which will remain, no matter what values are assigned as regular. Two devices obviously need to be tried. One is to teach children to read a phonetic transcription, and to turn to traditional writing only after the essential reading habit has been set up. The other is to begin with graphs that contain only one phonemic value for each letter—sets such as were illustrated above—and either to postpone other graphs until the elementary habit has been fixed, or else to introduce them, in some rationally planned way, at earlier points. The irregular graphs should be presented systematically (e.g. silent *gh: fight, light, might, night, right, sight, tight; a* for [ɔ] before *l: all, ball, call, fall, gall, tall, wall, halt, malt, salt, bald, false*). It may prove advantageous to use some distinguishing mark (such as different colors) for silent letters and for letters in irregular phonemic values. The methods of procedure, the order of presentation, and the various minor devices can be determined only by experiment; from the outset, however, one must know what one is trying to do."

Bloomfield prepared, at one time, an elementary reading text embodying these principles, but he encountered such opposition from vested interests, and such inertia even from those who had no special interests of their own, that he could get it tried only in one small parochial school. Reports are that the experiment was very successful, but apparently it was not repeated, and the text has languished in obscurity (not having even been published) since then. But if some such procedure were adopted and used, by teachers who knew the true relation of writing to speech, the learning of spelling could go so much faster that at least two years of every child's schooling could be saved. American elementary education takes eight years, in contrast to the six years it normally takes in schools in other countries. As a result, the ordinary American high-school and college student is two years behind the student of the same age elsewhere. This is at least in part traceable to the time we waste on English spelling, a difficult enough subject to acquire anyhow, and whose difficulties we aggravate by uncomprehending and inefficient teaching.

A striking demonstration of the ill-informed and unprepared state of the general public with regard to reading and spelling in our elementary schools was afforded in the middle nineteen-fifties by the controversy over Rudolf Flesch's *Why Johnny Can't Read*. This provocative book sparked a storm of protest against the prevailing unscientific way of teaching reading; but in a few years the outcry died down, and Flesch's book had little permanent effect. This was largely because professional educationists and publishers, with great sums of money invested in existing series of readers, conducted a tremendous anti-Flesch campaign to convince the public that his attacks on current teaching methods were unfounded. In doing so, Flesch's opponents dragged in such irrelevancies as the question whether the "Johnny" of Flesch's book was a real or a fictional child, and insinuated that to question the efficiency of our teaching of reading was to cast doubt on the validity of democratic education. On the specific question of teaching techniques, they countered his basically sound arguments with unsound ones, e.g. the logical fallacy that written words are perceived as units by adult readers and should therefore be taught as such to child learners. Unfortunately, the general public did not have enough linguistic knowledge to detect the unsoundness of such arguments, and Flesch, although his negative criticisms were quite valid, had not supplied his readers with enough linguistic theory to evaluate his opponents' replies. Consequently the Flesch revolt fizzled out and proved to be a kind of Wat Tyler's rebellion, in which an embattled group with a very just grievance and with right on their side were defeated by forces that had both greater material power and more tactical skill.

Once a pupil had acquired English spelling in a rational way, and with a good understanding of the relation of writing to speech, the way would be opened for him to study the real nature of the English language and to get an idea of its linguistic structure, at a slightly later point in his schooling (say, end of elementary school and in secondary school). It would be interesting and exciting to explore one's own language, to investigate and analyze and describe one's own speech-habits, in terms of what one really does. What is now a chore, a frustrating and confusing experience which serves only to make us insecure about our most basic and fundamental habits (those of speech), could become something live and real, something which would help the growing mind to see and describe and analyze objectively what is perhaps more easily accessible for observation than anything else in our surroundings, namely our language. This should be a fascinating activity for an age which loves to do experiments in chemistry and physics, and to pull automobiles apart and put them together. But we must first get rid of our normative preconceptions, we must substitute exploration for dogma, and we must be willing to examine all speech on a basis of equality without prejudice as to its value or social standing; and we must abandon the effort to cast English sounds and structure into any predetermined mold, that of Latin grammar or any other.

The further carry-over value of learning to explore our own language in this way is a matter which lies outside the scope of this discussion. One might venture to hope that objectivity, once learned for a subject so near to all our everyday life and activity as our language, might perhaps be carried over into other fields —economic, political, social questions, for instance—at least to a certain extent. It might also, by removing the cause of a great deal of needless difficulty for the majority of pupils, help to diminish their hostility towards the whole process of schooling, and to re-establish the esteem in which the schoolteacher and the school were once held by the public at large.

Is such a vision largely Utopian? Does the outlook for the future give any basis for hope that it may ever come true? The linguistic analyst, as he observes the present situation, is sometimes inclined to be pessimistic. Our schools continue, as before, to teach all the old shibboleths about "correct" language and "good" English, to inculcate value-judgments, to misunderstand the relation of writing and speech, to waste years of people's lives with inefficient teaching of a faulty system of spelling, and to either keep up the old Latinizing misrepresentation of English grammar or else abandon the whole study of grammar and thus throw the baby out with the bath. The findings of linguistic science are almost unknown and, even where known, disregarded. Yet, if we look farther, we find that there is a reason for this, as for everything else. Linguistics has been unknown and disregarded because, to date, we have not realized that it could give us any specific benefit; and, after all, every science—for instance, astronomy, chemistry, physics—has become known and recognized only in so far as it met practical human needs. As soon as our society comes to realize that its ideas concerning language, and its institutions based thereon, are defective and inefficient, and that linguistic science can help better them, we may look for the beginnings of improvement. And when our understanding of language is improved and our attitudes towards it are changed, we may reasonably begin to hope that the teaching of spelling and grammar in our schools may come to accord more closely both with the facts of language and with the democratic spirit that our society professes to aspire to.

12. Learning Another Language

The ordinary citizen who has grown up in an English-speaking home and has been taught in English throughout his school career, is what we call *monolingual,* that is to say, he uses only one language. Often, however, he may have occasion to use some other language. Some of us have been brought up in a home where our parents or grandparents spoke some language other than English. A person who served in the army outside of the United States may have picked up some of the language spoken in foreign countries; or ordinary traveling may have brought the same result. We often need a foreign language for some specific purpose. Our work may call for it in one connection or another: dealing with workmen whose language is not English; corresponding with foreign firms; traveling abroad or living in a foreign country. Scholars and scientists need to read books in other languages than their own. We may want to do missionary work in a foreign area, say South America or Africa or the South Seas, and therefore need to learn the native languages to preach in and translate the Bible into. Conceivably, we may get some of our recreation out of using a foreign language: as a radio ham, for conversation with foreigners, listening to the sound-track of foreign movies, or for leisure-time reading. Or, if we go through high school or college, we may be forced to take a foreign language course just because it is required, or because pressure is brought to bear on us to study it, whether we want to or not.

There are various ways we can set about acquiring a foreign language. One way is to get somebody who talks the language, and work with them, imitating and learning the language from them; of course, the more like a native speaker that person is, the better. The other way is to get a book and sit down with it, alone or in a group, with more or less speaking of the foreign language, but trying to get it by reading rather than by speaking. The first is the way that comes most naturally to the ordinary person, and is the way that people have, since time immemorial, learned the languages of other peoples. The second is the way that a literate society (or an over-literate one, as ours rather tends to be) is likely to go about learning a foreign language; if we think that the "written language" is the real language and that writing is more important than speaking, and especially if we want to do more reading than talking in the end, we are very likely to start out by trying to read and write before—or instead of—hearing and talking. A good part of the foreign language teaching that goes on in our schools and colleges has been, and still is, based chiefly on reading and writing.

Along with concentration on reading and writing goes, very often, the idea that the foreign language is to be learned by precept, by rules and regulations, rather than by examples. For some centuries, in learning both the classical and the modern languages, it was the custom to have beginners start out by memorizing sets of forms, like

mēnsa "a table"	*ich bin* "I am"
mēnsae "of a table"	*du bist* "thou art"
mēnsae "to a table"	*er ist* "he is"
mēnsam "a table" (acc.)	*wir sind* "we are"
mēnsā "from a table"	*ihr seid* "you are"
mēnsa "O table!"	*sie sind* "they are"

and also to have them learn and rattle off rules, like

"The verbs *utor, fruor, fungor, potior,* and *vescor* take
an object in the ablative instead of the accusative",
or "Seven French nouns ending in *-ou* take a plural
in *-x,* namely *bijou, caillou, chou, genou, hibou, jou-
jou* and *pou*". Grammar was (and, by some, still is)
thought to consist exclusively of this kind of memorization and repetition; this way of learning a foreign
language, the so-called "grammar approach", has gone
somewhat into eclipse in recent years, but it is still
with us to a considerable extent. Most people have
found that the "grammar approach" does not work
well. If the ordinary person starts out to learn a new
language by reading rather than speaking, or by memorizing sets of forms and rules, he is likely to get nowhere fast. A few people—I confess to being one of
them—enjoy very much the process of learning paradigms, and find that it does not interfere with being
able to come out with the proper form when called
upon to talk. But many, I should perhaps say most,
people find that it helps them not at all to memorize
a lot of forms and rules, that there is no carry-over to
actual speech, and that, if anything, the "grammar approach" short-circuits the process of understanding
and creates a block against bringing forth the foreign
language when the time comes to speak.

Likewise, it does absolutely no good to try to learn
to read and write without first forming speech-habits
on which to base the reading and writing. No one in
his senses would try to learn to read music unless he
had first found out what sounds the printed notes referred to, and had acquired at least an elementary
ability to make those sounds either with his own voice
or on some instrument. The same holds true for reading and writing a foreign language. Everybody, when
he reads, talks to himself, as psychologists have long
since found out; even if a person does not talk out loud

(as do children and unsophisticated readers), he in-
hibits the nervous impulses which would normally
lead to the muscular movements of speech, but the
nervous impulses are still there, and the reader is still
talking to himself even when he utters no sound. And
if I try to learn a foreign language and don't get a set
of foreign speech-habits, in terms of which I can interpret and understand what I read in the foreign
language, then I must of necessity give English
speech-responses (out loud or inhibited) to the foreign printed matter. Naturally, the English speech-
responses will not be very meaningful, and they will
come slowly and stumblingly. It does not make much
sense and is not very profitable to go through a painful
process of upsetting some foreign language into English in this way, as when I take, say, such a relatively
simple German sentence as this one from Thomas
Mann's *Buddenbrooks: Nun werden draussen die
Tropfen an den Bäumen hängen, und wir werden in
der Veranda Kaffee trinken,* and, after struggling
through it putting together a set of word-for-word
equivalents, come out with something like "Now will
out there the drops on the trees hang, and we will in
the veranda coffee drink".

Yet these were the approaches that much language
teaching had been taking for a long time, until the
early 1940's. There had been a few efforts at reform:
notably the "direct method", which systematically ex-
cluded all use of the learner's first language and attempted to have him learn the foreign language "just
as a child learns his native tongue"; and the "phonetic
method", which made extensive use of highly detailed
phonetic analysis and transcription, and also emphasized intensive oral practice before beginning to read
and write in conventional orthography. These attempts
to bring language teaching back to an oral basis had,

by and large, been unsuccessful, especially in this country, and by the nineteen-thirties most foreign language teachers had resigned themselves to doing nothing but teaching reading and a little grammar. The results were, naturally, not very encouraging; the teachers were getting more and more discouraged, and the general public's dissatisfaction was increasing. Time after time, I have had conversations with one person or another who had been exposed to language instruction, and whose complaints would run along this general line:

"I studied French [or German, or Spanish] for two years in high school and one in college, and what did I get out of it? Nothing. I can't speak French, I can't understand it, I can't write it, and I can't read it. When I went to France, I was totally lost. My teachers couldn't talk any French, and we never heard a word of French in the classroom. We learned a little grammar, but most of the time we spent reading a lot of nonsense that didn't have any meaning for us. The three years I spent on studying French were absolutely wasted. Will I have my children take French? Not if they still teach it the way they did when I was in school, I won't."

That particular paragraph is a composite, formed out of many people's statements, but it is a basically true picture of the general reaction to foreign language teaching of the nineteen-twenties, thirties and forties. The contrast between conventional language teaching in the schools on the one hand, and the commercial language schools, phonograph and radio courses on the other, became really painful. The professors often sneered at "Berlitz methods" and "jazzed-up" radio "vulgarizations"; the cold fact remained that the commercial teachers were successful and popular, whereas the professors were neither successful nor popular.

This contradiction was due to one basic fact: the commercial teachers were aiming at having their pupils learn to speak first of all, and were succeeding, whereas the academicians, putting the cart before the horse, were trying to teach theirs to read before they could speak, and were quite naturally failing to teach anything.

The situation was changed quickly and radically during the Second World War. Even before the war began, an organization called the American Council of Learnèd Societies (usually abbreviated to ACLS) had started a program to provide the country with what was termed a "stockpile of strategic language competence". Realizing that the country's supply of people who knew Japanese, Chinese, Russian, and other important "unusual" languages was woefully inadequate, the ACLS had put a number of linguistic analysts to work on analyzing such languages, and on implementing a program for teaching them to others. They soon found that a person with good training in linguistic analysis, even though he might be coming completely fresh to the language, could get a much clearer and truer picture of it and present it better to others, than could someone who might have lived in the country and spoken the language for years, but without any other knowledge of its structure than what an untrained learner might pick up or work out in terms of conventional Latinizing grammar. They also found that the best way to teach a language was to separate, if necessary, the functions of teacher and informant, the latter serving as a model for the learners to imitate and as a drillmaster to insist on good performance, and the former being in administrative charge of the course and doing the grammatical analysis as the course went along. If the language happened to be one on which the analyst, as well as the learners, was starting from scratch, they would all learn the language together, and the analyst would take his fellow-learners along with him in the process of exploring the linguistic structure of the new language. The linguistic analyst normally made much quicker progress than the others, and usually became thoroughly acquainted with the new language and its structure, so that when the course was repeated he was a true teacher rather than a co-learner.

From the fact that courses of this type were usually allotted more time than ordinary college courses, they came to be known as "intensive" courses; eight weeks' work, at four hours a day, would cover the ground usually completed in two years of college study. The Intensive Language Program (ILP) of the ACLS had already been under way before our entry into the war; and, when the United States entered the war, the armed forces were able to draw on its resources. In 1942, the Army decided to teach foreign languages—both the familiar ones and many unfamiliar ones like Russian, Japanese, Chinese, Burmese, etc.—to soldiers. Originally, the program was intended to be for a small number of officers, and its requirements were thought so exacting that only ten institutions in the country were at first considered capable of handling the necessary courses. The interest in such training was so great, however, that the Army expanded its language program far beyond the original intention, and, in its final shape, the Army Specialized Training (AST) Program of "language and area" studies needed the facilities of over a hundred colleges to put it into effect.

The soldiers needed to learn these languages for use in direct, everyday contact situations, with the people of the foreign countries, on the spot and by word of mouth; and they needed to learn them quickly. Besides, the Intensive Language Program's work had al-

ready shown that it was best to start out learning a
language by working at it orally and intensively.
Clearly, the "reading method", which at the time prevailed in most academic language teaching, could not
have been used. In its professed restriction of aim to
reading alone, it would have been insufficient to give
competence in actual use of a foreign language; and,
even with respect to the reading aim, the "reading
method" was by then too obvious a failure to be considered seriously. Fortunately, the ACLS's Intensive
Language Program was known to the Army authorities
responsible for the AST. They worked in close con-
sultation with the ACLS, and took over the principles
of the "intensive" courses which the ACLS had developed; and the ACLS undertook also to provide
teaching materials for the United States Armed Forces
Institute, based on these same principles and suitable for use in such courses. The "intensive" method
was introduced to the country at large, in an impres-
sive way, in the AST "language and area" program
of 1943–44. Since the general public had come in
contact with it only through the Army's program,
this method immediately came to be known as the
"Army method"—which, as we have seen, was a very
bad misnomer. Many people who were not in the
know had and still have the idea that the so-called
"Army method" was dreamed up by some colonels or
generals in the Pentagon and imposed on the language
teachers of the country by fiat; and, as we have seen
just now, nothing could be farther from the truth. The
"intensive method" developed out of a civilian, pre-
war undertaking, and its basic features were the out-
growth of the experience of skilled linguistic analysts (of all age-levels) in applying their knowledge
and techniques to the practical problem of language
teaching.

The directives that were issued for the AST program, to all the universities that took part in it, provided for the following principles to be observed:

1. A large number of instructional hours ("contact hours") in a relatively short period of time.
2. Small numbers of students per class.
3. Combination of presentation of language structure and conversational practice.
4. Emphasis on drill and on the formation of linguistic habits.
5. Phonemic analysis and transcription.
6. Employment of native informants.
7. Specific objective: command of the colloquial spoken form of the language. [This did not exclude reading, in fact reading ability came as a normal by-product.]

These are all, as we can see, eminently sensible principles, and based directly on the findings of linguistics as we have seen them in the central chapters of this book. Wherever they were carried out by people who knew them and who knew how to apply them, the results were extremely good. Unfortunately, the AST program was expanded far beyond its original scope, and many colleges and universities were drawn into the program that simply did not have properly trained and qualified personnel. At some places, therefore, the results were pathetically bad, due to the absence of trained linguists and to the non-observance of proper procedure.

Even while it was going on, and long after it stopped rather abruptly in March of 1944, the AST program of language teaching caused a great stir in the modern language world. To a certain extent, it was a tempest in a tea-pot, in that many disputes and debates arose over points that were not relevant to the main issue of how language should be taught, and war-time tension and nervous strain contributed to the bitterness of controversy. The true issues at stake were often clouded by a host of canards that gained widespread currency: that the ASTP was nothing but pure "direct method" or "Berlitz method"; that grammar had been completely thrown out of the window; that cultural values were being neglected; etc., etc. But, once due allowances were made for controversial exaggerations and for teachers' inertia and insecurity for their personal and professional futures, there still remained a basic disagreement among language teachers about the essential features of ASTP-type teaching and its approach. Many sincere conservatives were doubtful about the desirability of attaining a reading ability through speaking rather than reading at the start, and about the workability of "functional" rather than normative grammar. There were also administrative problems to be met, in any possible adaptation of the "intensive" approach to language teaching in civilian schools and universities, especially the question of getting enough time allotted to allow of a running start.

Yet, with all the difficulty and all the opposition, a start was made in the years after 1945, in the way of applying the so-called "intensive method", of the type originally designed for the Army's use, to civilian teaching, in a number of universities. Initial results seemed quite good. The general experience has been to date that beginning students in a semi-intensive oral course (of, say, 8 to 10 hours a week for two semesters, giving around 240 contact hours in the whole year) learn to read fully as well as do those who learn by either "grammar" or "reading" methods in the same total number of contact hours, and in addition get the extra benefit of being able to talk and understand.

The problem now facing progressive language teachers and the general public is rather, how can instruction of this kind be made available more widely —in universities and colleges, and in high schools and elementary schools as well? It would be a very wise and desirable thing to start foreign language learning much earlier than we now do—beginning, say, in the third or fourth grade, with at first a purely oral approach—so as to avoid the problems of adolescent self-consciousness and embarrassment that crop up at the high-school and early college level. Conditions naturally will vary widely from one school situation to another, and from one person to another; but, in general the intelligent person who wants to start learning a foreign language, or who is in charge of teaching a foreign language, will realize certain things about the nature of language and will want his course to fit the facts of language. By "intelligent person", we mean here one who is linguistically sophisticated, and who is not bound by traditional notions about the supremacy of Latin grammar or the absoluteness of "correct" speech. Such a person will realize that language is, as we've continually been emphasizing, an arbitrary system of auditory symbols serving for human communication; and that hence, the auditory aspect of language is basic, with writing secondary (though *not* unimportant!); that, since language is an arbitrary set of symbols, it has meaning only in terms of the world around the speaker, and that no one language is more "natural" or more "right" than another; and, finally, that language, being a system, consists of forms which have partial similarities to each other—that is to say, that linguistic structure has *pattern*.

In line with these basic principles, the intelligent learner will look for certain things in his language course and will avoid others. He will want to hear and speak first, and then start to read or write when he has a firm command of speech on which to base his reading and writing. How soon he starts to read and write, will depend on the difficulty of the writing system; with Spanish, Italian, or Hungarian, he can start practically from the beginning, whereas with Chinese or Japanese he will wait for a long time before playing around with written characters. He will want to learn the meanings of the foreign language along with the language itself, and in terms of situations rather than translations from one language to another. That is, he will try to build up foreign language habits in himself as responses to stimuli coming directly from the practical world rather than indirectly through his native language; when he has a certain feeling in his stomach, he will say (to himself or to someone else) *j'ai faim* or *ho fame* or *ich bin hungrig* rather than going through the English *I'm hungry*. As far as possible, he will try to forget his own language during the process of *learning* the foreign language; and he will try to get the new language as a thing that he has learned by heart, and—at the outset—as a set of conditioned reflexes, as something that he produces without even stopping to think about it at all, just as he does for his native speech. Naturally, he will want to learn the foreign language in complete phrases and sentences, not in isolated words, nor yet in grammatical sets like *ich bin, du bist, er ist;* after all, people talk and think in phrases and sentences, not in words or paradigms. He will also want to get everyday speech, as it's actually spoken, not stilted literary usage or artificial pronunciation that corresponds to spelling rather than to fact.

A learner of English, for instance, will insist on having *it's me* rather than *it is I* and should object violently if his teacher or informant pronounces *I do not want to go home* as seven separate independent items /'aj 'du 'nat 'wɔnt 'tu 'go 'hom/

instead of giving the normal rapid pronunciation of that sentence as /adoˈwanəˈgoˈhom/.

"But"—say many people at this point—"that's just having him learn the foreign language as an untutored child does, without any grammar and without any attention to correct speech. Is he to talk ungrammatically and like an uncultured speaker from the slums or like some country bumpkin with a rustic dialect?" By no means; nor is any such exaggerated conclusion justified at all by our approach. The grown learner—from, say, twelve years of age onwards—is of course no longer a child, and cannot learn by trial and error as a child does. Even if he wanted to he could not; because when a child learns the sounds and grammar of his native language, his mind is like a blank page on which new letters are being written, and he has no previous speech habits to conflict with those he is learning. This is where linguistics comes in, to make use of the analytical ability that the normal grown person has, and to help him to see just what the pattern of the foreign language is, in what ways it differs (in phonemes, grammatical structure, syntax, idiom) from his native language, and what special attention he will have to pay to points which will give him extra trouble because they are different. Moreover, the intelligent learner will want the linguistic structure of the foreign language explained to him by somebody who knows it and knows how to explain it—that is, by a trained linguist. As we have pointed out before, just because a person is a native speaker of any given language, like English or French or Navaho or Swahili, he isn't necessarily competent to analyze and explain that language; in the same way, I may be quite good at walking and running, but just that fact alone does not make me competent to explain the physiological processes by which I walk and run.

And, as we have been at great pains to make clear throughout our discussion, normal rapid speech is the basic linguistic activity of mankind, rather than over-careful stilted, or oratorical speech. Now, when people refer to "correct" or "grammatical" language, it is rather the latter kind that they mean (English expressions like *it is I,* or *I do not want to go home* all carefully spaced out and each word overemphasized). The sensible learner naturally wants to learn what will help him most, which is usually the standard language; but the true standard language, we know already, is what is actually acceptable, not what somebody thinks it ought to be. So, for the standard language of any country, the speech of any socially acceptable person is a perfectly satisfactory model—not, of course, that of a slum-dweller or of a country lout. Many countries, like the United States and Italy, have more than one regional standard, and the speech of any region is perfectly all right if it is generally acceptable socially. If I am acting as teacher or informant for my native English, I will do much better to talk naturally, as I always have, even if my native speech is markedly Southern or markedly Mid-Western or markedly New England, rather than to use some unnatural, artificial type of speech that I would never use in ordinary life. And, for the learner, it is much better to have an authentic regional coloring to his speech—showing that he imitated his informant well—rather than some colorless, unrealistic, non-existent "correct" but wholly non-native-like composite language.

What we have said about the intelligent learner's desires also implies certain things about what he is *not* looking for. Among the things we will try to avoid, if we have a realistic understanding of language and its nature, are: writing for its own sake (whether conventional spelling or any other kind of transcription),

translation equivalents for their own sake, sets of grammatical forms, and traditional grammar on the model
of Latin. There are also other subjects that people often
bring into language teaching, subjects which are very
good in themselves but which belong elsewhere: especially information about language in general, and information about literature. The learner's goal when he
starts out to learn the language is the language itself,
and other things belong in his work only as far as they
can be helpful; naturally, he can use the language later
on, when he is beyond the initial stages of learning it,
as a medium through which he can get information
about the country's culture, literature, economics, agri-
culture, religion, or whatever else he may happen to
be interested in.

Since he has these basic aims, there are certain
things that the intelligent learner will do when he sets
out to learn a new language. First of all, he will get
the best sources of information possible: for the language itself, a native speaker, or if such a person isn't
available, then somebody whose command of the language is extremely close to a native speaker's. (A
teacher whose main subject is German and who has
been told two weeks before school starts that she'll
have to teach Spanish instead, won't do.) And for the
structure of the language, a competent linguistic analyst, either in person or in what he has written about
the language. The native speaker and the linguist may
be the same person, in fact it is the most desirable thing
if they are; but such a combination is rather rare. Many
people have had instruction in the traditional grammar
of their native language, but, as we have seen, knowing
the traditional grammar of your language is usually
very far from making you a competent linguistic analyst. If the native speaker is not a scientific linguist, the
two can be different persons, and you will have two

different types of sessions: those with the native speaker to get the language from him, and those with the linguistic scientist to analyze it.

If I am an intelligent learner, the first thing I will do when I have gotten my native speaker and my linguistic analyst, will be to memorize, as thoroughly as I possibly can, a set of sentences in the foreign language. A large set, too: between one and two thousand, and if possible arranged so as to go from easy to difficult, and to include the most frequent words of the language, and all the basic, normal forms and constructions of everyday speech. I will apply myself with all the energy I can to repeating those sentences over and over again, imitating the native speaker just as closely as I can during the time I am with him, and working on the material on my own when I am not with him. There is great value in learning them absolutely by heart, until you know them forwards and backwards, and have not only learned, but *over*-learned them.

The intelligent learner will keep the distinction between native speaker and analyst clearly in mind, and will not spoil his informant by asking the informant questions he (the informant) cannot answer—like "Why do you say *j'ai faim* 'I have hunger' and not *je suis faim,* since *je suis* means 'I am'?" The informant cannot give a proper answer to such a question, any more than any one of us could answer the question "Why do you say *he has* instead of *he haves?*", except by saying "I say it that way because that's the way I learned it, and that's the way we say it in my language." The person to answer such questions is the analyst, whose job it is to tell how a sound is made with the organs of speech, how it fits into the phonemic pattern of the language, how an irregular form like *has* or *does* fits into the grammatical scheme, how and into what patterns words combine, and so on.

Once we have a set of sentences learned, and their linguistic patterns made clear to us, we still have a further step to take: we have to get practice in varying the patterns we've learned. After all, we are not parrots, and, although our first step should be memorization by imitation, that is only the first step; and the likelihood of our hearing others speak using exactly the sentences we have learned is rather remote. (One or two thousand sentences is not very many, in proportion to the millions, perhaps billions of different combinations which might occur in any given language.) So we've got to drill ourselves on extending the patterns, first by fitting different elements into a set grammatical mould, like these for English:

I'm —— (adjective referring to condition):
I'm hot.
I'm cold.
I'm hungry.
I'm thirsty.
I'm tired.
I'm worn out.

and so on. Gradually, we can pass to the give-and-take of conversation, first on set models and using only the sentences we've learned by heart, and then using the results of our pattern drill to make up new sentences of our own.

Reading practice will then come at a slightly later stage, depending on the difficulty of the writing system. We'll want to practice reading, first of all on material that's fairly easy and that is tied up with what we've been learning to understand by hearing—and a little later on material that brings in unfamiliar vocabulary, with special preparation for the new words. Finally, and not until some work has been done on this type of reading, the learner can pass to completely ungraded, unrelated reading matter. When he does, he will still have a lot to look up in the dictionary, especially at the beginning, but he can count on knowing a good part of what he reads, particularly the basic words and constructions, and on being able to guess a lot of the others intelligently without having to run to the dictionary for every other word. Writing in the foreign language and translation to or from one's own language are the most difficult of all, and come properly as the very last stage—not, as often happens, at the very beginning, where they only serve to confuse and block all but the person with a particular flair for that kind of approach.

This kind of course was the basic aim of the ASTP directives, and should be the basic aim of any person who knows what linguistics has to tell us about language, when he starts out either to learn or to teach a foreign language. In such an approach, the learner gets the essentials of the language he's learning, namely the ability to understand what he hears and to speak in answer, and reading follows as a natural by-product. How much time per week he will be able to devote to his work, and how much energy he will have available to put in on it, will of course vary. A "double course" in college, with drill periods comparable to laboratory work in science courses, seems perfectly practicable; and the American elementary and high school, with an hour a day devoted to language work for five hours a week, seems an excellent place to put in semi-intensive courses of this kind—once the resistance of conservative teachers and administrators can be overcome. But in any case, the learner will want to put in as much time and energy, especially at the outset, as he can; and if he approaches the new language in a sensible way, and treats language practice like he would sports practice or the acquisition of any other set of habits, he is likely to find language learning a lot more interesting, entertaining, and profitable than he had thought it could be.

13. One World, One Language?

Ever since Biblical times, people have been wishing that all mankind might talk the same language, so that —they've hoped—misunderstandings and quarrels and wars might not arise through failure of man to get what his neighbor was saying. We all know the myth of the Tower of Babel in the Old Testament, according to which all mankind did talk one language from the time of Adam until Nimrod presumed to build a tower to reach Heaven—and, to impede the project's completion, the Lord created diversity of speech among all the different peoples working on the tower. That myth is very significant from a number of points of view, especially (as we pointed out before) because it recognizes the basic rôle of language in human cooperation; it is interesting with regard to the universal-language problem, too, because it symbolizes the old human desire for a single language. This desire has always been present in human speculation; in the last two or three hundred years, not only has there been renewed talk of a universal language, but many plans have been made to bring one into existence.

There is a very good reason why interest and plans for a universal language have been intensified in modern times. We are decidedly worse off in this respect than were the Middle Ages. In those days there was one, and only one, language used all throughout the West of Europe by intellectual men, for their thinking, writing, and communication: Latin. This was of course

the Latin of the Church, not exactly like the Latin of
Cicero in "purity" or "correctness," but nevertheless
kept artificially alive by many generations of scholars
and grammarians. Not all the inhabitants of Western
Europe knew and used Latin, in fact very few did—
the members of the clergy, the lawyers, and a few
other intellectuals. And Latin had an intellectual tradition back of it, an extensive literature in religious and
profane subjects of then current interest, which kept
its use alive. Under these conditions—and only under
these conditions—it was possible to keep Latin "alive"
long after its popular developments, in the Romance
tongues, had changed so far as to become independent
languages. But for such artificial preservation of a
dead language, two things are necessary: 1) a very
small, highly trained number of users, with a conservative attitude and opposed to change more or less as a
matter of principle; and 2) a literature and intellectual
tradition to keep interest in it going.

A number of people in modern times have looked
back to the Middle Ages with regret and yearning, and
have wished that we might have a revival of Latin
as our international language. Some enthusiasts have
worked for revival and use of Latin as such; others,
realizing that Latin is rather different in structure from
our modern languages and that many speakers of modern languages find Classical Latin very complicated
and difficult, have tried to make a simplified form,
called *Latino sine flexione* ("Latin without inflection"). But these efforts have not succeeded, and more
or less naturally, since in modern times the two conditions we just mentioned as necessary, are no longer
present: a small number of conservative and meticu-
lous users, and a body of literature to arouse and hold
interest. The number of people who would use such
an international language, even if we restrict it to the

intellectuals (literary men, scientists, etc.) alone, would be far too great and of too varied a psychological make-up to permit of keeping the language unchanged; and everything dealing with topics of *modern* interest is written in languages other than Latin. These projects for reviving Latin have fallen through, more or less of their own weight, and have not commanded much popular support.

The chief alternative to use of a dead language is the adoption of some modern language as an international means of communication. Two or three hundred years ago, from about 1650 to 1750, France was the dominant nation of Europe politically and intellectually, and the fortunes of French as an international auxiliary language followed the fortunes of France. This was not due to any particular merit of French as opposed to other languages, but purely to non-linguistic considerations; later on, after French had risen to a dominant position, myths began to arise about its being especially "intellectual," "clear," "precise" and the like. English seems to have gradually been taking the place of French during the last two hundred years, due to first English and then American leadership in commerce, industry, and science. This kind of development is the natural way in which languages become predominant and widely used; people adopt the language out of whose use they can get the most benefit. But in the last hundred and fifty years, there has been another factor in the situation, working against English, French or any other real language: modern nationalism. From the time of the French Revolution and the Napoleonic Wars, the feeling of self-centered, ingrown, parochial nationalism has been growing ever stronger in almost all nations, large and small, and the people of each country have tended to use their own language as a symbol of their own nationality, the symbol to which they are perhaps more attached than any other, and which they are least willing to give up. So opposition to English or any other real language has grown steadily stronger, until people have tended to abandon almost entirely the aim of universalizing any specific national tongue.

If a national language, no matter how important, is going to arouse hostility when used as a means of international communication, then—some have reasoned—why not get a language that will not be connected with any specific nation and that therefore will not cause antagonism on that score? If a dead language like Latin cannot be revived, then—it has been said—let's create one of our own. For the last hundred years or more, many people have been fascinated by such an idea, and it has been estimated that over a hundred such artificial languages have been invented—averaging something like a language a year. Their inventors have given them all kinds of names, like Interlingua, Kosmos, Occidental, Parla, Spokil, Universala, and so forth. The three most successful to date have been Volapük, Esperanto, and Ido, of which the best known of all is undoubtedly the second. Volapük was invented by a Bavarian pastor named J. M. Schleyer, and first appeared in 1879; it was meant to serve as a world speech, and in it Germanic words appear simplified so as to be (supposedly) more easily pronounceable by all. For instance, the word *Volapük* itself stands for "world speech," and *America* appears in the form *Melop,* the letter *r* (and here it is a question specifically of *letters*) being replaced by *l,* since *r* is reserved for prefixes. Volapük achieved some fame and a number of adherents, but by no means as many as the language invested by a Polish physician, Dr. Zamenhof, which he called *Esperanto* (to the root *esper-* "hope") and made known to the world in 1887. Esperanto has a vocabulary and a grammatical system based essentially on those of Latin and the Romance languages, with a few words taken from Germanic and other sources. Its grammatical system is very much simplified over that of any real Romance language, all nouns, for instance, being made to end in -*o* and all adjectives in -*a*. Later, an international committee of Esperanto adherents recommended some changes in the language, which the inventor, Dr. Zamenhof, refused to accept; so the Esperantists split into two groups, the conservatives holding to the original Esperanto, and the progressives using a modified form which they called Ido.

Esperanto and similar languages have essentially failed to catch on, however, for much the same reasons we pointed out for Latin. In the first place, as soon as they come to be spoken by any sizeable number of people, they automatically start to change—whether unintentionally, due to the influence of the native language of each speaker and to internal organic change, or intentionally, as in the case of the reform made by the Idoists. There are by now a few people who are actually native speakers of Esperanto, having been brought up by Esperantist parents and using Esperanto as the normal family language from their earliest childhood; and in these people's usage, changes have already begun to take place. But by and large, the speakers of Esperanto are native speakers of some other language, and use Esperanto only by intention and with conscious effort; and in this fact lies a further difficulty. There are so few native speakers of Esperanto that they are not enough to serve as a standard for usage. And there is no body of material, oral or written, to serve as a canon, such as there is in classical Latin or Greek, or such as naturally grows out of the situation for any living language.

Recently, another group—the International Auxiliary Language Association, or IALA—has begun an ambitious program for the construction of still another auxiliary language of this kind. A number of competent linguistic analysts have aided in the work, by studying the types of concepts that are most frequently found, by analyzing the frequency of occurrence of the most important wordroots of the European languages, and so forth. The Iala language, when made available, may have a slightly more scientific basis to its choice of material than Esperanto or Ido; but, so far as can be told at this stage, it will still be the same kind of pick-and-choose affair, essentially consisting of selections from familiar languages, without any more authenticity than its predecessors.

Another objection to all the artificial auxiliary languages that have been constructed so far, is that they are essentially designed by and for West Europeans. A language like Esperanto, although supposedly simplified from our point of view, still keeps the essential parts of speech (noun, adjective, verb, etc.) of Indo-European, and the concepts and categories of meaning that our languages have made us familiar with. A speaker of—say—Chinese or Telugu or some American Indian language would have as much difficulty with the sounds, forms, and thought pattern of Esperanto as he would with those of French or English or German. And the more we study and describe the various languages of the world, the more different arrangements of linguistic material we find. To find a common denominator of linguistic material for all the languages of the world—that is, using only sounds and form-classes and constructions and meanings that would be familiar to every human being—would be a well-nigh impossible task, although it has repeatedly been tried, even by such outstanding linguists as Trubetzkoy. And yet, to base one's artificial language on any particular

language type—Indo-European, Semitic, or other—
implies inevitably a value-judgment of some kind,
whether reflecting supposed cultural superiority, or
mere numerical preponderance, or something else.

A still further solution is one that has been put forward in recent years—to recognize that a wholly artificial language is not likely to win great favor, and to try
to make a simplified version of some national language
already spoken. This is what happens without benefit
of any philosophical or philological guidance whenever
speakers of different languages come in contact with
each other and evolve a reduced version of one of the
languages, often with many borrowings from the other;
the resulting "minimum language" is called a *pidgin.*
Pidgin languages have developed in great number,
especially those based on Portuguese, French, and
English; just to limit ourselves to Pidgin English, there
are varieties of Pidgin spoken in China, West Africa,
Melanesia, and Australia. Most people have the idea
that a pidgin language is just a jargon, a hash, a "corruption" without any rules or grammar, spoken the
way an ignorant American might try to talk to a Chinese laundryman. This is a wholly mistaken idea.
Pidgin English, although reduced in grammar and vocabulary from its base, has nevertheless a true linguistic
structure of its own and is a language in its own right—
but one which has gone its own way. Careful study of
a pidgin language is something which ought to repay
anybody trying to construct a simplified version of a
major language, to see along what lines the simplification might well be made.

In the following discussion of Melanesian Pidgin, we shall use
the German missionaries' transcription, in which the vowel letters
have their "Continental" value. It is highly inadvisable to use
ordinary English spelling in citing pidgin forms, since the reader
is likely to get the false impression that these are merely or-

dinary English words being misused; the more we realize that Pidgin English is a true language in its own right, the better we will understand its structure, and a non-English spelling will help us to this realization. The theoretical linguist will want, for more advanced discussion, to go beyond the missionaries' transcription and use a fully phonemic writing, based on IPA or some other phonetic alphabet.

Melanesian Pidgin, for instance, has taken the English word *fellow* and has made an adjective suffix *-fela* out of it, so that "big" is in Melanesian Pidgin *bigfela*, "this" is *disfela*, "three" is *trifela*, and so forth. Likewise, the users of Melanesian Pidgin made the object pronoun *'im* into a verbal suffix, indicating transitive meaning of the verb (the presence of a direct object): *rait* "write" refers simply to the activity of writing, as an intransitive verb, but *raitim*, means "write it," and has to be used whenever there is a direct object either expressed or implied: *mi raitim* means "I write it," and if I want to say "I write the letter" I have to say *mi raitim pas*. Interesting changes of meaning have taken place, and some words have been greatly extended beyond their original English use, in a way which is perhaps superficially amusing to speakers of English, but which has its own logic and sense. Thus, we're likely to be amused at first when we find that "hair" is expressed by *gras bilong hed*, literally "the grass of the head" (*bilong* is a preposition, meaning "of" or "for"). But, when we consider that the natives knew the words *gras* "grass" and *hed* "head", it was the most logical thing in the world to compare the hair to grass growing out of the head, and easier to make the phrase *gras bilong hed* than to learn a completely new and separate word for "hair". In the same way, in Melanesian Pidgin the word *ars*, originally "buttocks," has had its meaning extended to cover any kind of "bottom"—for instance, *ars bilong diwai* means "the bottom of the tree"; and, in transferred meaning, *ars* also means "reason" or "cause": *em i-ars bilong trabal* means "he is the cause of the trouble".

But makers of reduced versions of modern major languages do not seem to have wanted to bother with pidgin languages, perhaps because of their low cultural and intellectual standing, and have instead sat down in their armchairs and excogitated their reductions on *a priori* philosophical principles, with little attention to reality. The results are usually far from what they are cracked up to be. The best known of these reduced languages is of course Ogden and Richards' *Basic English*. This language is strictly limited in vocabulary to 850 words, chosen by the sponsors of the language, plus 18 special auxiliary verbs or "operators" such as *get, do, be,* etc. Ordinary English spelling is used, and little attention has been paid to the phonetic side of the problem; apparently it was assumed that foreigners' difficulties in learning English nouns were of little or no weight, and the language seems to have been envisaged primarily as a means of written communication. Although the number of individual words is limited to 850, the number of compounds and combinations in which they may be used—in ordinary English patterns—is enormous; so, as Basic English uses the separate words *fancy, dress,* and *ball* (in all the different meanings which standard English attaches to those words), it is permissible to use also the combination *fancy dress ball*. Hence, despite its professed limitation to 850 words, the actual number of possible combinations, and the range of meaning covered by Basic English vocabulary is very great, and all according to the patterns of standard English.

Basic English has received a great deal of attention —especially due to the "plug" which Winston Churchill gave it in a speech at Harvard in 1944—and has made a number of converts, some of whom have gone about spreading the new doctrines with more enthusiasm than understanding. Unfortunately, the basis on which Basic English is established is not of the soundest, and, as a reduced version of English, it is definitely unsatisfactory—much less satisfactory than, say, Melanesian Pidgin English or Chinese Pidgin English, both of which are quite serviceable auxiliary languages. The choice of the 850 words of the Basic English vocabulary is quite arbitrary, and includes such a relatively unimportant term as *sticky*, while omitting others that would be far more serviceable. The meanings, both literal and transferred, are simply those of ordinary English vocabulary, without regard to the fact that for speakers of most other languages, our range of meaning for any particular word would be quite unheard-of: the speaker of Russian, for instance, would never find it natural to speak of the *leg* of a table or the *foot* of a mountain. Similarly, our combinations of words into compounds and set phrases with specialized meanings could never be accepted as normal, without considerable explanation, by speakers of any language but English; a phrase like *fancy dress ball* would be quite meaningless to a speaker of, say, Spanish or Hungarian. The auxiliary verbs or "operators" constitute one of the hardest parts of Basic English for any non-speaker of English, since such words as *get* and *do* are among the trickiest things in the English language. In short, Basic English is quite without the ease and simplicity that has been claimed for it, and has been put together naively and without realization of the linguistic problems involved.

Well, then, what is the answer, after all? A dead language won't work; nor will a completely artificial one, nor an artificial language made up like a hash out of various elements of different modern languages; nor will a naive and unskillful reduction of a major language. We might perhaps think of making a better job of reducing a major language, taking lessons from Pidgin English and trying to see in what way our language could be reduced and simplified to make it usable by people of other speech. The trouble is, we would have to not only simplify it phonetically and grammatically—with true simplification, not pseudo-simplification like that of Basic English—so far as to reduce its phonemes, forms, and constructions drastically, but also change the range of meanings of its words, in such a way that it would be almost unrecognizable to speakers of English itself, and incur their hostility and rejection in much the same way that Pidgin English does. There's no way out along that path, either.

When we get to an impasse of this kind, it is always worth examining the matter anew and seeing whether, perhaps, the problem has been approached from an unproductive angle to begin with, and put in unfruitful terms. When we look at the whole quest for an international language, we notice one thing above all others: the desire for *ease* in learning, an ease greater than that of learning an ordinary major language. This has been the avowed force behind the international language movement; in the words of Otto Jespersen, the great Danish linguist, one of the backers of the Ido movement, "The best auxiliary international language is that which in all points offers the greatest ease to the greatest number of people." But this assumption is questionable, at best; it seems likely that ease of acquisition can be gained only at the cost of impoverishment of form or of content. Although a pidgin language is a perfectly workable and usable form of communication, and you can convey in Melanesian Pidgin, say, any idea that you can in standard English, it often takes longer to do so just because of the limited means; what you gain in simplicity, you lose in richness and directness of expression. A major living language is of course a complicated affair; as Herman Collitz, one of the great American philologians of the first part of this century, pointed out, "They [living languages] may be compared to an armory or a big store in which everybody may find the kind of uniform or suit just to fit him, and a different suit for every occasion." Slang, jargon, humorous words and turns of phrase, and even everyday expressions like *kids, cop, stag party,* all contribute their share towards not only accurate denotation but also delicate shading of connotation; and, as Collitz pointed out, cutting down the abundance of a living major language to reach the level of an artificial language "would amount to nothing more than moving from a palace into a poorhouse."

Furthermore, the difficulty of acquiring another language is something which has been greatly exaggerated, and of which most people have a totally unjustified fear. It is understandable that we should think it almost impossible to acquire a foreign language well, as long as inadequate methods of teaching prevail, and years of students' time are wasted without accomplishing anything. But improved methods of language teaching, with the help of linguistics, have made it clear that any ordinary person *can,* with proper desire and application of time and energy, acquire a second language without waste and inefficiency. Greater "ease" of learning an artificial or reduced auxiliary language, we now see, is something largely illusory, and certainly not worth the price in loss of communicative power as contrasted with a real language.

Then why not all agree on some one language as *the* language for the "one world" which many of us have yearned for, and everybody learn that language at least as a second language, with the hope that perhaps eventually the whole world might shift to it as a first language? I confess to having entertained such notions at one time, and to having felt that I would willingly give up my native English for any other language that might be chosen, be it Chinese, Russian, Arabic, or Malay. Yet it is an impossibility, after all. Even if we could reach some ideal condition where nationalistic feelings did not preclude adoption of some one national language as a world means of communication, we still could never attain world linguistic unity. To attain and keep linguistic unity, the whole human race would have to be much more capable of accepting and following rigid rules—in regard to all aspects of language: sounds, grammar, vocabulary, meanings, and even spelling—than they are or give any sign of becoming. As the chosen language became more and more widespread, it would automatically be differentiated into dialects, since it would be learned in somewhat different form and adapted somewhat differently by the speakers of each different language. These dialects would soon move farther and farther from each other, both through internal organic change and through borrowing from each other, until after a few centuries we would simply have another set of different languages again—and the whole problem of translation, foreign language learning, etc., would start in over again.

Furthermore, hasn't the problem perhaps been ascribed to the wrong causes? Those who advocate an international language usually assume—whether they say so or not—that misunderstandings and international quarrels and wars are *caused* by differences in language. This is far from being necessarily so, as we can easily see from two kinds of examples. There have been plenty of instances in which people of the same language have fought each other bitterly and long: just think of our Revolutionary War, our Civil War, all the wars between different countries in Latin America in which both sides speak Spanish, or the religious wars in almost every European country in the sixteenth century. On the other hand, we can see from the example of Switzerland that speakers of four national languages (French, German, Italian, and Rhaeto-Romance) can live together and get along extremely well, on the whole, in one nation, and in a rather cramped and restricted territory, at that. The Swiss get along together, neither because of nor in spite of their linguistic diversity, but because they have common interests in the economic and political and cultural sphere—in non-linguistic matters, in short—that they are willing to take the trouble to cooperate about. The conditions for peace and harmony are essentially non-linguistic in nature; two people of almost identical speech can hate each other to the point of strife and murder, whereas two people of completely different speech can get along well enough to cooperate wholeheartedly.

The whole international language question, then—the idea that, to have "one world," we must of necessity have one language, and the debate over how to attain and spread that one language—is illusory, and based on an unrealistic assumption to begin with. We do not need linguistic unity in order to attain world peace; the problems besetting the world as a whole are non-linguistic in nature, and use of a single language would not help solve them in the slightest. First reach an agreement, not so much on actual points of disagreement, as on attitude towards disagreement itself, and get a willingness to agree; what language you then use to agree is of relatively minor importance. We will still continue to need more than one language, both for everyday use in our own communities, and for international use; and the present major internationally used languages (English, French, Spanish, German and—more and more—Russian, Chinese, Arabic, Malay) are perfectly satisfactory for the purpose. Besides, the variety of languages spoken throughout the world is an asset to the human race as well as, or perhaps even more than a liability; for, after all, a language is one way of organizing and classifying human experience, and we certainly have no right to say that our ways of organizing and classifying human experience have reached such perfection that we can afford to throw out all but our own. Multilingualism is with us to stay, in short, and there are good reasons for not regarding it as a curse and trying to get out of it, but, quite the contrary, for accepting it as a blessing and trying to turn it to our best advantage.

14. There's Nothing Wrong with Your Language

> "Folks are dumb where I come from,
> They ain't had any learnin';
> Still they're as happy as can be,
> Doin' what comes natur'lly."
> *Popular song of the 1940's.**

In 1945, the distinguished anthropologist Ralph Linton published a book named "The Science of Man in the World Crisis," a collection of essays by 22 anthropologists and sociologists on what their particular branch of the science of man could contribute to solving the world's problems. Although linguistics is basically a branch of anthropology, no discussion of its contribution, such as we have been trying to give in this book, was included in Linton's volume; as a reason for this omission, Linton said in his preface: ". . . linguistics is still unable to make any great contribution toward the solution of our current problems. For that reason it has been ignored in the present volume."

How justified this statement was, the reader may be able to judge for himself from our discussion in the last few chapters. We have seen how linguistics can help us reach a conclusion on a number of points which are concerned in whatever crisis exists in our culture at present: on the questions of education and interna-

---

* From the copyrighted composition by Irving Berlin, "Doin' What Comes Natur'lly". Copyright 1946 Irving Berlin. Reprinted by permission of Irving Berlin Music Corporation.

tional understanding, as reflected in the problems of teaching our own language, of spelling (items which waste at least two years of every school child's life!), of foreign language learning, and of an international language. These are matters which concern, not only the specialist's technique of resolving particular problems (such as methods of teaching and writing textbooks), but the general public's attitudes towards the problems. The teachings of linguistics can help us all to save energy, time, and money by seeing the situation in better perspective and applying our efforts more effectively.

But that is not all; for, even though linguistics has definitely a practical application to these problems of language learning, literacy, and international languages, those are still simply specific problems. If that were all the contribution linguistics had to make, it would still be on the level of technology and "applied science" without any more general implications. Linguistics and its results, however, have very broad implications for all of our daily living, and for our attitudes towards many of the problems that beset us even when we don't realize, perhaps, that they exist. All of our thinking, as such, involves the use of language, and if we have no clear notion of the nature of language and our use of it, we are bound to get confused on the nature of our thinking itself. What we say and how we say it is dependent, to a certain extent, on what we know about our language; and, even more so, our attitude towards what other people say and how they say it.

On this score, linguistics has a message which is largely in direct opposition to what we get taught in schools and in other sources of opinion (newspapers, magazines, and the like). Many people uphold, and (perhaps) most people accept, the notion that it is just "common sense" to insist on "correct" speech, and to hold it against people if they do not speak "correctly." Untutored and natural speech is very often made an object of reproach and condemnation; the general attitude towards talking naturally, the way we learn to from family and playmates without benefit of schoolmastering, is usually that it shows ignorance, neglect, carelessness, or stupidity. A person who talks a nonstandard dialect is apt to have the same attitude of self-depreciation (usually serious, sometimes humorous) that is shown in the popular song we quoted at the beginning of this chapter.

The amount of snobbery and social discrimination which goes on in the name of "correctness" is enormous; each one of us can think of many instances in his own experience. The case I remember most clearly is the one in which two ladies condemned a girl thoroughly, and held her in quite low esteem, simply because she said *Armitice* for *Armistice*, *buffet* (rhyming with *Miss Muffet*) *dress* for *bouffé dress*, and made similar substitutions. She was not a very bright girl, and the two ladies justified themselves by claiming that "her speech reflected her personality traits." In fact, there is no correlation, and many other more intelligent and likeable persons might make the same "mistakes." The point is that the determination of her intelligence and merits ought to have been made on some more rational and analytical basis than by the mere catchword of "correct" speech. Plenty of people have been turned down for jobs just because they said *ain't* or *it's me*, and others of inferior worth accepted because they said *is not* or *it is I* instead. If we make decisions on such a basis as this, we are cutting off our noses to spite our faces, and we are setting up an artificial, superficial, meaningless basis for separating some of the sheep and goats from others, rather than using our intelligence to get to the bottom of the matter and find out what people's true worth is, and really learning how to tell sheep and goats apart. This misdirection of our energies is probably due to at least two factors: 1) desire for some easy criterion on which we can base a judgment instantly, the minute somebody opens their mouth—which is essentially a lazy man's criterion; and 2) desire to satisfy our own egos by setting up our own ways as superior to others', and looking down on others because they do not conform to our standards.

Linguistics, on the other hand, points out that such standards, although they have a perfectly real existence in many people's behavior, have nothing to do with language itself. They are criteria imposed from the outside, for motives of laziness and snobbery, as we have just suggested. The real reason behind condemning somebody for saying *Armitice* or saying *buffet dress* is the desire to put that person in his or her place. The further conclusion is twofold: first, as we suggested in Chapter 11, that if we find it necessary to change our speech from non-standard to standard, we should do so by objective and rational means rather than by making a stab at it in the dark, and we should have a clear-eyed recognition of the fact that we are thereby trying to change our social status, rather than with a false humility and needless self-depreciation; and second, that it is up to users of standard speech to be less snobbish, less overbearing, and less rigorous in their insistence on a false "correctness." What does it matter if someone says *Armitice, it's me,* or *the minute somebody opens their mouth,* or splits an infinitive, or does one of the hundred other things the grammarians object to but everyone does? The merit of what a person says or does is not in any way affected by the way in which they say or do it, provided it is the most efficient way of saying or doing it; and to accept or reject someone just because of "correct" or "incorrect" speech is to show oneself superficial, lazy, and snobbish.

The damage done by this kind of attitude on the part of standard speakers is incalculable, and extends much farther than we may think at first glance. The non-standard speaker, when he meets up with this kind of snobbery, is at first perplexed and then badly thrown off the track. He is usually at a disadvantage for economic reasons, and finds that he has to change his natural speech-patterns to conform to those of the people that have more social and economic prestige and who hence have power over him. But when he tries to conform, he finds that it is by no means easy. Very few people can tell him what to do in order to conform, and those who do try to tell him, do it rather by invective ("your English is bad," "your language isn't English") and by preaching ("Saying *it ain't me* shows that you are neglectful and careless and sloppy in your speech; you should say *it is not I*"), than by objectively telling him what is not acceptable in his speech and in what way it needs to be changed.

The psychological harm thus done is very great. The non-standard speaker is made insecure, and this insecurity shows up in many ways. It is evident in all the over-corrections to which such speakers are prone, as when they say *between you and I*; they have been preached at for saying things like *you and me done it*, and they carry the substitution of *you and I* too far. The use of *whom* is gradually dying out in English, and would probably be completely lost by now (and no harm done) if it had not been for the over-zealous exertions of purists; as it is, many speakers to whom the use of *who* comes natural in all positions, have been confused on the distinction between *who* and *whom*; such a speaker will tend to use *whom* by over-correction, even where it does not belong, uttering such sentences as *Senator Blank, whom it is well known is opposed to the proposal* . . . and the like. (Edward Sapir has a very discerning and penetrating discussion of the *who–whom* question in Chapter VII of his book *Language,* which ought to be read by everybody interested in the question of "correctness.") This insecurity shows up especially at crucial moments, as when a speaker is in front of a microphone, or orating at a banquet, when he is more likely to pull a "boner" than on any other occasion—a thing that would not happen if he had not been made needlessly insecure about his speech by browbeating and excessive insistence on "correctness."

It shows up, too, in the extreme vulnerability of the ordinary person to those who offer to sell him instruction on "correct" speech. Our newspapers and magazines are full of advertisements of individuals and institutes offering to teach "good English," and of syndicated columns in which supposed "authorities" put forth their views on what is right and what is wrong. Dictionaries, grammar-books and "guides to good usage" are sold in bookstores, with claims on the jackets and in the books to an authoritative basis for their pronouncements. But, as we have seen, any claim to being "right" or knowing what's "correct" is, by the very fact of its being such a claim, a pure fake and an imposture. Anybody who tries to sell you his own dictum about "good English" as being authoritative or correct, is cheating and defrauding you, fully as much as the unscrupulous physician or drug manufacturer who tries to sell you a patent medicine guaranteed to cure this, that, or the other disease. It has not come yet, but we may look forward to the time (probably some centuries hence!) when a claim to dispensing "correct" speech will be treated as being equal in fraudulence to a claim to dispensing a cure-all in medicine; when anybody who sets himself up as an "authority" on language without any scientific training and competence will be prosecutable under law in exactly the same way as a person who tries to practice medicine without proper training; and when newspapers and magazines will, simply as a matter of common ethics, refuse advertisements for correctness-mongers and vendors of "authoritative" pronouncements in the same way they now refuse advertisements for quack physicians and fraudulent patent medicines.

But such frauds are able to live by battening on ordinary people's insecurity; if I do not know whether I should say *it's me* or *it is I,* and am insecure about my present behavior in that respect, I am an easy victim for somebody who comes along and offers to set me right—for a consideration, of course, whether it be a fee paid directly or a fraction of the price I pay for my evening paper. Of course, the way to get rid of such victimization is to get rid of the insecurity, and to reassure the person being victimized that he doesn't need to be. This means that we must realize, all around, that—as I put it in the title of this chapter—there's nothing wrong with our language, and that we had better find other and more serious things to worry about. It means that those of us who start out our lives speaking non-standard English have nothing inherently wrong about our speech, and that any change we make in our speech-patterns later on need be only such as we feel necessary. It means that those of us who are brought up on standard English have no right to lord it over non-standard speakers just because of our language, and that we would do better to take an attitude of humility towards our own speech and tolerance towards others', with a willingness to accept deviations from our own practice.

"Well"—it may be objected at this point—"by destroying standards in this way, you're simply removing all barriers to people's talking any way they want to, and if we don't try to preserve the language from corruption, within fifty years everybody'll be talking his own language and nobody will understand each other at all." I have heard this objection made numerous times; but such an argument fails to take into account the cohesive, centripetal forces of society, as well as the disintegrative, centrifugal forces at work. That is, abandonment of absolute standards does not necessarily mean abandonment of all standards (as we have already pointed out), and just because we tolerate deviations from our own practice, we do not have to expect everything to fly apart immediately. As a matter of fact, the pressure of human need for communication will always insure people's keeping their speech reasonably uniform; the difficulty arises mainly over certain moot points (like *he did it* vs. *he done it*, *it's me* vs. *it is I*) which normally do not make any difference in communication and which simply serve as criteria to determine social and intellectual standing. Relaxation of over-rigid and absolute standards would bring no harm at all to mutual communication and understanding, in fact would rather improve it by removing sources of needless disagreement and friction.

Once we have cleared the ground by ridding ourselves of prejudices of "correctness" and the like, and by substituting a relativistic for an absolutistic point of view, we begin to see some further considerations with regard to human speech as a whole. We begin to realize that our own language is nothing special in comparison to other languages, nothing particularly God-given or superior or peculiarly fitted for higher intellectual activity, any more than our own dialect of our language is better than any other dialect. Our own language—English—and all the other so-called "civilized" languages are civilized only in that they happen to have been spoken by particular groups of people who achieved enough technological progress along certain lines to build "civilizations," that is, more complicated cultures. There is nothing about English or French or German or Italian that makes them more especially fitted to be the vehicles of civilization than any other languages; if we think so, it is just because we are committing the logical error of reasoning backward from the events.

In fact, our West European languages are almost all (except for Hungarian, Finnish, and Basque) of only one language family, the Indo-European, and represent only one basic type of language structure. There are many other types, all of them equally fit to be used for "high" civilizations if the need should ever arise. In many languages, there are distinctions of form and meaning that we do not have in our familiar languages, and that it would actually be very useful to have. The Hupa language of northern California has tenses for its nouns; and Hopi, a language of Arizona, has in its verbs a special form to indicate that the action takes place in repeated segments.

Thus, the speaker of Hupa can make such a distinction, in speaking of a house, as that indicated by the following forms:

> *xonta* "house now existing"
> *xontaneen* "house formerly existing, i.e. in ruins"
> *xontate* "house that will exist, i.e. not yet built"

The following pairs are examples of Hopi verbs, in each of which the left-hand form refers to action taking place at a single point of time, and the right-hand form refers to action taking place in repeated segments:

hóˊci "it forms a sharp acute angle"	*hocícita* "it is zigzag"
wála "it (e.g. a liquid) makes one wave, gives a slosh"	*walálata* "it is tossing in waves, it is kicking up a sea"

ríya "it makes a quick spin"	*riyáyata* "it is spinning, whirling"
héro "he (or it) gives out a sudden hollow gurgle from within"	*herórota* "he is snoring"
yóko "he gives one nod of the head"	*yokókota* "he is nodding"
rípi "it gives a flash"	*ripípita* "it is sparkling"

Benjamin Lee Whorf, the linguistic analyst who first observed this distinction in Hopi verbs, said of it:

"All this . . . is an illustration of how language produces an organization of experience. We are inclined to think of language simply as a technique of expression, and not to realize that language first of all is a classification and arrangement of the stream of sensory experience which results in a certain world-order, a certain segment of the world that is easily expressible by the type of symbolic means that language employs. [In other words, a grammatical process of one kind or another serves as a symbol for—in this instance—vibratory phenomena.] In other words, language does in a cruder but also in a broader and more versatile way the same thing that science does. We have just seen how the Hopi language maps out a certain terrain of what might be termed primitive physics. We have observed how, with very thorough consistency and not a little true scientific precision, all sorts of vibratile phenomena in nature are classified by being referred to various elementary types of deformation process. The analysis of a certain field of nature which results is freely extensible, and all-in-all so harmonious with actual physics that such extension could be made with great appropriateness to a multiplicity of phenomena belonging entirely to the modern scientific and technical world—movements of machinery and mechanism, wave process and vibrations, electrical and chemical phenomena—things that the Hopi have never known or imagined, and for which we ourselves lack definite names. *The Hopi actually have a language better equipped to deal with such vibratile phenomena than is our latest scientific terminology.* [Italics mine—RAHjr.] This is simply because their language establishes a general contrast between two types of experience, which contrast corresponds to a contrast that, as our science has discovered, is all-pervading and fundamental in nature. According to the conception of modern physics, the contrast of particle and field of vibrations is more fundamental in the world of nature than such contrasts as space and time, or past, present, and future, which are the sort of contrasts that our own language imposes upon us. The Hopi aspect-contrast which we have observed, being obligatory upon their verb forms, practically forces the Hopi to notice and observe vibratory phenomena, and furthermore encourages them to find names for and to classify such phenomena. As a matter of fact the language is extraordinarily rich in terms for vibratory phenomena and for the punctual events to which they are related."

This is news indeed—a "primitive" language, spoken by a tribe of supposedly ignorant, backward Indians that live in pueblos on top of mesas in Arizona, without any of the benefits of civilized education, commerce, science, religion, or plumbing, and yet which is better equipped to deal with vibratile phenomena than the very languages of the peoples whose scientists have (so they thought) "discovered" these phenomena after long and laborious analysis! What has happened to these supposedly "superior" and "civilized" languages, that they have been outstripped by a "primitive" language in this way? For a short while, we might be tempted to reverse the scales, and in our new realization that our own languages aren't all we think they are, exaggerate in the other direction, proclaiming the superior merits of "primitive" languages. That would be just as bad an exaggeration, however, since it would be simply a continuation of our previous technique of applying value-judgments to languages, only turning things upside down. That will hardly do either. But, as soon as we stop applying value-judgments to languages as wholes, we see something important: that no one language symbolizes, either in its grammatical forms, or in its meanings, all the different ways in which our universe might be analyzed. That would be impossible, just because of the sheer number of different possible items to be symbolized, if we took into account all the various possible analyses. Each language picks out only certain ones of the possible contrasts that are to be found in the universe around us, and symbolizes them, leaving the others out of consideration or expressing them with relative difficulty. Hopi is better than our West European languages for symbolizing vibratory phenomena; but our languages are better for symbolizing some other things, like time relationships. (Don't be misled into saying "But time relationships are more important than other relationships, aren't they?"—because our notion that they are more important is just a conclusion that we have reached because they are emphasized by the structure of our languages and by certain aspects of our mechanized culture.) In the last analysis, one language turns out to be just as good as another in the long run, and here again we need to adopt a purely relativistic point of view.

We see, moreover, that there is no reason at all for assuming that a language reflects in any way—even, as

we can see from the Hopi example, in its vocabulary—
the degree of complexity of its speakers' civilization.
If this were true, we might expect the Hopi to have
been far out in front of us, in investigation and analysis
of the vibratory phenomena of physics. Actually, we
know that they are far behind us; but the grammatical
inadequacy of English, French, German, etc., has not
kept our scientists from working on these phenomena
and arriving in the end at a recognition and classification of wave-like motion, oscillation, vibration, etc. The
point is that the differences between West European
and other "higher," i.e. in some respects (e.g. mechanically) more complex, cultures on the one hand, and
so-called "primitive," i.e. less complex cultures on the
other, have been brought about by differences in technology, not by differences in linguistic structure.

Once we realize that all languages are equal in merit,
we are in a position to stop treating language differences as something to worry about, something to condemn, and something to eradicate on nationalistic
grounds. It is a common habit of mankind to think that
difference in speech must necessarily imply difference
in nationality, and that hence the first thing to be done
to assure national unity is to enforce linguistic unity.
Central Europe, as we all know, has been a stamping-
ground for this kind of linguistic nationalism. One of
the worst offenders was the old Austro-Hungarian Empire, whose two parts—Austria and Hungary—conducted a ruthless campaign, before 1914, to Germanize
and Hungarianize their respective parts of the empire.
Languages of subject groups were given a less favorable standing in the political and educational system,
and the government did all it could to force its subjects
to talk German or Hungarian, instead of their native
Slavic or Roumanian tongues. The pre-1914 German
Empire was even more savage in its attempt to eradi-

cate minority languages, like Danish and Polish. There was no justification for these campaigns, which served no useful purpose, were an expression of nothing but the brutal domineering of the ruling nations, and in the end caused immense damage.

What naturally happened was that the subject peoples—Czechs, Croats, Serbs, Roumanians, Poles, etc.—developed, as a result of this uncalled-for oppression, a fierce and utterly unreasoning love for their own languages, as opposed to all others, an emotion equally unjustified on an objective basis, but quite comprehensible in terms of psychological reaction. And after the First World War ended in 1918, the successor states like Czechoslovakia, Yugoslavia, Roumania, and Poland tried to turn the tables on their former oppressors by stamping out German and Hungarian with equal ruthlessness. This, of course, only aggravated the trouble, since Germans and Hungarians resented the stigmas and disadvantages placed on their languages, and the evil thus returned for evil contributed greatly to the German and Hungarian desire for revenge and renewed dominance which led to the Second World War.

We have already mentioned Switzerland as a good example of a country whose citizens are fully as devoted to their native land as those of any other, yet who speak four different languages. This example in itself is enough to prove that there is no necessary connection between language and nationality or patriotism. The popular notion that there is such a connection is quite mistaken; to win and hold the affection of its citizens, a government does not need to ram the majority language down the throats of all its minorities. Actions, here as elsewhere, speak louder than words, and decent, fair treatment is essential rather than enforced linguistic unity. Following this principle, there is no harm in the majority language being treated as a foreign language—though a favored one, due to its special position—in schools wherever necessary. Some Spanish-speaking regions under United States rule, such as Puerto Rico and New Mexico, have suffered from politicians' misconceptions on this point. Nationalistic politicians in Washington have insisted on English being taught in Puerto Rico in just the same way it is taught in schools on the continent to children who are native speakers of English, despite the fact that the language situation is wholly different in Puerto Rico and that over 99 per cent of the island's population are native speakers of Spanish. Puerto Rican education has suffered badly from this wrong emphasis, the children's learning of English being very much reduced by inappropriate teaching and their knowledge of what they learn in Spanish being also reduced by much-needed time being wasted on poorly taught English. Why not teach English as a foreign language, which it certainly is in Puerto Rico? That would indeed be the most sensible thing to do; but can you persuade a United States politician of such a self-evident truth? No; because he is sure to come back with the argument—which seems to him unanswerable—"Puerto Rico is American territory, isn't it? Then they have to speak English there; and if we let them learn Spanish in the schools and treat English as a foreign language, they won't be good American citizens." An argument which is based, as you can see, on the fallacious assumption we have just been demolishing, that good citizenship depends on linguistic unity.

The contribution that linguistics can make to the world's affairs is roughly parallel to that which any other branch of the science of man, such as cultural anthropology, can make. This can be in the fields of analysis and of practical application, and in the latter, both within our own society and in the relations of our own with other societies or nations. Just as cultural anthropology and sociology analyze the structure of social groups, linguistics analyzes the structure of language systems, giving us a technique to make exact statements about languages as they exist and as they change in time. Of course this analysis will never be absolute; linguistics is like other sciences, in that it is cumulative, each generation builds on the work of preceding generations and goes farther, and the frontiers of knowledge are always being pushed ahead more and more. That is the way it should be, if linguistics is to remain truly scientific; otherwise, it would petrify into a theology, like traditional grammar has become in the last two thousand years. Present-day linguistics will undoubtedly be obsolete a hundred years from now, just as the linguistics (or chemistry or physics) of a hundred years ago is obsolete now. But the principles that linguistics seeks to follow are the only ones that can help us to get a real understanding of what language is, what rôle it plays in our lives, and how we can use our knowledge of it in improving our living.

But most linguistic analysts have been so concerned, until now, with working out their technique that they have not had much time to devote to practical considerations. To date, they have not made it known, as they should, that linguistics can tell us what notions about language that are prevalent in our society—such as "correctness" and our misconceptions about writing —are wrong, what harm they do in our society, and how the situation could be improved. Our society should know that linguistics can also tell us what part language does and does not play in inter-society and international relations, showing us for example how the "international language" problem can best be resolved, and how false ideas of linguistic superiority have misled nations into needlessly imposing their languages on other nations or groups. Here, too, there is a parallel with applied anthropology, which shows us how we can use the findings of anthropological and sociological analysis in dealing with such problems as race relations and with cultural minorities like immigrant groups; and, on the international level, in determining the proper understanding of how colonial peoples and tribes live, and in interpreting the cultural and psychological backgrounds of national "character" and behavior, as Geoffrey Gorer did in his study of American psychology.

But to return to our basic point: the message that linguistics has for our society at present is primarily this: Don't Meddle Ignorantly With Your Language! Any meddling with our language, by ourselves or others, in the name of "correctness," of spelling, or of nationalism, is harmful. As we mentioned before, this message is both negative and positive. It is negative, in that it warns us to give up, to abandon entirely the old dogmatic, normative, theological approach of traditional grammar and of social snobbery; and to substitute the relativistic, objective approach of scientific study and analysis. It is positive, in that it tells us, once we've cleared the ground in this way, to go ahead and find out for ourselves what the facts really are, to analyze and describe them as accurately as we can, and then to apply the knowledge we have obtained in that way. In both these respects, the contribution of linguistics is simply a part of the effort of all science in modern democratic society, to find out the truth and to act upon it; in this sense, the linguistic analyst, like other scientists, may take as his motto that noblest of all slogans: "Ye shall know the truth; and the truth shall make you free."

Appendix A: Some Useful Books

This does not pretend to be a full bibliography, even of books on general linguistics. The books are listed, not in alphabetical order nor yet according to the year of publication, but in order of ease for the beginner.

1. *A Course in Modern Linguistics*, by Charles F. Hockett (New York, Macmillan, 1958), is definitely the best introduction to the whole field of linguistics. It is thoroughly and carefully planned in a highly logical series of short chapters, each provided with definitions of new terms and with exercises. Hockett's style is easily understandable to the ordinary reader. His book is especially strong in its discussion of widely different types of linguistic structure and in its treatment of the relation of linguistics to anthropology. After Hockett, the next book might well be:

2. *Language*, by Edward Sapir (New York, 1923; reprinted in the Harvest Books series, No. HB7, 1955). This is perhaps the best written of all the general treatments of linguistics; Sapir was a great stylist as well as a great analyst, and his discussion of language is extraordinarily keen and perceptive, with many flashes of illuminating comparison with other fields of human knowledge. Sapir knew a great number of languages, and drew on that knowledge for the examples in his book. The book is somewhat anecdotal in treatment, and does not give a complete picture of all linguistic analysis. Another valuable discussion by Sapir is his article "The Status of Linguistics as a Science", in the

journal *Language*, volume 5, pages 207–214 (1929). After reading Sapir, it is time to go ahead and tackle:

3. *Language*, by Leonard Bloomfield (New York, Holt, 1933). This is far and away the best book on the subject written in the twentieth century. It contains a thorough discussion of all aspects of linguistic analysis, descriptive and historical, and has served as a starting point for almost all work done since 1933. Nearly all of what Bloomfield says is sound, although some of his discussion (especially that on descriptive linguistics) has been superseded by more recent advances. The book is not always easy reading, however, since it has some of the characteristics of a mathematical exposition: the reader is expected to understand fully each point before he goes on to the next, and to keep in mind what has gone before. Bloomfield's style is often disconcertingly simple, in that he never wastes words and always means exactly what he says, no more and no less; this often causes difficulty to readers who cannot rid themselves of traditional attitudes and terminology.

After reading these three, you can then go on to other works, either older or more recent. Bloomfield's bibliography contains a listing of the major works that had appeared up to 1933; of them, the most useful to the general reader will probably be:

4. *Language*, by Otto Jespersen, the Danish linguistic analyst (London and New York, 1923).

5. *Language*, by Joseph Vendryès, a French philologist (English translation, New York, 1925).

6. *Cours de linguistique générale* (Course of general linguistics), by Ferdinand de Saussure, a Swiss linguistic analyst of great insight and depth of understanding (Paris, 1915 and later editions; now translated into English, New York, Philosophical Library, 1959).

A more recent work which exemplifies the approach and technique of some modern analysts is:

7. *Outline of Linguistic Analysis,* by Bernard Bloch and George L. Trager (Baltimore, Linguistic Society of America, 1942). Methodologically valuable, but so terse and condensed as to be most difficult reading.

Two recent popular books of considerable interest are:

8. *Language in Thought and Action,* by S. I. Hayakawa (New York, Harcourt, Brace, 1949). An application to language problems of the approach of Count A. Korzybski and the "general semanticists," with a useful discussion of the relation between language and human behavior.

9. *The Gift of Language,* by Margaret Schlauch (New York, Dover Publications, 1956). One of the best popularizing books on linguistics now available; it is weak on descriptive linguistics and contains a number of factual errors, but is very good on the relation of language to society and to literature.

There are a number of books dealing specifically with English, among which we may recommend especially:

10. *What Is Good English?,* by C. C. Fries (Ann Arbor, 1940; first printed in 1927). An excellent, easily readable and understandable discussion of the problems involved in finding and using "good English," with an objective, scientific point of view.

11. *American English Grammar,* by C. C. Fries (New York and London, Appleton-Century, 1940; English Monograph No. 10, National Council of Teachers of English). An application to English of the principles of descriptive analysis; not a complete description of American English, as the title might seem to imply, but a discussion and presentation of actual usage on certain moot points, based on analysis of

many thousands of letters in the War Department's files.

12. *The Structure of English*, by C. C. Fries (New York, Harcourt, Brace, 1952). A thorough discussion of English syntax, presented clearly but in quite unorthodox categories; based on many hours of telephone conversations recorded and analyzed by Fries.

The Fries approach to English syntax, often combined with the Trager-Smith phonological analysis, has afforded a foundation for a number of presentations of modern English grammar, including especially:

13. *American English in its Cultural Setting*, by Donald J. Lloyd and Harry R. Warfel (New York, Knopf, 1956).

14. *Patterns of English*, by Paul Roberts (New York, Harcourt, Brace, 1956).

15. *Introduction to Linguistic Structures: From Sound to Sentence in English*, by A. A. Hill (New York, Harcourt, Brace, 1958).

Two books need especial mention as something to be avoided:

16. *The Loom of Language*, by Frederick Bodmer and Lancelot Hogben (New York, Norton, 1944); and

17. *The Story of Language*, by Mario A. Pei (Philadelphia, Lippincott, 1949). Both of these attempts at popularization cater to all the traditional misconceptions we have tried to refute: prescriptive dogmatism, misunderstanding of the relation of writing to language, and ethnocentric value-judgments. Both are pretentious, full of out-of-date notions, misinformation and misinterpretation, and are wholly misleading.

Appendix B: Additional Phonetic Symbols

The type-books of presses that specialize in linguistic work list hundreds of special symbols, all of which have their application in transcribing one language or another. Here we give only a few of the symbols of the International Phonetic Association which are used for well-known languages other than English.

SYMBOL	DESCRIPTION	EXAMPLE
β	Voiced bilabial fricative	Spanish *haba* "bean" ['aβa]
ç	Unvoiced palatal fricative	German *ich* "I" ['iç]
γ	Voiced guttural fricative	Spanish *haga* "(that) he do" ['aγa]
ɥ	Voiced front-rounded semi-vowel	French *huit* "eight" ['ɥit]
ɨ	High central unrounded vowel	Russian *byl* "he was" ['bɨl]
ʎ	Voiced palatal lateral	Spanish *calle* "street" ['kaʎe]
ɲ	Voiced palatal nasal continuant	Spanish *bañar* "to bathe" [ba'ɲar]
ø	High-mid front-rounded vowel	French *peu* "little" ['pø]
œ	Low-mid front-rounded vowel	French *peuple* "people" ['pœpl̩]
x	Unvoiced guttural fricative	German *Bach* "brook" ['bax]
y	High front-rounded vowel	French *pu* "been able" ['py]
ʔ	Glottal stop	Danish *hus* "house" ['huʔs]

Italic letters or hooks under consonant letters are used to indicate palatalized sounds, in which the tongue is close to the palate during the articulation of the consonant: e.g. Russian *byity* "to beat" ['*bit*] or ['ḅiṭ].

A til [͌] over a vowel letter or a hook under it indicates nasalization: e.g. Portuguese *bom* "good" ['bõ] or ['bǫ].

A small circle under a letter indicates that the sound is unvoiced, as in French *peuple* "people" ['pœpḷ]; a vertical stroke under the letter, that the sound is voiced, as in slow colloquial French *en face de la gare* "opposite the station" [ãfaṣdəla'gar].

A dot under a consonant letter indicates that the sound forms a syllable, as in English *button* ['bʌtṇ].

A small capital consonant letter is used to distinguish alveolar consonants or those pronounced with the tip of the tongue turned backwards in the mouth (*retroflex* consonants), if necessary: e.g. Sanskrit *paṭṭanam* "port-town" ['pʌTTʌnʌm].

Other devices may be used as necessary, e.g. special fonts of type or special marks placed near the letters.